Africa Beyond Wars, Diseases & Disasters.

Answers to the 101 Most Commonly Asked Questions

Ebonics. Rap Music. Homosexuality. Polygamy. Female Circumcision. Teenage Pregnancies. Do's & Don'ts in Business. The People. Cultures & Traditions.

by

Primus Chukwuemelia Igboaka

authorHOUSE

1663 LIBERTY DRIVE, SUITE 200
BLOOMINGTON, INDIANA 47403
(800) 839-8640
www.authorhouse.com

First published by AuthorHouse 12/21/04

ISBN: 1-4184-6120-2 (e)
ISBN: 1-4184-5174-6 (sc)

Printed in the United States of America
Bloomington, Indiana

This book is printed on acid-free paper.

"It is not what you call me, but what I answer to that matters."

– Ibo proverb

DEDICATION

MOTHER,

MARY IGBOAKA, (1930-2004)

Table of Contents

PART II

IT TAKES A VILLAGE

PART III

"Certain African situations cannot be judged by our criteria."
– Pope John Paul II

ACKNOWLEDGEMENTS

I want to thank many people across the United States, curious minds of different races, shades, and sizes, old and young—Blacks, Caucasians, Hispanics, and Asians—who wanted to know about the origin of my accent. When I revealed who I am and where I came from, they wanted to know more about my African heritage. Without you, this project would not have taken off.

I also want to thank all the people that have invited me to talk to them about Africa—families, churches, teachers, and organizers of black cultural festivals and events. You may not realize how you have helped me in reaching out to many people and sharing with them my knowledge and experiences about Africa. As a newspaper correspondent who has traveled extensively, and having had first-hand experience of the beauty called Africa, I am proud and pleased to tell you about the people, cultures, and traditions that I know too well.

In spite of Africa's problems, the people are wonderful people, as any visitor or immigrant would testify. They are deep-rooted in spirituality, which has helped them to cope through troubled times.

What I am telling you is not about hearsay. It is not all about traveling for a week or months, coming home, compiling and comparing notes, and writing my story. It is all about practical experiences that spanned over four decades and beyond.

Special thanks to my wife, Vickie, and our three sons, Somto, Ify, and Nnaemeka. Without you, this project would not have succeeded. To Dr. Austin Lado, a professor of Business Management at Cleveland State University; thanks for your encouragement. Alice Lorante, Mrs. Higgins, Ms. Arka, Mr. Richard Homzy of Lorain Avenue, Cleveland Public Library branch, you were always available to render help when I needed it most.

To my father, Ogbuehi Simon, and my mother Lolo May, you have been pivotal in forming my outlook of life and I owe everything to your kindness, your warmth, dedication to duty and belief in power above; your philosophies about life – especially life beyond materialism. To my sisters and brothers especially Carol, you've always been an inspiration to me. Dr. A.B.C. Orjiako, Sam Mba & Dr.

Chris Azoro - childhood friendship will always outlast new ones. My other friends too numerous to list here, you have made tremendous impact in my life. Thanks to John & Faith Ball; and Sister Angele of Royal Oak, Michigan. Isaiah Ismail—thank you for assisting me in putting my ideas into powerful graphic images, as seen on the cover. Special thanks to my editor, Stephanee Killen for your comments and queries. I am responsible for any oversight in this book.

Thanks to *Concord Press,* my former newspaper in Nigeria, for the opportunity to travel across Africa, Europe and United States.

Finally, to all agents and publishers that have felt strongly about my book for years but who have repeatedly sent out rejection letters. Your positive comments and, at the same time, your inability to accept and publish my book fired me to go ahead and make this dream a reality.

PREFACE

Africa is not a single country teeming with poor people, as media images portray. It is a diverse continent of fifty-three independent nations. It is a continent that holds roughly one-eighth of the world's population.

Africa is a continent that has the largest deposit of untapped diamonds, gold, silver, and petroleum—mineral resources that will have a potent and lasting influence in the world's global economies. These assets buried underneath seabeds, ocean floors, hills, mountains, and plateaus will continue to provide wealth to Africans (if managed and accounted well). The resources could equally be squandered, misappropriated, and end up in private accounts in foreign banks. It is therefore necessary for Africans to vigilantly provide the necessary checks and balances to ensure that they are adequately accounted for and managed.

African countries comprise some of the world's most lucrative untapped markets for trade and investments. For example, in Zaire alone, buried under her rich soils is the world's largest copper deposit, stretching almost 3,000 kilometers. This is the same area that has produced more than 14 million tons of copper and is known to have the world's largest deposits of other minerals, including diamonds, gold, gems, and petroleum resources.

In Nigeria, crude oil production is expected to increase from its current 30 billion barrels to 40 billion barrels—about four million barrels per day—by 2010. Revenues from oil alone will double the $400 billion Nigeria has realized from its export of petroleum since the 70s, when oil exploration began in the country. The U.S. Energy Department forecasts that U.S. global oil imports from Africa are expected to increase from the current 15 percent to over 25 percent. The United States' energy import from the continent, especially liquefied natural gas (LNG), is also expected to increase substantially over the next decade.

Finally, Africa's spectacular range of granite hills and mountains, which straddle the borders between states, her wildlife, and her seasonal "flaming forests" filled with beautiful flowers will continue to draw tourists and visitors from across the world.

This project was a great challenge. Africa is a huge continent and a heterogeneous collection of people with different religious beliefs and customs, making it very difficult for me to avoid generalizing about her cultural practices. Africans, for example, speak different languages in different countries. Hausa language is spoken in thirteen nations; Somali is spoken in twelve countries, the same as Swahili in twelve countries. Because of Africa's various languages and cultural and religious overlaps, there were instances when I struggled not to over-generalize. I bear all responsibilities for any misunderstanding this might create. Feel free to point out these mistakes, as future editions will address these oversights.

Of course, there is no denying that Americans are accustomed to seeing only famine, wars, and diseases in media reports about Africa. I was not surprised that the majority of Americans I interviewed in the process of writing this book have widely held stereotypes of Africa and her people.

It is, for no other reason, a direct consequence of the accumulated negative images in the news—including documentaries—that never showed the real Africa to their audience. Africa undeniably has its problems, but it is not a continent disfigured by wars, diseases, and famine, as is unrealistically portrayed in the headline news.

I am not suggesting that the media created these bad situations in some parts of Africa. That would be false and irresponsible. African leadership bears the greatest responsibility for Africa's image and state of affairs in the continent. However, the media plays a major role in shaping the world's perception; therefore, it has the duty to report events objectively and responsibly.

Unfortunately, the selective emphasis on wars, diseases, and disasters about Africa puts the media in a position of determining subsequent world behaviors towards Africa. The pervasiveness of the media cannot be overstated. From the curiosity of my sincere questioners, there is no doubt that the accumulation of negative images projected to the viewers about Africa has perpetuated certain beliefs and stereotypes.

Some critics argue that the media panders to uninformed sources. As a journalist myself, I do not think so, but I have not seen the media strive to add the opinions of Africa's intellectuals and middle-class to views expressed about Africa. When the media depends on the opinions of so-called pundits, some of them for undisclosed reasons, they do not give objective and balanced views on issues about Africa in the news. As a reminder, there is a large population of Africa's Diasporas that could give balanced opinions (positive or negative) about what is actually going on in Africa rather than the present, subjective, biased, and unbalanced approach to reporting and interpretation of news from the continent.

Critics have also argued that diverse African opinion in the news would no doubt enable the public to decide who is telling the truth and what to believe. Others warned that objective and balanced news about Africa with detailed analysis and official comments would be difficult to come by because media and news managers won't allow that to happen. Their reason is that apart from the difficulties of getting African authorities to speak, the negative image of Africa already in the perceivers' minds (the audience), and spread across the world for more than four centuries, would be very difficult for reporters to correct. Their conclusion is that it would be difficult to change negative images of Africa for very long, unless the person encounters experience that would contradict already held opinions. But I disagree completely.

It would, however, be unfair of me to write off every media outlet as subjective, biased, and unbalanced about reporting Africa. According to the survey, there are few media sources that report news about Africa and do not concentrate on wars, diseases, and disasters. These organizations have showed that objective and well-balanced reporting of Africa is very possible in the Western media. These genuine attempts to report news, good or bad, have added diverse perspectives to real issues, problems, and the life experiences of Africans, offering angles to news reporting and analysis that are often missing in the mainstream media.

Public Radio International (PRI) is among few news sources in United States for now that reports real experiences of Africa to the world; the station tells about the "normal" people of Africa—their traditions, customs, and cultures—in a more serious and in-depth analysis without the caricatures, innuendoes, and stereotypes daily seen in other media (even though much still remains to be achieved).

Africa is not about spectacular isolation and poverty. It is ironic that millions of Americans are not aware that Western European economies and the United States have, for centuries, depended on Africa for raw materials, cheap labor, and other commercial imports dating back to the tenth century. Trade with Africa, before and after European exploration, boomed with native Africans exchanging mainly gold, spices, and ornaments with European merchants.

Before Europeans came to the continent, Africans traded with Arabs and the Chinese. Between the tenth and eleventh centuries, large quantities of African products were reaching as far as China through India. As of today's modern Africa, trade with Europeans, Asians, and Americans still thrives, even though it is unfavorable on Africa's side and under-reported in the mainstream media.

Africa is as big as China, the United States, Europe, India, and New Zealand combined. It is 30,343,551 square kilometers in area, while these nations combined add up to 29,412,690 square kilometers *(see appendix)*. Unfortunately, Africa is seen in the eyes of almost all my questioners, even the most educated, as "One nation state," and the shape of Africa in many maps contributes to the miseducation of people about Africa's real size.

Several people find it difficult to trace African countries on the map. Egypt, an African nation, is seen as a nation in another Gulf region near Baghdad. Egypt is Arabic, but there are nations within the African continent that are Arabic and Muslim.

Africa has its own share of men and women of goodwill—hard working and ambitious. She also boasts of royals, academia, and intellectuals of international repute, as well as engineers and computer scientists, doctors, teachers, businessmen, students, and of course the under-class. The poor we are very familiar with because they are always Africa's emblems on our primetime network news. They have become the representation of everything Africa.

Africa's economic growth has improved in the last five years in such countries as Botswana, Mauritius, Mozambique, and Seychelles. Democracy has taken root in more nations in Africa than elsewhere in Central Asia and the Middle East upon the setbacks in Sierra Leone, Liberia, and the Congo. According to IMF economists, the fastest growing economy for the last thirty years was Botswana, a state in the southern part of the continent. As one of the largest suppliers of diamonds to the world's market, it remains a rich nation by local and international standards.

I have tried to offer a little knowledge on subjects we are familiar with, which are often on the headline news. I have tried to handle them more elaborately to correct some distortions. I have also discussed subjects that are untouchable in most African cultures, such as homosexuality, sex, female circumcision and nudity. I never had second thoughts in discussing them as my own way of informing my readers, rather than leaving them to understand these issues and subjects from rumor mills which Africa's culture of superstitions and secrecy do not help in any ways. As a reminder, I have made these contributions from the perspective of a reporter, not as a commentator or a judge. As an African, I have the advantage to see Africa's reality from the vantage point of her real self. I have learned from the process of listening to thousands of people—at shopping malls, churches, mosques, temples, post offices, at my work place, at college cafeterias, and in classrooms—that they want to know what is happening around the world, including Africa.

Africa is not simply a continent with problems, and neither should African people be viewed as those in the vicinity of ghettos. It is a very large continent with people ready to interact socially, politically, and economically. They want to do business with the rest of the world. It is also a continent with over 10 percent of its population in the upper (middle-class). This population, which controls about 30 percent of the wealth in their respective countries, travels overseas and can afford goods and services like their counterparts elsewhere in the world. That population alone (even though it is unfortunate that wealth is limited to few hands compared to the United States or Western Europe) translates to about 80 million people that crave and could afford to buy goods and services based on forces of supply and demand. Economically speaking, that population, to any marketer, is a huge segment by any standard.

Some African nations account for the world's largest producers and exporters of cocoa, coffee, yams, cassava, peanuts, cotton, spices, and ginger, just to list a few of the products that have markets overseas—even though they are still under-priced or have no steady market in global economy. Some African farmers that seek overseas markets have faced barriers, including closed doors to their products, high tariffs, and their inability to compete with farmers—whose products are subsidized by their governments

This book offers you insight about Africa, her people, cultures, traditions, and unsung promises from a perspective never before addressed. I have also included the political, social, economic, and leadership problems that continue to burden new leadership strategies and efforts to alleviate poverty and put African nations on the track to economic posterity.

FORETHOUGHT:
THE RHYTHM OF AFRICAN WARS

Why is it that there is always a country in Africa at war or experiencing violence and instability at any time?

Taking a general view of present and past conflicts around the world, whether in Bosnia, Northern Ireland, Cambodia, East Timor, Philippines, Colombia, Indonesia, Kashmir, Middle East, Rwanda, Sierra Leone, Chechnya, Afghanistan, Iraq, Congo, Liberia, or Somalia, the lesson drawn from these conflicts is that we have, regrettably, not shown an understanding of managing conflicts before battle lines are drawn. Yesterday, it was Haiti, and as I am about to go to press with this project, Haiti was burning until President Aristide agreed to flee the country. But the world waited for three weeks and watched more than 100 Haitians die. All that these conflicts suggest is that unlike species in the animal kingdom that struggle over territorial control—dominance, food, and mates—and know there is time to cool off, human beings have not learned much from our own experiences or from that of others to avoid repeating the same mistakes of history. We have, unfortunately, witnessed the same or similar political, social, and economic problems that cause global instability recycling all over, either in new places or in places where they were once "resolved." Directly or indirectly, we contribute to these conflicts through policies and actions that we take, which affect our people and our neighbors in a global village.

A look at the world as a global community, and based on the number of unresolved conflicts, shows that we are still learning when and how to give peace a chance. Conflict management has failed humans in many instances of history. Some problems that purportedly would be better if micro-managed through dialogue and negotiations have been allowed to escalate, as is the case in most African tribal and religious clashes and of course, wars. When early intervention is not forthcoming, and the longer the wait, the more arms and ammunitions are acquired and reactivated; the more battlegrounds are established; and the more soldiers are recruited, including child-soldiers. Some of them drugged and dazed, and with fingers on the trigger of their loaded AK-47, everything in front of them becomes a target, not just on the side of the enemy. By the time the intervention forces finally arrive, million of casualties, mostly women and children, are found on the streets. Villages are raided, razed and no hope of rebuilding them anywhere in the future.

It is unfortunate that this is the reality of Africa's situations, which of course reveals the darker side of human history—not just Africa's account. It is hoped that lessons learned from conflicts, racism, tribalism, abuses of human rights of minorities, and ethnic cleansing would improve our relationships and contribute to a peaceful and harmonious co-existence for our future generations. History has yet to prove us right that we learn anything from these ugly events.

There is no particular part of the world that could be exonerated from savagery. Today there is no safe haven anymore as far as threat to global security is concerned. There is also hardly any region on the face of the planet where anyone can point a finger and declare that the region is totally free from tribal, racial, religious, or political commotion. What we have made of our environment, and brought to ourselves, is yet to be determined since many nations have yet to recover after years of war, as evidences of failed states and depleted economies have shown.

On the average, thirty to forty hot spots across the world are in turmoil every year. Most of the world's hot spots don't get any attention, and unfortunately, they may never get attention. The worst atrocities in the world occurred in Europe before Rwanda and in small villages and hamlets; today, tribal conflicts of huge magnitude are taking place without much attention.

Africa's harsh realities in terms of conflicts and people's reactions to them have shown the resilience of African people in troubling times. As people always stereotype, "Nothing changes in Africa." But this is not true. Africa is in tune with the rest of the world. They want development; they want better standards of living, not just for the rich but also for themselves and future generations. They are abreast with every development around the world, but what is still lacking is development in health care, science, and technology.

Pope John II said in 1980, when asked about his relations with some African dictators, "Certain African situations cannot be judged by our criteria." He indicated that his statement "does not mean tolerating abuses." (This was in reference to visiting African countries with "dictators" as leaders.) The Pope was right, because Africa cannot be viewed from the same standpoint as the West in many ways. That mistake resurfaces all the time in the way the media writes and often misinforms the public on several African issues that need thorough analysis.

It is also very difficult to understand, in some situations, why blood is shed to resolve problems that would have worked well with dialogue and negotiations. It becomes more difficult to fathom why so many people are ready to die when we are not wearing the shoes of a "Freedom Fighter" or a "Gorilla Fighter." Peace will always remain the best alternative to any conflict, no matter the cause and justification for any war. That appears to be the mantra that the new African Union is promoting and working hard to establish throughout the continent.

The role greed, hate, tribal intolerance, and the lack of compromise also plays in African conflicts cannot be underestimated. Critics have rebuked some African leaders that flag colonialism as the reason why Africa has been embroiled in endless conflicts, and also why Africa has not done well economically. Yes, it is undeniable that slavery and colonization of the land, the people, and their minds were evils that badly impacted the continent. But of equal consequence were policies and abuses of human rights by some African civilian governments, as well as dictators.

Africans can relate themselves to the degradation people suffered under colonialism. It hurts when African administrations, expected to protect their people, inflict injustice and deprivation on the same people they are in office to look after. In short, it is the worst crime to be treated inhumanly by your own so-called leaders. Under the brutal regimes of the past, many Nigerians strongly believed that no colonial government would rule in the 80s and 90s with an iron hand while the world simply sat, silently watching, as they did during those darker days of tyranny. Of course, critics claimed these regimes lasted as long as they did because they were Africans. More so, they were serving the interests of others that benefited from their staying in power—their extremely poor human rights records notwithstanding.

Some African leaders used to blame colonialism for Africa's worst problems. But African critics have said, "Wait a minute…if you have problems with colonialism, why do some of you African leaders stifle Africa's poor and hoard corruptly-acquired wealth belonging to the same poor people in bank vaults around the world?" It does not make sense that the so-called people they are protecting—the poor—are in dire need of basic amenities, yet these billions of dollars of illegally acquired money are hidden in foreign banks.

The irony of this political propaganda is that the same poor people are being told that one of the reasons they are poor is because of the evil of colonialism. It makes no common sense. Anyone familiar with Africa knows that it is not a poor continent, and therefore should not have poor people.

Another question raised by concerned Africans on colonialism as a reason for Africa's deplorable economic state is why not encourage indigenous entrepreneurs by awarding billions of dollars in business contracts—road construction and rehabilitation jobs—to African business men? That has not been the culture in African road, railway, and airport construction programs; almost 99 percent of these major contracts are awarded to foreign, multi-national construction companies.

Capital flight from Africa is a serious threat to her economic growth and development. The behavior to corruptly deprive people their wealth and then run away with it to foreign banks is deliberate. It is a decision made by the person depositing the money in these overseas banks and not by any compulsion as to blame "colonialism." What is painful is that the majority of people whose money was siphoned had no good roads or reliable electricity. In short, it is ironic that rather than investing the same money to generate more jobs, build industries, award scholarships, grant loans to young and new entrepreneurs, or to attract joint partnerships or ventures with multi-national companies around the world, these billions of dollars are in banks, generating little or no extra income to the depositor. In fact, it is generating minimal CD interests of about 1 percent, while the same banks are loaning the money out to investors, and other loan applicants like you and me, at rates of between 5 percent to more than 18 percent annually. Of course, the losers are the same poor people, who are deprived of their wealth; the same poor Africans whose images are plastered everywhere in the media by non-profit agencies soliciting for money for the same poor people, the refugees, and the destitute, created of course by poor management and decision of few that have deprived Africans their wealth and ran to deposit huge sum of wealth in foreign banks.

Of course, the middle-class and the poor in Africa don't know much about colonialism of the 21st century other than that a few corrupt politicians are depriving them of money that could have been used to pay their salaries and pensions, or used for loans to start businesses or award scholarships (since there is nothing like student loans in Africa).

As at December 2002, United Nations Secretary General Kofi Annan disclosed that for the sixth year running, developing countries made a transfer of financial resources of almost $200 billion to developed countries. This is a typical example of carrying coal to New Castle. Many agreed with the Secretary General that such a situation lacked common reasoning, especially as these funds could be used to promote investment and growth in countries where they were taken away.

Africa, of course, accounted for a large number of such transfers upon recording the nations with the worst and the highest number of "poor people" in the world. The majority of this wealth was allegedly money corruptly acquired and siphoned to private accounts by the same African leaders that want the people to believe that colonialism left Africa and the people in shambles. In fact, critics disclose that the claims of colonialism as the cause of Africa's problems have lost their meaning (when it should not, because it is still relevant), and serious attention it undeniably deserved because politicians are using it when it is suitable to them or politically correct to do so.

However, with this said, colonialism cannot be entirely ruled out as major part of Africa's problems today. Turning a blind eye to the evils of colonialism is absolute ignorance and relegation of history. Colonialism has its own consequences, especially in most

African countries that lacked the willpower to recover from the psychological, political, economic, and social destruction it brought on the continent. That poverty is prevailing in some parts of the continent today is also attributable to neo-colonialism, which in the 21st century, comes in different forms and shapes – including trading of stocks and movement of investment funding globally. Unfortunately movement of investment funds and capital will continue to play a part in global politics and economic development of nations around the world.

On the side, Africa has all the human and natural resources it needs to shift economic gears and lift the continent to economic prosperity. It is unfortunate that corruption, selfishness, and greed have prevailed. These vices are still taking their toll on new democracy and the economy.

The evil of corruption never originated in Africa, but it has permeated some societies so strongly and unfortunately hurting some African nations so deeply that it would take extraordinary efforts, and the willpower of the people themselves rather than government, to fight the vice. Both under the military as well as civilian regimes, Africa's enormous wealth continues to be siphoned away, and it is preventing Africa from building wealth internally and sustaining economic growth.

No doubt, colonialism depleted Africa's self esteem to such a level that its people no longer believe in her or in the capabilities of her human resources, which today are spilling across the globe in the name of brain drain, benefiting Europe and the United States. Holding colonialism entirely responsible for 21st century Africa is like a child crying for spilled milk. Reasons I explained in my responses to questioners may shade more light to what I seriously meant.

Colonialism disfranchised people by strengthened caste and class-consciousness among a very small percentage of the ruling class. The system supported isolation of the people from what was going on at the center—the seat of government—and prevented the people (except the privileged class) from benefiting from wealth that belongs to all. Africans were never presented with any "Marshall Plans," nor was any financial assistance in place to improve devastated African economies after more than 400 years of slavery and colonialism. These are indeed part of Africa's problems, which cannot be dealt with through the continued poor management of resources by some leaders of the continent.

Let us also not forget that the British were used to class-structured system, and the training of early African leaders in British political schools promoted this objective. The legacy and mentality it bred still persists today among most African leaders. Military or civilian—no administration is ruled out of this weakness. The system reinforces class structure to the exclusion of the poor. In some instances, when the people resist this situation, the consequence is the clash between the police and the masses on the streets.

Though war is not the answer to human problems, looking at each case of Africa's wars and violence on their "merits" or "demerits," as presented by some of the "Liberation Fighters," it seems that both sides have their reasons for taking arms or for suppressing the insurgence. However, on a second look, one realizes there is nothing worth more than dialogue in conflict resolution, accommodating the views of opposition even when it seems to "have no meaning" to the other side. After all, in most wars, the civilians often pay the ultimate price—death. Such wars often and permanently leave scars on the poor, mostly women and children, for the rest of their lives.

In reality, there are African wars that were fought for the right reasons—purposefully as a deterrent, for territorial security and protection. Some were fought to stop the abuses of a citizen's right to live freely and express themselves in their own country. Others were fought for the liberation and independence of the "people" from the shackles of dominance, colonialism, tribalism, and dictatorship.

Instances abound in countries where dictators cling to power and suppress ethnic minorities, and resistance to these abuses seemed the only way out. This has often led to revolts or civil wars. Cases also abound where because of colonialism, tribes with nothing in common other than black skin were merged together. In others, tribes with a common heritage and history were torn apart, or joined with tribes with which they had nothing in common. Unfortunately, some of these tribes that either separated or merged had independence in their own quasi-democratic system of government before they were lumped together. In tribes where these powers of autonomy have been stripped away, and the people now find themselves as the minority, the struggle to gain recognition brings its own resistance and conflicts of various dimensions.

Prior to Africa's partitioning and the new experience, tribes had maintained peace and order in the usual traditional dialogue and negotiation styles. Wars in tribal villages were not ruled out, but anarchy was a taboo in most of these cultures.

The European amalgamation of villages, towns, and states for easy administration of territories became a problem when they left. As is presently witnessed in countries with weak political systems, when no strong infrastructure is laid for the democratic process to take root, the consequences will always be anarchy, conflicts, tribal clashes, and civil war.

Furthermore, when the Europeans finally left Africa, postcolonial rulers never put in place a concrete master plan to hold people together. The frustration of these merged or separated tribal people became worsened when power, known to be exclusive to one tribe, was taken away and given to another tribe—maybe to the minority. The problem of inequitable distribution of power, the aftermath of the "Divide and Rule" colonial system of government, continues to play a role in Africa's crisis and wars.

The cold world era built dictators to buffer communist intrusion or invasion of territories that were of interest to the West. The culmination of these events and the participation of Africa against Russia for the interests of the United States—including promotion of dictatorial regimes, armed to the teeth by these two countries to resist internal challenges—are partially (not entirely) responsible for some of the "confusion" most states in Africa face today. Many have yet to overcome these conflicts of interest and damages left behind at the end of the cold war. With no assistance from either the West, in terms of Marshall Plans, or Russia—which also left Africa, as soon as the West gained the upper hand—Africa was left to struggle on its own.

Ibos in Southeastern Nigeria have a history dating back 6,000 years. The society has no king or ruler; instead, it has a village elders' council that is nominated by the people who represented the masses with either the chief at the head or a leader nominated by the people's representatives. Where chiefs are nominated or appointed, people always ensured that the chief never abused his position or the institution he represented. The power belonged to the people. The masses had little or no recognition for the institution at the center to control their lives, other than to lead the people in times of distress or for a common good. Other than that, they also believed that honesty, hard work, the pursuit of excellence and success, and a commitment to immediate and extended family are the norms for the common good of the society. Once everybody in the society plays his or her role well, the society needs a leader, not a ruler—a team builder to achieve success for the community.

One of the new era problems that Africans face today, often not mentioned in the media, is the adoption and duplication of Western democracy across Africa without the infrastructures and strong economic foundation that have sustained the United States or the French and British democracies. The replication of these systems hurt rather than help Africa.

Of all the systems of government, democracy is no doubt the most beneficial to the people, and the most beneficial in terms of freedom of expression, human rights, and enterprise. Examples of countries that have adopted democracy, and the level of their successes, are testimonies to the positive benefits of social equality. These successes of nations under the system have proven that of the worst of all political ideologies, democracy remains the best. Regrettably, the system is not working in Africa as it does in the West. It is because of many geo-political, economic, religious, and environmental reasons. First, the present economic and political environments in most African nations are not conducive. Weak economic infrastructures are antidotes to breeding democracy.

Secondly, democracy is expensive. Africa is not disposed to maintain and service the huge number of institutions that the system sustains and still have money to face the reality of her real problems. In the midst of budgetary deficits, there is unemployment, nations spending all resources on servicing IMF/World Bank loans, and there is poverty. There is a limit to what a well-intended leader can do to satisfy the yearnings of his people, especially under the messy economic situations that have prevailed decades before the leader probably came into office. The point is that institutions and infrastructures to build and sustain everlasting democracies are not well developed in most African states. And the money to build them is not there because of the scope of other problems.

When the infrastructures that promote democracy are absent, undoubtedly what we have are frustrations and violence. These are not good precursors for democracy. That explains why the African Union—especially leaders of South Africa, President Thambo Mbeki, and his Nigerian counterpart, President Olusegun Obasanjo—spends more time quelling crises, tribal clashes, military coups, and civil wars in the continent than administering their respective countries.

The solution is that Africa needs "African democracy," with traditional and modern institutions combined; the two interplaying roles in administering policies, law, and order. In essence, maintaining peace and an environment devoid of corruption where citizens are free and crime rates are down. This would take the form of a grass root leadership involving traditional rulers, village councils, traditional courts, and some of the old institutions that were vital in the old Africa. Some states are gradually experimenting with this system. This does not, in any way, dispose modern leadership infrastructures or systems of legislature that are found in Western democracies, but they should be tailored to be affordable to the people and the state.

The high interest on IMF/World Bank loans has left many African nations incapable of paying their debts. They are unable to provide basic services to the people and still maintain and service the institutions that "democracy" has created.

The transition of African governments from one system of government to another without weighing the costs and consequences of a new system is a big problem. Similarly, neglecting to clear the garbage of the old system before jumping into a new one simply because it worked in the West (or elsewhere) presents the greatest danger to every democratic initiative. Africa needs a democratic process that evolves internally while recognizing the inhibitions and benefits of, at times, rigid and often conservative African way of life.

Traditional African governments were centralized with kings, traditional rulers, chiefs, obas, or emirs as leaders in the village elders' council. Depending on what name was given to the institution by the tribes, decision-making, however, flowed from bottom to top and gave every representative of the village a voice to contribute to the governance of the people. The chiefs provided leadership on matters of civil, traditional, and cultural relevance. African democracy must recognize the roles traditional institutions play in respective tribal societies and merge them into African democracy.

Colonial administrators operated like the feudal lords with every autonomy, power, and initiative that neglected the people in decision-making. The powerful minority lords it over the majority. Till date, that arrangement still exists. In Africa, where wealth is in the hands of government and controlled by the central authority, wealth meant for all only benefits the rich, close to government, with little or none at all left to provide basic amenities for the poor.

When colonialism ended, Africans with the same style of leadership were educated and trained in Europe. They inherited power without election; where elections were held, they were overwhelmingly elected with the backing of the powers behind their appointment. In fact, shady elections were held where cronies were put into office to maintain power by every means, at all costs, including of course with support from outside. They followed the master's style of leadership that was beneficial to his (master's) interest. The consequences included a repetition of the mistakes of the colonial masters—wealth that benefited the few, this time the pockets of leaders. Thus, the continuity of what could be described as circle of titular, power-manipulating bureaucrats who continued to rule and disrupt economic planning and growth, just for personal aggrandizement and self-serving egos. The system left the rest of the people to feed from the master's table—if anything was left over.

Since democracy is served by the existence of a healthy and prosperous economy, Africa's economy, badly weakened by colonialism and shredded by past leadership mismanagement, corruption, and "squander-mania" during Africa's oil boom eras, has continued to weaken and endanger democracy.

People's material and social welfare has been abandoned. There is a lack of jobs; there is no good drinking water; there is poor housing or no housing policy at all; and roads are not maintained. In the confusion that arises from these neglects, tribalism is played by leaders in power like Nazism to overshadow these real, undermining problems. In some instances, the opposition capitalizes on these loopholes. They in turn preach to every ear that wants to hear that they are the "messiahs" to remedy these problems. In the real sense, it boils down to the fact that these parties do not actually care for the people. The opposition wants power by all means. The party in power plays the "tribal card," not the race card, this time to maintain its base and keep power. Behind the scenes, the opposition is persuading people to join the forces that push for destabilization of the state in the name of the crisis that you see repeatedly in Africa.

As one African diplomat told me inside a London flight, "Democracy is founded on full bellies and by peaceful minds." An example of an African country where good leadership prevails, and the majority of the people are benefiting from the sale of their resources and diversification of their economy, is Botswana. It is example of where people are "full bellied" from diamond resources, and the difference it makes is glaring in every facet of the society—including health care and employment.

It is always difficult to mobilize people when they are hungry. There is hardly any problem anyone with an empty stomach, who is frustrated by decisions that do not impact his life or that of his children, could solve. Africa remains one of the places on the face of the planet where there is no welfare for the poor—where people are not able to afford subsidized medicine or free health care, food stamps, and subsidized housing. The lists of programs benefiting the poor in the West or developed nations are so long that listing them here may take another page or two.

In Africa, there are also problems with blood diamond money – wealth generated by illegal sales of diamond by warlords to fund wars. Arms' trafficking is a multi-billion dollar global business, and it benefits the few that want money for personal enrichment and the maintenance of their money machines (huge profits). Recently, the United Nations blacklisted more than 150 companies involved in sponsoring or benefiting from war in the Democratic Republic of Congo, and to be honest, these companies were just the tip of the iceberg.

Since the end of the cold war and the independence of breakaway nations in Eastern Europe, it is estimated that over 350 million illegal rifles are floating around these regions. Where, and in whose hands, these dangerous weapons finally end up; we may not be able to tell. However, from global events and trends, it would not be surprising to find that they may end up in Africa's war fronts or in the hands of criminal and terrorist groups.

For all the reasons in this book—be it to remedy the wrongs of colonialism and slavery; be it to assist Africa through transparent open market and equitable trade agreements; be it to dismantle the walls of subsidies and tariffs, so that Africa can have a fair share of the global export markets in developed nations; be it the reduction of poverty through collaborative African-International community initiatives—Africa must not be left alone to handle these problems. The world is a global village—politically, socially, and economically. There is a huge prize we may all pay one day if we neglect Africa's problems. We have the power to avoid the price, and it can be done.

PART I

LANGUAGES, DIALECTS, CULTURE, AND SOCIETY

QUESTIONS AND ANSWERS:

WHAT IS IN A NAME?

1. Question: I am a frequent traveler to Africa. I still recall my first experience when I addressed a Senegalese as African. I had the same experience with a Nigerian. Why does addressing a Nigerian or Senegalese as an African draw such an awful rebuke?

Answer:

When I am asked (as is often the case), "Are you an African?" my response is always no. This is because in Africa, a person is recognized first by his name. Most of the time, this is a traditional or Christian name, depending on the person's preference. A family's name and a person's tribe follow other names. Many prefer to be identified by their tribe or country rather than as an "African," the name of his or her continent. People are often embarrassed and confused when addressed as "Africans."

I have always put this test to people with good intentions. Let's assume that, yes, I am an African—how would the questioner feel when I ask him, "Are you a North American?" In all sincerity, that is the same way a person born in the continent of Africa feels when this question is asked.

Put it this way, it sounds meaningless to ask a person whether he or she is from Africa or whether the person is an African. But this is more commonly used in the United States than in Europe—where people are more identified by their countries, even tribes, than by the name of their continent.

Whenever I am confronted with this question, I have always tried to explain to the questioner that I am a Nigerian from the African continent. In fact, no one identifies a person by his or her continent.

Africa is not a country rather a continent made up of fifty-three independent nations. Africans prefer to be identified by their tribes or native countries rather than by the name of their continent.

AFRICAN TRIBES, LANGUAGES, AND DIALECTS

2. Question: I learned that there are many tribes in Africa. If you don't mind . . . how are tribes formed, and how do people become members of a tribe?

Answer:

I find this question very interesting. I recalled that this question was asked after I delivered a speech about tribes in Africa in one of my public speaking engagements.

One is not just born into a tribe as a member. Either one or both parents must come from the tribe you are born into. In matrilineal societies, you are a member of a tribe that your mother comes from, and the reverse is the case in patrilineal societies.

That a person is a permanent resident of a town or a village either by immigration or other ways does not make the person or his family a member of that tribe. No person makes the choice by himself. You are either born into a tribe or adopted into one, but belonging to a tribe as a result of adoption is very rare.

Marriage does not automatically confer membership of a tribe to a person. When a woman marries, she is married to the tribe of the husband, unless in some situations, say for example she decides to relocate to her father's house after her husband's bereavement or other circumstances. However, in matrilineal societies, a child born to a daughter, same as married to the daughter of another tribe, has the chance of being accepted as a member of that tribe. An in-law for example, who migrated to take refuge in the village of the wife, may decide to settle in his in-law's village and could be accommodated under special provisions as a tribal member of his wife's tribe. In other words, he may have the privileges or rights that other tribal members have in the village.

A tribe is a group of people – descendants from one large family tree, often spanning centuries, who share the same customs, beliefs, cultures, traditions, and most of the time, the same religion. They share common values and language. A tribe is a human community developed by a very long association of families with the same customs, beliefs, and values. A tribe starts just like a family and gradually grows and spreads out over time.

There are instances where tradition and customs allow a child to be accepted into a tribe. A child for example, born to a mother that divorced or that decides to return to her father's house because of bereavement, assuming she does not want to remarry, can be accepted into the tribe. The son has the option of choosing which tribe (the mother or father's) he wants to belong to or identify as his own.

In the last circumstance, mutual agreement with the families of the former husband may allow the child to be accepted into the mother or father's tribe. Another way of becoming a member of a tribe is a grandson that decides to resettle in his mother's birthplace due to certain circumstances. It may be the grandfather has no heir apparent or male child as a patriarch. The son of his daughter may be accommodated as a member of the tribe for this mission to be accomplished.

As earlier disclosed, a person cannot belong to tribe just because he wants to be a member of that particular tribe. You can only be born into a tribe or by circumstance of relationship to either the mother or father's side.

PROUD HERITAGE

3. Question: I am proud of my African ancestry. In my African arts and culture class, I read about African *griots* and *grioles* and their roles in African societies. Are there still generations of these men and women alive and active today in Africa? If there are, what roles do they play in modern Africa?

Answer:

Grioles and *griots* are storytellers. They tell stories to pass along information about oral traditions. In traditional African societies, the best way of people knowing their history and passing it on to the next generation is by storytelling. Therefore, *griots* and *grioles* (along with elders in the village) were conveyors of this oral history, traditions, and cultures. They were not just limited to these roles. They performed at various functions in traditional African societies. They were also inspirational storytellers who occasionally used their traditional string instruments to compose music about specific events.

Griots and *grioles* compose poems and music for various occasions and events. They also tell history through songs and poetic rhymes. They sing about ancestors, about wars, and tragedies; they sing praises to kings and queens; compose music for traditional weddings and inaugurations; and sing at the coronation and installation of chiefs, funeral ceremonies, rite of passage ceremonies, and other village festivals. They sing about the living—friends and neighbors. They can be inspired by events happening in their immediate environment. From these events, they can compose and play songs and recite poetry with their native instruments.

Griots and *grioles* in traditional African societies are great social psychologists of repute. They are the go-betweens for the king and the people, in some instances, in villages where they lived.

In modern Africa, one could count a handful of existing *griots* and *grioles* in such countries as Senegal, Guinea, Gambia, and Mali. Most *griots* and *grioles* today are either descendants or people influenced by old generations of these talented men and women. Unlike the orthodox *griots* and *grioles,* the modern artists have discovered new ways of rendering their messages and playing and entertaining different audiences. However, most of them perform today in ceremonies within the confines of their tribes and their countries. New generations or descendants of *griots* and *grioles* in places such as Senegal and Mali have stepped ahead to popularize their songs and continue to improve on the talents of their forebears. Their traditional songs can be heard mixed with rhythms of blues and jazz. Few have made it commercially big, but locally they are more than music celebrities—they are custodians of history, traditions, and cultures.

Africa's top musicians such as Mali's Ali Farka Toure and descendants of *griots* started by listening and playing a traditional *njurkel,* a native, one–string horsehair lute instrument used by *griots.* In spite of clashes between musicians of the traditional *griot* caste, and modern musicians of blues and jazz that wanted to adopt the original styles and tunes of *griots,* the relationship between the traditional music of *griots* and modern music continues to be present in modern compositions and in different genres of music.

4. Question: I am an American, and I am also very proud of my African ancestry and heritage. I often wear African dresses. Is it true that African dresses, and their designs, make cultural and social statements? Could you explain?

Answer:

It is true that African dresses make social, cultural, and of course fashion statements. By this, I mean that every traditional African dress has a story it tells. It depicts where the dress was made and sometimes the tribal origin of the person wearing it. It could also depict the occasion—maybe the event or the ceremony the dress was made for. The designs on them could equally tell their own stories. Of course, there are royal ceremonial dresses and expensive materials that also tell the social class of the person wearing the dress. Unlike ordinary shirts and trousers (pants), African dresses are not just for covering the body. They make statements, as I have earlier said, that could be interpreted to answer many cultural and traditional questions.

Of course, there is no question that African dress also gives a sense of African pride. It is a trademark that whenever anybody sees an African dress, a person familiar with African history, tradition, and culture could easily trace the person wearing the dress to a particular tribe or region in the continent.

There are African dresses that have spiritual attachment. Kente cloth, for example, has royal, religious, or spiritual significance. For other African dresses, their beautiful graphics, traditional dyes, colors, designs, and the materials used in making them tell their own stories.

Royals in the Ghana (Ashanti) Empire adorn Kente on special occasions. On these special appearances, gold ornaments and precious jewelry are worn to suit Kente—one of the most expensive materials in Africa.

Weather, culture, class, and the status of the person wearing an African dress influence the type of material and style of dressing.

Overall, in some cultures, certain clothes are designed and tailored for special traditional and cultural events.

In Southeastern Nigeria, the Ibos have particular dress codes different from the Hausas in the North, the Yorubas in the West, and the Ijaws in Midwestern and Southern Nigeria. Different tribes wear dresses made in styles that identify their tribes. The most popular traditional dresses of the Ibos include chiefly red caps with caftans. The Hausas wear hand-woven and decorated caps with flowing caftans. The Yorubas wear decorated caps, with embroidered traditional dresses and *agbadas.*

Overall, there are regalia, caftans, tunics, and specially made dresses designed specifically for kings, queens, and chiefs.

AFRICA'S FLOATING DRESSES

5. Question: While I was in Africa, I witnessed that most traditional dresses for men are flowing—*agbadas, dashikis,* and caftans. Why are African traditional dresses huge, baggy, and floating? How true is it that baggies (pants) and bigger dress styles trace their origins to Africa?

Answer:

Weather determines the type of materials used to create African dresses. Climate also affects the pattern and style of African dresses. Don't forget that Africa is almost divided into two equal parts by the equator, and the weather condition along the imaginary line is a tropical climate. In essence, temperatures are warm almost throughout the year.

In the West Africa region, the rainy season is often warm, except for intervals of cool, westerly winds that descend occasionally from offshore, bringing cold air from the Atlantic Ocean into the coastlines and hinterlands.

Harmattan is dusty and has cold-dry temperatures. Cooler temperatures are in the range of 30 to 40 degrees Fahrenheit, and at the peak of sunny and warm weather (summer), temperatures could scale over 90 degrees. An average temperature in Lagos for example is 76 degrees Fahrenheit. In Kenya, temperatures could reach 80 degrees maximum and 60 degrees minimum. Therefore, dresses are made to reflect these weather patterns and changes, with flowing gowns, *agbadas,* and caftans (with spaces for easy flow of air) made from local and imported materials.

At the desert and sub-desert zones, accessories such as scarves and bandannas accompany these floating dresses. Dresses such as gowns, *agbadas,* and assorted styles of other beautifully hand-made robes are common dress patterns of Africans.

Another important factor that determines what and how Africans dress are religions affiliations. Christians and Muslims alike are influenced by religion. The conservative values of both religions ensure that a man or woman dresses appropriately for every occasion, not just religious events. What I mean here is, for example, the Muslims dress in flowing white or caftans of different styles, colors, and materials. For the Christians, there are appropriate dresses that are meant for church services and other events, even when the dress-style is caftan and *agbadas.* Women in particular do cover their heads with scarves, even when ordinarily they may not do so publicly. Men cannot come to church in shots, slippers and rarely on sandals. For women, dresses that partially reveal or expose certain parts of the body, not just private are not decent to be worn publicly.

Before baggies became very popular, African flowing dresses and loose-top shirts were popular. I witnessed the dress styles when I was growing up in the 60s. Dress styles from the caftan to the *dashiki,* embroidered gowns, tunics, and *agbadas* have all been part of African dress culture. Traditional attires from tribes of the Bantus, Madigos, Ibos, Yorubas, and Hausas, even the Maasai, are all floating dresses and are made in beautiful colors.

Cross-cultural influences make Africans appreciate their tradition and cultures. Different African dress styles and cultural attires are gaining worldwide appeal. African-inspired designs have continued to show up on runways in international fashion shows. There is no history of the origin of floating pants and shirts that I know that could be traced to Africa, but many of the designs that inner city and suburban youths wear today have African cultural history, from what I observed growing up in my village. Whether it is a mere coincidence, I cannot explain.

6. Question: I am proud of my African and American heritage, but I am often confronted by conflicts between the two cultures. One is prominent and the other latent, I may say. They occasionally worry me. My parents don't make the situation any easier for me. They are head and toes "Africans" (although we are Americans) and have just recently visited Africa for the first time. How do children of Africans born in the United States deal with this dilemma of culture clash?

Answer:

This is a very important question. I will, as usual, respond by reflecting on my personal experience. What my experience spells may not apply to others, especially other Africans from different backgrounds and cultures. However, most Africans I have talked to have either passed through a similar experience or have known someone who has gone through it.

I never realized what a huge cultural difference there was between the West and African cultures until I settled down in Cleveland. In spite of the many good friends I have made, imagining that I could integrate easily into the society was wishful thinking for me; it never worked as easily as anticipated. However, it is very unfortunate that a person has to do the learning, acclimatization, and assimilation by him or herself. Of course, like any hard road to travel, some stumble and do not get up; others stumble, get up, come up wiser, and even become facilitators in the area of cultural diversity.

Initially, for many, the culture shock may be difficult to deal with, but as the years pass by, they have adapted. Overall, dealing with culture shock is very difficult, especially when one is not prepared or informed on how to deal with it. Experience is always the best teacher, but many have discovered that the philosophy has several setbacks, as far as learning and adaptation to the environment or situation is concerned. Unlike psychological problems, which may require medication or counseling, there is no prescription for a victim of culture shock.

For Africans in particular, our traditional value system, and the conservative views on almost every subject, adds to the problems of integrating and relating African and Western cultures. A person's behavior and public conduct are defined by customs and traditions, with listed punishments for violating these values. On the religious side, both the traditional religion and Christianity have moral norms, which on their own impact on one's accepted behaviors in the society. The combination of these values provides the wide path to what is accepted and what is not accepted or tolerated by the society.

In short, one is entangled by this long web of cultural differences cast around himself or herself when struggling to adapt to Western culture. The battle to release oneself from the mesh either by living one culture or combining the two is a big problem people face when they arrive in the United States or Europe.

Just be aware that both cultures have their very good sides. Blend them and you are on the right track. As the saying goes. "When in Rome, behave like the Romans." For children born to African parents, the interplay and mixture of values from two cultures will affect behaviors. Yet, as many have discovered from their personal experiences, children do overcome the difficulties of exposure to two cultures more easily than adults. Speech problems are the most common problems children face at their early childhood ages.

7. Question: I have an African mask my grandmother gave me. She said it was from the Ivory Coast, and she made me understand that the mask symbolizes "power over evil...that it gives strength to overcome turbulent tides in one's personal life." Are all masks symbolic in Africa?

Answer:

In African traditional religion, some objects such as charms, statuettes, and figurines of different shapes and sizes are items of worship. These are symbols, and they are revered in traditional religious cultures. They also serve different purposes in traditional worshiping.

Carved images of deities and gods existed in the homes and shrines of traditional worshipers while we were growing up.

Christian converts would often discard any symbol of traditional religion. Discarding a statuette, a mask, or other items of traditional religious worship served as a vow to uphold Christianity. It also guaranteed that a convert would not go back to his or her traditional beliefs.

In Africa, where Christianity (there are more than 380 million Christians in the continent) is deeply rooted, in villages in particular, these statuettes are still seen as a symbol of idol worshiping among Christians. Christians are forbidden from having them. They either give them away or destroy them. There are Africans that still follow traditional religion. There are about 92 million ethnic religionists—traditional believers. Statues, masks, and other symbols (representing deities) still remain their symbols of worship.

There are also masks made purposely for decoration. There is a huge difference between masks made as religious symbols and those for decoration. Adults and young children playing "masquerades" and some dancing traditions require wearing masks. Some masquerades are just for entertainment, while others are symbols depicting the faces of ancestors whose spirits are believed to be alive and living among the people. These spirits are respected and celebrated as reminders of their omni presence among the living in the society. And since individuals are not supposed to see the faces of these spirits or any part of their body, they wear special masks.

I do not know whether your mask is just a decorative mask—one that can be purchased at art shops in markets or roadside shops, hotels, and resorts in Africa. From what you described to me, it seems that it is not, but one can always distinguish decorative masks from those placed at the altar of shrines or in a traditional worshiper's home. It depends on where and from whom the mask was bought, or who gave it to your grandmother. In addition, spiritualists, native doctors, and voodoo priests all use different objects, including statuettes and masks, for different purposes in their altars of worship.

RITE OF PASSAGE FOR BOYS AND GIRLS

8. Question: I have heard much about rite of passage initiation ceremonies for African teenage boys and girls. Is "Rite of Passage" an annual event? And what responsibility, if any, does the initiation confer on the celebrants? How does the initiation prepare African youths for adulthood?

Answer:

The traditional, African "rite of passage" marks the transition of teenage boys and girls into adulthood. We all celebrate birthdays—the 18th birthday in most societies being the turning point in a person's life. At this age, we are telling everyone that wants to listen to us that we are prepared to shoulder responsibilities as young adults. First, to ourselves, and then to the society. But in African cultures, where the community comes first, it is that role to the society (and self) that the rite of passage celebrates.

For boys in the rural villages, it entails initiation into social and cultural associations, including adult cults. Rite of passage transcends tribes, cultures, and religions. In African societies where religion (be it traditional or Christianity) plays a very significant role in shaping attitudes, the rite of passage is celebrated to reflect these values that religions teach—but not refraining from traditional values.

Ceremonies that celebrate rite of passage vary across geographic regions, ethnic groups, and nations. In some societies, enormous rituals are performed, as is the custom and tradition of that ethnic group. Overall, the essence of these ceremonies is one thing: to prepare teenagers for the challenges ahead, and to let them know their responsibilities and obligations as young adults. Summarily expressed, the rite of passage is a celebration where young adults take an oath of allegiance to be responsible citizens of the society.

British Prince William's choice of Africa and the theme, "Out of Africa" for his for his rite of passage ceremony that took him to Kenya when he turned eighteen is a reminder of importance attached to young people and beginning of new phase of life as responsible adults. Rite of passage is an exceptional event in life of teenagers and young adults in cultures where the ceremony is still celebrated. It could be recalled that Prince Harry in first week of March 2004, began a two-month vacation, and camped in mountainous South African kingdom of Lesotho. He lived among teenagers and young adults and in rural villages; he and other teenagers and young adults assisted in the usual busy lives of African young people assisting in constructions of farmhouses, fences, helping the needy and in several community projects.

Young girls use the initiation ceremony to undergo circumcision in some cultures, a practice that has been criticized around the world by human rights activists and women's rights advocates; however, in societies or tribes where female circumcisions are still carried out, they have yet to be convinced of what is wrong with the culture. They believe that it prepares their girls to be in a "form" that is accepted by their traditions and cultures before they move to another phase of life. Marriage is a very important obligation, and these societies don't accept single motherhood or unmarried lifestyles. In these societies, an uncircumcised woman is not accepted as a potential spouse.

In the fattening rooms, the young women spend weeks or months learning domestic duties, such as cooking, mending dresses, cleaning the house, breast-feeding, and mothering roles in general. Teen girls in their primes are housed in secluded hostels, served the best meals, and during the same period pampered and "spoiled" by maidens that provide everything from food to washing their dresses and doing their chores. The girls are expected to perform no other roles during this period, except learning about their roles as mothers and other lessons that will be particularly useful upon completion of the initiation ceremony, where they will face real life challenges.

Christianity's strong hold in 19th and 20th century modern Africa has affected the way most of these traditions are observed and celebrated. In rural societies, the custom still exists in its original form, but Christianity has interceded in many aspects and eliminated the activities in these ceremonies that are reminiscent of ritual or idol worshiping. As alternatives to some of these ceremonies, the church has established social centers where young men and women learn trades—craft making, technical skills, sowing, cooking, and domestic science—including etiquette and mannerisms that would sustain them as adults.

In some villages, the rite of passage ceremonies have ceased to exist in any form due to Christian influence. But as more and more Christians want African cultures integrated into the church, and vice versa, those with strong attachments to African traditions and values are undeterred in their struggles to include traditional ceremonies without suspicion that they are reincarnating "idol worshiping."

KWANZAA AND AFRICA'S INFLUENCE

9. Question: Do Africans observe Kwanzaa? If Africans do, when and in what ways is the festival celebrated?

Answer:

Africans don't celebrate Kwanzaa. However, some Africans do join the 13 million people that observe the holiday in the United States during the week of December 26–January 1st every year. As you may be aware, all the ideas, the recipes, fashions, and home decorating for this important celebration are reminders of our African roots and rich, cultural heritage. Also, the seven principles of Kwanzaa that serve as a guide for daily living—as they relate to family, community, and culture—are continuums of customs from the motherland.

The goal behind the creation of Kwanzaa by Dr. Maulana "Ron" Karenga in 1966 was first a cultural one, which he single-handedly created to enable blacks in the Diaspora (African-Americans) in particular to look back at our African heritage and to pay tribute to the rich, cultural roots of Americans of African ancestry. It is neither a cultural creation nor a religious or political movement.

The main theme of the ceremony, which is cultural reaffirmation and reflection on cultural heritage, is based on values that Africans observe and cherish always. It is based on the seven fundamental principles, which are referred as *Nguzo Saba*. These principles are self-determination, collective work, shared responsibility, economic cooperation, creativity, and faith. And most importantly, the principles that remind us of our purpose here in America and on Earth.

Take the libation aspect of Kwanzaa for example. Every event or occasion, including offering kola nuts to a visitor in Ibo culture, involves pouring libation.

Also, lest we forget, we live in a global village where Africans in the Diaspora have taken motherland cultures and traditions to different parts of the world. Cultural activities on one side of the world are carried over to other corners of the planet, and as such there are people that celebrate Kwanzaa as a part of the global African-American community in Africa. Since there are growing African-American populations in many parts of the motherland and across the world, Kwanzaa has, in recent years, gained international recognition and celebration.

Kwanzaa is not celebrated elsewhere with the same excitement with which it is celebrated in the United States. Nigeria and South Africa have large populations of Africa's Diaspora now living permanently in the motherland. It is not unusual to find families observing and celebrating Kwanzaa during the month that it is celebrated in the United States.

AFRICAN FOODS—MOTHER OF SOUL FOODS

10. Question: What are the common foods Africans eat?

Answer:

African foods come in a variety, as climatic conditions that favor their growth vary from one region to another. Also, ethnic nationalities (some tribes don't eat certain foods), religion, cultures, and traditions determine which foods are available on dinner tables. Climate remains the most important factor, however, determining what particular food crops will be planted and in what period of the year. Certain foods and meat products are forbidden in some tribes.

In most African countries, the old farming method of crop rotation is still practiced. The condition of the soil, depending on weather, also determines which crops are planted at what time of the year and their availability in the local markets.

In my small village, one specific type of food crop—another form of potato known as *Ona*—is forbidden, while in neighboring villages, it is a delicacy. These differences spot and criss-cross cultures, villages, and towns. The lists of foods that people don't touch and eat are not many. Other reasons for some tribes not eating certain food crops may be a result of allergies or food poisoning in the past, which may have scared people away from eating that particular food crop.

Foods come in a variety, such as grains, tubers, stems, and vegetables. Most soul foods found in menus can be traced to the motherland. They include okra, black-eyed peas, sesame seeds, and peanuts. Africans, depending on where you are coming from, have species of plants, grains, and vegetables, most of them grown by subsistence means in small family farms.

Africa's tropical rainforests provide a good environment for plants of different species to grow well. Fu-Fu is prepared from Cassava. It can be prepared into pastry and eaten with soup. Rice, Millet, Sorghum, Yam, and Cassava (Tapioca) are prepared in different ways and consumed in most homes, either cooked or pounded. Stew or soup is the accompanying menu.

Foods abound in forms such as roots, fruits, and vegetables. Tropical foods are mainly rich in carbohydrates. However, foods rich in proteins and fibers are also available. Favorable weather conditions prevail in most regions across the continent, all year round. There are exceptions—the few months of dry seasons. Yet, the season provides time for harvesting certain crops planted during the rainy season.

Tropical weather favors most plants, such as tubers and vegetables. That explains why grains such as maize or corn, rice, beans, and root crops such cassava and cocoa yams are the most common foods produced in the continent. Bananas, papaya, or paw-paw, oranges, breadfruits, and peas are others that grow well in tropical weather conditions.

Africans were traditionally farmers, fishermen, herdsmen, and hunters. The majority of Africans still keep the farming tradition of our forebears. The problem hindering the development of Africa's agricultural sector lies in its dependence on old and traditional methods of clearing the bush, planting, and tendering and harvesting farm products. African farmers also rear cattle, goats, sheep, and chicken. Families rear domestic animals for meat and for their hides and skins. The trapping of animals in the forests in the name of hunting is a hobby and is still very popular in rural villages. Pigs are not popular in some African tribes, since religion and customs forbid touching or eating pork. However, people rear pigs where customs and cultures do not abhor eating pork meat.

Chickens, goats, and "bush meat" remain the main sources of meat. Goats are reared in almost every home in the village. They stay in their pens and are rarely allowed to roam about in the compound.

Africa has no spring, winter, or fall. Year-round good weather conditions produce a good harvest of vegetables, roots, and cash crops. Before the discovery and exploration of gold, diamonds, and petroleum, the economies of most African countries were sustained by trading on agricultural products. Presently, even with the low pricing of African products in the international market, resulting in a very unfavorable balance of trade, African countries still remain one of the world's largest producers of yams, palm oil, coconuts, cocoa yams, cassava, bananas, peanuts, cocoa seeds, coffee, and tea.

EBONICS AND AFRICAN ORIGIN

11. Question: During the controversial Ebonics debate on whether Oakland California Public Schools should allow the use of Ebonics by inner city youths as acceptable "English" in classrooms, the public learned that the language originated from West Africa. Do Africans speak Ebonics?

Answer:

West Africans don't speak Ebonics. As a person from the region, I first heard the word Ebonics during this debate. Africans speak different native languages. West Africans speak English, French, and Portuguese as second languages. These languages are spoken in about fifteen countries that make up the West African region. In English speaking countries in the region, "Queen's English" is spoken with a mix of African accents.

In other countries in Eastern Africa that speak English, Kenya for example, no one speaks Ebonics; however, some West Africans speak "Pidgin" or "Broken English" in addition to both correct English and native languages. People that have not attended any formal training or engaged in any learning process in the use of proper English found it very convenient to use Pidgin English to communicate with others who don't speak native languages. Therefore, broken English became a "language," which these people use to communicate with the rest of the English-speaking public.

Broken English has limited use, and merchants, traders, and day laborers speak it predominantly. But educated people still have to learn to speak the language to be able to communicate with them. It is a mixture of more than one language because of native slang and vocabularies introduced into the language when natives speak it. But English remains the intended language of communication. Advocates that claim that Ebonics has an African origin are wrong. Without being drawn into the controversy, I am certain that the speech pattern of people that speak any language has something to do with their heritage—call it their roots. I doubt if the accent of our forebears that migrated to the Americas 400 years ago is still present in any of the new generation African-Americans.

While Ebonics was coined in 1973 in the United States, "Broken" or "Pidgin English" existed in West Africa long ago. It does not, in any shape or form, resemble Ebonics—either in structure or in syntax.

Because Pidgin English has an unofficial, common use in daily communication with various segments of people, their vocabularies continue to expand. Broken language has also gained critical reviews in linguistic and language classes in colleges and universities. It has attracted scholarly reviews among African academia. But as far as the space between Pidgin or Broken English and its usage and applications are concerned, it is limited only to communication outside homes, schools, and any formal situation where proper English language is not strictly a requirement. Parents and teachers restrain their children, pupils, or students from using Pidgin English formerly, even when they are speaking to friends in an informal environment. It is perceived as a language that has limited usage, and it is not universally accepted since it would not take the speaker anywhere, other than the confines of the narrow space where the language is used.

RAP MUSIC AND AFRICAN ORIGIN

12. Question: As an African who was born into the diverse cultures and traditions of the continent, is it true that rap music originated from Africa?

Answer:

Not quite true. But growing up I heard the beats and rhythms of traditional singers and entertainers that modern rap seems to have emulated. The beats were played at social events or at funerals. Speaking from experience, I can tell you that the rhythms of songs that I listened to traditional entertainers play were not different at all from the voices and rhythms I hear today in the form of rap music. But I have told people in several forums that in every aspect of life in Africa—social, religious, and even political—songs, music, and dancing are integral parts of the people's culture.

We should not lose sight of the fact that the cultures of African people moved with Africans that left the motherland for America and have since stayed alive and well in black cultures across the world, not just in the United States. It is therefore no wonder that cultures of the people of West Africa still have influence in the lives of people of all races. These influences are reflected in music, dancing, aerobics, fashion, and religion. The same could be said of the lifestyles of Haitians, Caribbeans, Jamaicans, Afro-Cubans, and Afro-Brazilians. Popular Latin and Cuban music has African roots, and the mixes have produced some of the best music produced by stars with African roots.

Hip-hop, Jazz, and R&B all have traces of their origin in Africa. Rap, in the style and form in which it is rendered in Africa, usually tells stories about life, revolutions, disasters, and predictions—and equally entertains. A rap musician in the context of African music is a storyteller. There are no foul languages, no loud voices, no gyrations depicting sexual innuendoes and moral laxity. Rap in my culture falls into the category of rappers that have proven that the music genre is a form of art and does not have to depict the stereotypes often associated with the music.

"Afro Beat," made popular by the renowned musician Fela Anikulapo Kuti, is another genre of music from Africa gaining global recognition and fans. Afro Beat is a mixture of jazz, funk, and African high life. Fela's music speaks against social injustices and corruption in the society.

AFRICAN NAMES AND CULTURAL SIGNIFICANCE

13. Question: I am *Bobo* **and my son's name is** *Taku.* **My parents told me that our names are African. I learned that names are not just given to a child for identity purposes—that they are always meaningful. How significant are names in African cultures?**

Answer:

Every African name has a meaning. Africans do not give names just for the sake of identification. Most names, especially Christian and Muslim names, always reference God. Even with Christian names, most Africans bearing baptism names have their names after apostles and angels of God. In my tribe, people have not just one name but at least three names. The day the child was born in the native calendar, which has four days; the traditional name given during the customary naming of the child; and the religious name, assuming he is a Christian. These names notwithstanding, grandparents on either or both sides could equally give a child different names from the ones other people, including his or her parent, have given the child. However, what matters most is the name given by the parents, be it a traditional name or a Christian name. Parents do occasionally give the names given by the grandparents.

Names always relate to the positive experiences of the child's parents or the circumstances of birth. They may be memorable experiences of the family, what the family expects the future to hold for their child, or most importantly, the child could be named after heroes and role models. In the part of Africa that I came from, native names are referenced mostly to God. The reference of names to God indicates spirituality and the recognition that nothing is possible without God.

All names reflect good qualities and virtues. It is forbidden to name a child after something ugly or something bad. No parent would want to do that.

In Gambia, among the Mandingos (just as you could find in other cultures), it is the custom for a father to name the first son after himself and a daughter after her mother.

WILLS AND INHERITANCE

14. Question: Is it true that the first male child, or sons, inherits the parents' property in Africa?

Answer:

African cultures ensure that no individual is denied rights of inheritance as willed by a deceased parent or relative. There is always an executor to wills. In most instances, the senior brother of the deceased or relatives that the person trusted and empowered to execute the will, will do so.

Cultures vary depending on whether social groups are centered on the mother or father's side. In other words, there are always differences in the ways customs spell out who gets what.

In patriarchal societies, the first male child inherits the father's property, along with his siblings, in the order of seniority, but most importantly, according to the way or order that the deceased person has enlisted the beneficiaries of his or her wealth—including property. It also depends on the amount of wealth that was left behind. But all debts must be paid before any property left over is given out.

In some tribal cultures, it is not just the first son that inherits the father's property; the rest of the children do have shares of the inheritance. In male-dominated cultures, the women mostly share their mother's property, and the last male son inherits the mother's property, where she resides at the time of her death.

In Ibo culture, the first son inherits his father's house while other male siblings also get their own share of property—most of the time, land and other tangible assets. In the same tribe, first daughters inherit the mother's jewelry and other substantial items, excluding land (which I earlier disclosed is willed to the last son in the family). Females in the family also inherit property, depending on how much wealth is left behind.

Africa is not a monolithic society, so there are variances on how different tribes establishes who and then how much a beneficiary is entitled to receive. It all depends on traditions and cultures and how they define these obligations. In tribes such as the Ashanti tribe of Ghana, where lineage is traced through the mother's side, inheritance flows along that same pattern of ownership rights. The right to inherit the father's property rests on the grandson of the first daughter, not the first son of the man.

In patriarchal societies, there were instances where a grandson, especially a father without a male son, has inherited his grandfather's property. At times, it entails the son re-locating with his family to the village where the mother was born.

In polygamous families, for instance, and depending on the will of the father, the responsible first son gets a bigger share of his father's property. Others share the property among the children of wives according to order of seniority. Wives in polygamous relationships may re-marry, but most prefer to stay in their husband's place. Under that circumstance, the first son carries the responsibility of keeping his deceased father's house intact, including the position of the wives in the family and what roles they play.

15. Question: I've heard about Africans' deep spirituality and the influence Nature has on everyday life. What makes this deep spirituality bloom? Do African traditional religious backgrounds, the people's cultures, and traditions have anything to do with it?

Answer:

I tell this to my questioners, especially those that have not traveled to Africa. You will be amazed by the different pictures of Africa you come home with after visiting or living in the continent—impressions different from the negative images on the television we are used to seeing of distressed nations and ghettos of poor people.

If there is one spot in Africa where there is war or violence, there are ten other countries or more where there are laws and order, and people are living normal lives. Even in countries where we are repeatedly shown footage of child soldiers fighting with AK-47 rifles, there is life for people going on in countrysides and villages where the war has not touched. I tell people that Africa is a very large continent, and the impression we get of a continent always at war with itself is wrong. Most African wars are internal insurrections, but what stories and their props suggest is a continent embroiled in wars.

A Western journalist traveled and returned from Sierra Leone. Even after the war that ravaged the country, he was overwhelmed by what he'd witnessed—the high spirit of people to come together and work harmoniously towards rebuilding their nation. What he observed is no doubt the true spirit of Africans, irrespective of situations that rear their ugly heads, while an outside observer watching the conflict unfold (real or on television) may think that the situation is irreparable.

In 2004, Nigeria was rated as the most religious country in the world by British (international) survey groups. With over 90 percent of people going to church and praying more than twice every day, there is no question that any visitor to Africa would see the same pattern of faith in other parts of the continent. The deep spirituality of Africans sustains the people from being extinct from wars and diseases that confront the people when they least expected these situations. That same spirit saw the people survive the worst dictators that ruled and ruined the people, shattering dreams and economies. That same spirit is seeing the continent through this turning point in Africa's history with HIV/AIDS infections and deaths.

African enthusiasts attribute the attitude to the strong tradition and deep, religious faith that emboldens Africans to deal with the reality of these problems. Some claim it has advantages and disadvantages, since it may have the effect of minimizing the problem, thus preventing the person needing help from ruthlessly attacking the problem whenever it repeats or learning from the ugly experience to avoid it repeating.

In the case of an African infected with disease, relying on his or her spirituality alone as a panacea for problems, observers claim, is very risky. For instance, a patient with a serious medical problem may not be able to go to a doctor because the person assumes that his or her praying and fasting will cure or heal him or her. The consequences are deaths in the thousands. There is no doubt that combining high spirituality with adequate, routine medical care is more beneficial for good health than an over reliance on spirituality alone. Overall, Africans' deep spirituality runs through every tribe, ethnic subgroup, and nationality.

Traditional rituals still reflect in prayers when Africans communicate with God, even among Christians. For example, kola nut is a sacred fruit, a stimulant, but it is traditionally used to toast and welcome a guest. Traditional recitations mixed with Christian prayers are said before the breaking of the kola nut.

Beliefs vary; however, traditional African religion believes that ancestors live among the people as spirits, and that the Supreme Being communicates through the spirits of ancestors to the living. Just as ancestors watch and protect the land, they also play the role of guiding and protecting the village from dangers, diseases, and disasters.

Africa's spirituality makes Africans see hard times as awakening moments to hold strong to their faith, unity, and affirmation. Faith in particular plays a big role in the lives of the poor and the rich alike.

AFRICA'S RAINFOREST – HOME TO HERBS, SHRUBS, AND MEDICINES

16. Question: The Africa I see on TV is endowed with rain-forests and a huge landmass of unpolluted landscape. Jungles, as we know them, are homes to millions of plant species and wildlife in Africa. I also learned that most medicines are derived from herbs, most of which are found in the tropical rainforests of Africa. How involved are African governments in develop-ing alternative medicines to meet the health care needs of the people, especially the poor, dying from diseases as a result of inadequate supplies of modern medicines?

Answer:

For good or bad, we have scrutinized the idea that modern medicine provides all remedies to every health problem and it has been debunked. A look at the shelves across the United States and the world will tell how herbal medicine has advanced in spite of the bad rap it has received from groups on the other side of the aisle. It is not only herbal medicines but also acupuncture, yoga, and other forms of traditional healing that have become accepted and adopted into modern health care.

All too well, Africans know from ancient times that tradi-tional medicine provided a panacea for most ailments, but not in all cases. Overall, the benefits from herbal medicines, irrespective of critics, cannot be underestimated.

The location of major global pharmaceutical and drug man-ufacturing companies in African countries (and the huge amount of medicine they spin out from their factories) does not impact the number of Africans that still depend on traditional medicines as a cure for ailments such as headache, arthritis, fever, and cold. But these companies have their markets for consumers that rely on noth-ing other than modern medical care—and can afford the cost.

The long trials and "reliability" that traditional or herbal medicine has provided to patients that patronized herbalists could be traced back to centuries of use by generations of Africans. These patients passed this patronage to their children. There are also new generations of Africans that have resorted to traditional medicines because of cost, since their income is not enough and there are no government subsidies to alleviate the financial burden of meeting these costs. Traditional medicine has, therefore, become the most popular source of medical care for the majority poor and large populations of the middle-class.

There is no question that herbal medicines should be regulated. Meanwhile, it is an indispensable part of Africa's health care. Therefore, running away, or denying these realities, is only worsening Africa's health problems.

In fact, leadership mistrust and a lack of motivation of the people to probe into herbs and roots may be responsible for the neglect that this area of medicine has faced over these years. Opponents contesting the reliability of traditional medicine have vehemently opposed the introduction of the practice, and herbs into the health care system. They have, on every score, won without providing any alternative to the high cost of modern medicine that is far from the reach of the poor and the middle-class.

A look at the shelves of herbal medical shops in the United States and Europe will tell you how far industrialized nations have explored what some of Africa's leaders have long mistrusted, feared, and neglected. In fact, herbalists in Africa have made claims to finding cures for serious infections and diseases like HIV/AIDS, and yet the government finds it very discomforting to accept the need to investigate these claims. It was not until recently that the government opened its eyes to the reality that investigating and incorporating the group into its medical policy could benefit the poor in the long run. It is a common culture in Africa to dismiss the claims of herbalists regarding medical cures including ailments that modern medicines have yet to come out with drugs to combat them.

There are evidences of collaborative efforts between herbal and modern medical practitioners to see how they can harness resources to find cheaper and genuine medicines for the cure of diseases in Africa. Governments and health agencies in Africa have shown great interest in bringing relief and a reduction of deaths from

HIV/AIDS by combining both the orthodox and modern methods in fighting the epidemic.

AFRICA'S FUMING MOUNTAINS

17. Question: Rarely do I hear the news of climatic disasters in Africa. What major weather problems does Africa have? Does snow fall in Africa?

Answer:

Snow rarely falls in Africa, except at the peak of Mount Kilimanjaro, Tanzania. It stands at a height of 19,340 ft (5,892 meters) above sea level and has snowcaps on the tip of the mountain. Unfortunately, the snowcap has melted about 4 meters from its previous measurement, a problem that experts claim is related to global warming.

In South Africa, it was news in 1999 when snow fell in the country. The unusual weather conditions add to the controversy regarding whether weather changes are really the effects of global warming or a "make belief theory," as some dissenting opinions have suggested. But it is not just in Africa that these weather-related changes are occurring; they are also occurring in other parts of the world.

In Nigeria, located directly above the equator, temperatures reach extremes that were never experienced before. Heavy rainfall causes gullies and overflowing riverbanks, eroding beaches and flooding offices and homes.

There are notable active volcanoes in Cameroon Mountain, which erupted in 1999; Nyiragongo and Nyamuragira in the Congo erupted in 1994 and 2000 respectively; Doinyo Lengai, in 1996; Fogo, in 1995; Cape Verde Island, Karthala, Comoros, in 1991; Lake Nyos, Cameroon, in 1986; and Erta-Ale, Ethiopia, in 1995.

With a landmass of over 30 million square miles, covering rainforest, Mediterranean, grasslands, and deserts, African nations have different weather conditions. However, known seasons on the West Coast of the continent are rainy and dry.

Seasons are not divided into four seasons—fall, winter, spring, and summer—as in the West. Africa's rainforest supports the growth of trees and dense forests. In the Northern region is the savanna and Sahara desert, the largest desert in the world, stretching over 3,000 miles; and the Kalahari desert covers over nine countries.

Dust storms, as witnessed during the Iraq and Coalition war in the Middle East, occur in the Sahara desert. Desert storms could be felt as far as Texas and Cuba. The Savanna is a smooth plain, flat land over 600 miles in the continent. Tall grasses, shorter trees, and shrubs are part of this vegetation.

African climates support cold weather in some parts of the continent at some periods of the year. That explains why some parts of Kenya, South Africa, and Jos, in Nigeria, with seasonal, mild and cold weather (close to spring in the Western hemisphere), are attractive vacation spots for residents and tourists alike that love mild, cold weather.

Earthquakes are rare occurrences in Africa, but there have been reported incidents of earth tremors lately in East Africa and North Africa in Algeria, just like the one that occurred in May 2003, almost two decades after the last one happened. In 2004, an earthquake occurred in Morocco, claiming more than 500 lives.

Heavy rain causes major havoc and natural disasters like erosion, mudslides, landslides, flooding, and typhoons in Africa. Ocean drifts, especially the overflow of tidal waves on the shores of the Atlantic Ocean, continue to cause huge loses in property along coastlines, where most commercial cities are situated.

Mozambique flooding is a typical example of the havoc many cities located by the sea and close to ocean beaches will face in the 21st century. Lagos Bar Beach, washed by tides from the Atlantic Ocean, has repeatedly experienced overflow of its banks into the commercial capital city of Lagos.

Another danger of imminent consequence on African seas and waterways is the growth of a water plant called the water hyacinth. In the past decade, it has spread so widely that it was affecting Africa's trans-Atlantic shipping and transportation. However, recent African and international collaborative efforts and initiatives to get rid of these water plants from African waterways are signs that the problem may be overcome. Meanwhile, it remains a major setback to sea and ocean navigation and transportation.

18. Question: How close is the African continent to Europe?

Answer:

Africa, from the Straight of Gibraltar, is about eight miles from Europe. From the city of Tangier in Morocco, it is about 100 meters to the city of Spain.

You may recall that in July 2002, a handful of Moroccan soldiers almost clashed with Spanish forces when they later mounted the Moroccan flag on the Island of Gibraltar. That shows how close Europe and Africa are from that point on the map.

It took international mediation for soldiers from both sides to leave the island on the agreement that none of the neighboring European and African nations lay claim to it.

DEATH, TRADITION, AND CULTURE

19. Question: When an African dies, what are traditional funeral rites? How do Africans bury tribal heroes, ordinary people, and "outcasts" or a bad person? Does traditional religion believe in life after death?

Answer:

Death in African religions and traditional belief systems is a transition to another life. In other words, death is understood to mean a continuity of life in another spiritual level. Africans of traditional beliefs believe strongly that a good person would always join the spirit of the ancestors in "enjoying" eternal rest, peace, and happiness. In reincarnation, such a person will assume the personality of any person he or she wishes and will come back to any family that favors him or her.

In reflection of this culture, African funerals are elaborate. In cultures where religion makes such funerals brief, there is the strong belief that the soul is gone to rest, and the body must be laid to rest as soon as the spirit is gone. The loss of a person is mourned and accorded all the traditional burial rites befitting the person's status and the individual's achievements while alive.

A morally bankrupt person, lawbreaker, or a criminal is expected to live a life of despair when he dies. Committing suicide, killing, and abortion are abominations. A person that commits suicide is not accorded any funeral rites; rather, he is treated as an outcast. There is no funeral for a person killed for stealing or robbery. A person who dies from any act that the society considers a taboo is said to have died a "shameful death."

It used to be custom that villagers who died this way were either thrown into "evil forests" or buried hurriedly, without any traditional funeral rites—maybe in the middle of the night. The custom is symbolic because the society frowns at evil, and throwing a person that commits suicide into an "evil forest" served as a message to others that taboos must not be violated. Christianity has changed these customs, and they are no longer practiced.

Christianity and Islam are two important religions in the continent. They perform different burial rites for the dead. In some tribal cultures, a person is buried the same day he died. In other tribes, "befitting burial," another word for an elaborate and expensive burial, is a proof to the society of how well the person lived before he or she passed on. Costly traditional rites, vigils, singing, and dancing with long processions mark these ceremonies. Critics have called for moderate and less expensive funerals, since some claim that families "waste" money on funeral rites and ceremonies. Some critics also affirm that money spent on "celebration of death" would be better spent when the person was alive.

There are situations when living relatives, after these expenses, go bankrupt, leaving the family in debt for several years to come. Critics of expensive funerals claim that they serve egoistic purposes, because some people have abused the traditional ceremony, turning the events into unnecessary avenues for a flamboyant display of wealth. Present economic downturns notwithstanding, there are people that spend all their life savings to perform these expensive funeral rites. For the middle-class and the poor, big funeral ceremonies are expensive and unaffordable. Insurance never covers funeral ceremonies (except for the very few with life insurance or accident insurance, which is a drop of water in an ocean). The family offsets all costs.

Africans are very spiritual people, and spirituality is most pronounced by the ways people live and attend religious events. Christianity notwithstanding, traditional values still prevail. They shape people's lives irrespective of failures and other influences.

The loss of a person is seen as a transition to heaven or hell. Traditional African religion emphasizes the worship of one supreme God. The small gods or deities are messengers to the bigger God or "Almighty God." Religious beliefs accommodate the worship of local deities and reference to ancestral spirits who are regarded as the souls of the dead in the community and believed to be omni present. They are believed to be actively involved in the fortune or misfortune that daily life brings to the village and community. Not every soul that has a spirit is believed to be reincarnated. Individuals who have not lived up to the moral standards of traditional beliefs when they were alive are believed to be in hell, and their souls cannot re-incarnate.

However, no matter the type of burial rites accorded to a person, there is always a church service for Christians, prayers for Muslims, libations, and long rituals for traditional worshipers. Some traditional funerals last four days, while others may last a week or two, with ceremonies stretching at times into months after the death of a person.

It is perceived as a bad omen for parents to witness the death of a son or daughter. Christianity dismisses this superstition as un-true.

TATTOOS, TRIBAL MARKS, AND OTHER BODY

PIERCINGS

20. Question: What tribe wears marks on the face and parts of the body? Of what significance, if any, are tribal marks or tattoos in traditional African societies?

Answer:

Few people are tattooed in the village. But dying is more common cultural and artistic expressions. Tattoos are not just for decorating the body, but tribal marks are traditional symbols that serve various purposes. The significance varies from one culture to another, as well as with tribes. Tribal marks are tribal identity. They also signify a person initiated into a social or warrior class. In other tribes, they do signify a person of repute—maybe an outstanding member of the village who has excelled in feats such as war, sports, and other competitions. It was a "badge" of achievement that distinguished the people wearing them from the rest of the villagers. Tattoos are known in some tribal cultures to depict symbols of religion, social group membership, art forms, and the drawings of folklore characters, mostly animals and birds.

Dyes are common ingredients applied to decorate the body. Special events and occasions demand the use of special dyes; some dyes are rubbed all over the body, in particular, the face, hands, and the legs. Most dyes are washable; others stay until they are scrubbed away with special herbal ingredients.

Cascading lines or strings of tribal marks on the forehead, cheek, and chin are no longer performed in tribes such as the Ibos and Yorubas in the West and Southeastern Nigeria, but there are tribes that still exist in Africa where tribal markings are used. The Mandika and Mandingo tribes are among several people of Africa that wear tattoos and tribal marks in various shapes and sizes.

The stripes, or the "thickness and narrowness" of these tribal marks, equally tell their own stories. Some are wide, others narrow. Tribal marks may be single, tiny strokes on the sides of the lips or a line on the cheek or chin. It may cover the whole face. The part of the body and the size of the tribal marks may distinguish a super man from the rest of the men in the village. For instance, facial marks that run from the forehead in a tiny string of patterns down to the chin distinguish a titled man or a warrior from the rest of the population. Women are exempted from this painful process of tattooing or wearing facial marks.

A man initiated into a special class for his achievements may have different strokes of tribal marks. Some patterns cover the whole face in a very long, painful incision exercise. It tests the endurance and stamina of the person. Being able to withstand the pain from these cuts is the sign of a warrior, and warriors are respected and admired as heroes in traditional societies.

"Hold down the progress of your neighbor, and you are indirectly endangering yourself, your family, and the entire village."– Ibo proverb

21. Question: What tribes wear necklaces, bangles, and have their body parts pierced? It seems that images we see on television about these tribal people clearly indicate that they are living in isolated hamlets. How is it that we don't see ordinary Africans like you and others mingling with them? Does it mean that these tribes are disconnected from the general population?

Answer:

Women (in particular) wearing jewelry are part of African culture that is as old as the continent.

It dates back to early man's tools-making skills and his ability to carve, cut, mold, bend, and twist metals into various shapes and sizes. We are of course very familiar with the images of the Maasai tribe and their beautiful cultural trademarks, assorted sizes, and colors of necklaces, bracelets, and bangles. The Maasai represent one of the few tribes whose culture is still intact, even as it is constantly threatened by external influences.

In my village in Southeastern Nigeria, growing up I witnessed titled women wearing beautiful earrings, necklaces, and arm bangles made of silver, gold, and ivory. Gold necklaces and ivory bangles were decorative ornaments of choice, and they were very expensive luxury items. Local goldsmiths, even during the time when I was growing up, abound in market street shops. Most women make their jewelry from these goldsmiths. I also witnessed women wearing heavy ivory bangles on their ankles. Women who wore these ivory bangles were highly respected members of the society.

Body piercing is not common except in some rural tribes such as the Maasai in Kenya, where it is part of their culture. Even at that, these tribes are battling the "invasion" of the outside world and struggling to keep their culture alive.

Images of tribal people that are repeatedly shown on network television, cable, and satellite television broadcasts with expanded ears or mouths depict rare, remote villages, most times isolated from the majority of the people. The difficulty experienced by most Africans in connecting with these remote tribes could be attributed to distance and logistics.

Africa is a huge continent; villages located far from the general population are fewer when you compare and contrast with the many that live close to one another. The other reason why isolated tribes don't connect well with the rest of the African tribes is because the tribes are "self-sufficient." The first contacts these tribes often have with the outside world are with government officials, journalists, missionaries, tourists, and oil exploration teams.

It is often a problem when we want these tribes to change overnight and look like the rest of us. By doing so, we are unknowingly violating their old traditions and cultures. Already, human activities—such as mining and deforestation as a result of felled trees for various purposes, exploration for oil and gas, and tourism—are endangering tribal virgin lands and people who would prefer to keep their environment and cultures intact.

22. Question: Do you speak Swahili? I was thinking that all Africans speak Swahili.

Answer:

Africa has the largest number of languages spoken by any group of people in any continent in the world. There are more than 1,500 major languages, an indication that more than two-thirds of the languages spoken in the world are in Africa. From South Africa to East Africa and West Africa, different languages are spoken. Swahili is the original language of Tanzanians, and is spoken in twelve other African countries.

Kenyans speaks Swahili, Arabic, and other native languages. Like Nigeria, English is Kenya's lingua franca, just as French is in Cote d'Ivoire and Senegal. Arabic is spoken in Egypt, Morocco, Algeria, some parts of Sudan, and Portuguese in Equatorial Guinea.

In Somalia for example, there is Somali, a Cushitic language by the Somali race. Northern African countries, such as Egypt, Algeria, and Tunisia speak Arabic, among other native languages.

Arabs live in Egypt and a large part of North Africa. However, Arabs have dispersed over the years across the continent. They have also assimilated into these Sub-Saharan African countries and adopted the native languages and cultures of their host countries. Today, most African countries, in particular Liberia, Kenya, Congo, Sierra Leone, Ghana, South Africa, and Nigeria, host a large Arab population.

The Hamites, the Hottentots, and the Bantus can all be found in the continent. Swahili (like any other African language that is spoken by a large population of African tribes) is also the language of the Bantu people living in the Zanzibar of South Africa. The language is similarly a lingua franca in some parts of East Africa, just as Hausa and Yoruba languages are spoken in many West Africa countries, with English as the lingua franca.

In Northern Africa, Arabic is the dominant language spoken. The Arabs and Berbers in Morocco speak Arabic and Berbers dialect, while French and Spanish are other languages spoken in North Africa. In Egypt, they speak Arabic, Greek, Hebrew, and Berbers.

Africa's linguists and scholars have been brainstorming to fashion a common language that every African could speak and understand. Call it Africa's lingua franca. This dream has yet to materialize.

PART II

IT TAKES A VILLAGE

IT TAKES A VILLAGE

23. Question: The African proverb, "It Takes a Village," was overshadowed by commercial and political campaigns when a book with that title was launched in 1996. From your African perspective, could you explain the significance of this African proverb? How do the values expressed by the proverb impact on African societies?

Answer:

The proverb explains what communal life is about in a typical African village. It illustrates the shared responsibilities of raising a child in an African village. In an African village, a child does not literarily belong to just the father and mother. The child belongs to the community, and it is the responsibility of the community to raise a responsible adult. Just as tending to a tree starts early, raising a responsible adult starts from childhood.

In Africa, neighbors know one another for generations. Children grow up in close-knit families where there are brothers, sisters, uncles, grandparents, and neighbors living together—who by the dictates of society's value system are participants in guiding and ensuring that children are brought up well. It does not also have to take the father or mother of a child to tell the child straying or doing wrong to be on the right course. In fact, "It takes a village" to steer a child going astray. Of course, in every society, a child growing up has various routes—good, bad, and some ugly paths to follow. You do not have to know a child to correct a child and tell him that what he or she is doing wrong.

One of the tenets of African cultures is the belief system that emphasizes spirituality, good name, conservative family values, and virtues. The emphasis is always on good morals and ethical values. They are priceless.

The community dictates what is right. Every individual is made to conform to tribal values handed over by generations of ancestors and promoted by elders in the village. It is the duty of every person in the community, and for the common good of the society, to uphold these values. Every individual in the village therefore avoids acts that would not only tarnish the family's name but also the village's reputation. Images that stigmatize are avoided, including those that give flesh to the stereotypes that clans and tribes hold against each other.

A village life is better lived than described. The beautiful memories still linger in adults, especially those of us that have traveled across different cultures around the world. Children know their roles and elders ensure that everybody plays his or her part in the family as well as the community.

The burden of keeping the society morally and ethically responsible rests on every shoulder in the village. Children know their roles, and parents in the family and elders in the village ensure that everybody plays his or her part, not just to the family, but also to the community. Village shares the success and failure of a child, because the village begins with the child and family. It takes both the child, adults as well as everybody that lives in the village to make it work. None could function well without the other. In villages and communities, families strive hard, even amidst deprivation or subsistence living, to guard and protect their good names. Since society is comprised of the people in a community, the actions of a member reflect on the family and the community.

Traditionally, villages have norms—codes of conduct derived from evolving customs and passed on from one generation to another. Every family tries to live according to these tenets. These tenets are not spelled out in stone tablets or mounted on the rotundas of the public arena or village square; however, they are prescribed in simple forms, mostly orally, in small bits and pieces.

It is the belief in some tribes that violation of a taboo casts evil spells on a family or the village that lives with the family. Christianity has changed the way people accept some beliefs and customs. However, to an average traditional believer, the values of traditional religion are the foundation of values preached by Christianity—except in most instances the enforcement of punishments. Therefore, most Christians still hold strongly to traditional beliefs and values, even as the church preaches against mixing the two.

Almost like an extension of the same ethics and moral values that spell the evil from good, stealing, adultery, fornication, disrespect for elders, lying, conversion of neighbors' property, greed, and deceit are village taboos fiercely observed till now. Violators take serious punishment. They may face a traditional court of justice, as well as the state justice. Social ostracism and fines are some of the punishments. Depending on the severity of the offence, a perpetrator may be, voluntarily or by mandate of the community, forced into exile as a punishment and also to clear the village's name. The law does not provide full proof against violations. However, it is rare for any person to commit a crime or violate the law without heavy and severe consequences.

In Africa today, the exercise of law and order, including enforcement, lies with the traditional courts, but with constitutional provisions for civil or criminal courts to weigh in on matters outside the jurisdiction of the customary courts. The law is far from being the final arbiter on matters involving customs, traditions, and cultures. A perpetrator of crime must face the villagers and serve the punishment stipulated by custom for violating the village "taboos." Critics call it double jeopardy, but villagers don't think so.

Age groups, elders, and social organization are vigilantes by creations of traditions and cultures. They police the community not by wearing uniforms or carrying swagger sticks or concealed weapons (guns) but by acting as "Neighborhood Watch" groups and reporting any suspicious person or activities in the village to elders and authorities.

"It takes a village" for a disobedient child or straying adult to be realigned to the cultural norms and values for the common good of the society. The task is not just for the parents, or the authorities, because none could do the job perfectly in isolation of the other. It takes the community. It takes the village. That is the village concept of African life, and it has survived tremendous threats from other cultures and influences. It is a real life experience, as well as a proverb.

"Pushing a son or daughter into the dungeon is an abominable crime, but if the action is the outcome of the unanimous

decision of the villagers, the gods will ignore it rather than be angry." – Ibo proverb

IT TAKES A VILLAGE AND MORE

24. Question: I have heard that generations of Africans of the same lineage still live in the same compound and answer to the same last name. Does this mean that Africans inherit large acres of land to accommodate all of these generations of extended family in one compound? What happens when the family grows too large for one family compound?

Answer:

Yes, it is true that generations of African families still live together in the same place or close to each other in a family compound. Close–knitted family structure, part of African culture, is responsible for this style of living, but it is not without setbacks.

Families do rarely move or re-locate from the main compound or village where the person is born. When the family tree has grown many branches; so large that it could not be accommodated in one compound, most families have reserved pieces of land, which they may be using for other purposes, such as farming, or maybe it is fallow. When there is such pressure, it becomes compulsory that some members of the family must leave the compound to migrate to the family land elsewhere. But these lands are, most of the time, located in the same vicinity as the old compound. They may only be a distance of a few kilometers.

Today's modern Africa and its changing environment have influenced and changed the old family system of the same family living together in one compound. The search for jobs and migration patterns has changed. People are not always aware that Africans migrate from village to cities for different reasons, some of which include affiliation with other family members, and the increasing shortage or lack of availability of land because of inequitable distribution of land. However, irrespective of the reason for families leaving the big compound, people do not forget or abandon their family compounds where they were born in the village.

Land in Africa is a property rarely leased or sold in the village. It is like that gift that grandpa gives to a grandson, and he wakes up often to look at it and appreciate the gift. Land or inherited property is an indispensable asset. That explains why hundred of thousand acres of land across villages in the continent are fallow and not properly or effectively put into any use. It also explains why people live in clustered villages, towns, or cities. It is a culture that has remained with people for centuries and has become very difficult to change by legislation. In fact, politicians know what to do, but none dare do it. Every one of them seems to shy away from acquiring village lands or privatizing land property in the villages. Yes, in the towns and cities where government has the authority to do so, it is possible that they could acquire lands in exchange for citing projects in the village.

African families living together also enable others to keep in touch and maintain records about everybody and every important historical fact in the village. Africans, of course, have for centuries depended on oral historians in keeping and passing on history to new generations. There were few known written records of Africa's past. So, knowing family members even when they have grown and dispersed to towns and cities is very important. These members of the family coming back to the village once in while, especially during seasonal celebrations, like the traditional festival time or Christmas, help in keeping these records convenient.

Apart from maintaining family records for historical purposes, it is a taboo in most African cultures (including my Ibo tribe) to marry one's relative—even a distance cousin or niece. A family knowing their family tree, their history, keeps relatives close to each other and prevents such marriages from taking place. In short, Africans living in the same compound reduces the chances of marrying family members, especially as family trees grow and expand. That is why, in case a relative migrates to another country for instance, the elders usually use the family's oral history and family tree to trace the missing link.

It is also true that families answer to the same last name, to second or third generations, depending on the choice of the people involved. First generation Africans, in some tribes answer to the same last name. Depending on the circumstance, or personal choice, a family member may decide to opt out of answering to the same family name; however, this is a rare occurrence. Such a person often must choose the name of either a grandparent or his parent's name.

Family names are important in African customs and tradition. They are like social security cards, without the cardboard. They are not adopted without genuine, convincing reasons. Hardly are names discarded, too, just for any reason.

Close-knit African families create support systems that ease the demands of life generally and most pressures as a result of stress and depression. The demands of life in Africa are generally not as complicated as they are in Western cultures. The family support system (and it is customary) makes life less difficult in terms of one person carrying the burden on his or her shoulders alone. The same support translates into taking care of the elderly. In Africa, it is the duty of the parents to financially care for his or her children, and when they are aging, it automatically switches around for the children to take care of their parents. The social net that families living together provide cannot be measured in terms of dollars and cents. It remains a valuable and intangible asset to Africans. Succinctly put, children are social security for the elderly in Africa.

25. Question: How does an African spend his or her leisure time?

Answer:

In the wave of global competition and fluttering economies, the struggle for families to keep food on the table, especially the middle-class, has taken deep cuts into the lifestyles people live. But no matter the circumstance, Africans share the tradition of community life. It starts with a person's appreciation of immediate family and their interpersonal relationships with friends and neighbors. Also, a deep belief in the powers above helps in drawing people very close to God and energizes the deep spirituality inherent in most people. Do these values play into people's daily lives, leisure time, and happiness? Of course they do.

Recognition of a family as an important asset to African life entails going out with family to visit neighbors or relatives living in another village or town; it entails attending various traditional ceremonies and social activities. As I explained before, every aspect of African life is celebrated with music, songs, and dancing accompanied with drumming and other traditional musical instruments. There is hardly any village activity where these elements do not come into play. It is as entertaining as going to any opera or a Broadway show. There are also musicians, some of them of international repute, who fill stadiums with their fans. Africans love to be entertained, and they go all out to ensure that there is no hold up in that aspect of the people's lives. Of course, there are wresting matches, games, masquerading, and sports—including field and track. Soccer, the most important game in the whole wild world, has a large following in Africa.

Daily life activities revolve around schedules, some tight and controlled, others not. When it comes to spirituality, the devotion to religion occupies the life of an average African. In essence, Africans spend their leisure times visiting people, participating in meetings and religious activities, and celebrating at festivals.

Many Africans share similar traditions—they are very hospitable and friendly people. A neighbor can walk into a neighbor's house without a prior call. A visitor can come from a long distance without notice and may decide to stay overnight or as long as it is convenient to both parties before returning back to base.

Dancing and singing are inculcated into every social and religious activity, including fellowship and worship, and Africans have several festivals and events that attract people from far and near villages and towns. They are forums for interactions and socialization, especially between individuals, families, or groups of people that have not been seen for a long time.

During annual events, most of which revolve around traditional festivals—such as fishing festivals, the new yam festival, traditional wedding ceremonies, the coronation of a chief, homecoming during holidays such as Christmas, school graduations, masquerading and naming ceremonies, burial ceremonies, and church activities like bazaars and church building projects— people travel long distances to neighboring villages and towns to celebrate. These events are scheduled at different times of the year, and every community has its own calendar for when they celebrate these festivals and events.

The impact of these lifestyles has been recorded in the recent worldwide survey titled "World Values Survey" and published by a United Kingdom's magazine, *New Scientist.* Its research found out that, "Nigerians are the happiest in the world." Of more than 65 countries that participated in the survey, Nigeria scored the highest of all categories measured by values that make people happy. The rating by the magazine placed countries in a percentage score based on many variables, and it showed Nigeria with the highest percentage of happy people, followed by Mexico, Venezuela, El Salvador, and Puerto Rico, while Russia and Romania have the fewest. Any immigrant, tourist, or visitor that has been to Africa—not just Nigeria—will agree that the survey results reflects reality of life on the ground in Africa, It also supports other studies that have shown that material wealth does not make people happy.

But the study also disclosed that what makes people happy may vary from one nation to another, with self-expression and personal success being seen as most important in the United States, while in Japan, fulfilling expectations to family and society is a value most appreciated, just as it is in Africa.

26. Question: What is daily life like in an African village? What is the aspiration of an African teenager growing up in the village? Images I have seen here in the U.S. on television do suggest (if I am wrong, please correct me) that many African children and teenagers are victims of war and disease, and the majority are conscripted by warlords to fight African wars. What can I learn from you about African teenagers and their growing up in Africa?

Answer:

There is the misconception about Africa that I have been dealing with from the first chapter of this book—and that is that war affecting one part of the continent or region affects the whole continent. Yes, to some extent, but not to the level that abruptly stops economic activities or people from pursuing their goals and ambitions. Fighting does concentrate on capital cities, but this does not give the impression that people are not affected by wars.

What I am saying is that life in places where there are no wars or disasters is peaceful. For a working class family, daily activities start very early in the morning—as early as the first cockcrow. Since comfort technology provided to people in more developed countries are limited to those that can afford the luxury, the majority of Africans perform most activities by manual labor. That means rising early in the morning to do most things, including household tasks.

For an average school child in elementary or high school, life in the village is far different from city life. At the village, schools are located within miles to the residence of a pupil or student. In essence, children go to schools near their homes, except by the choice of parents to send their children or wards to particular schools. Therefore, distance is not an important consideration. But as I disclosed, most children walk to school. There are schools with buses, but their usage are restricted to official matters such as transporting students to games or intercollegiate events. Students can live in the hostels or apartments near the school, or they can come from their parents' homes if they chose to do so.

Elementary education is free and compulsory in most African countries. In countries like Nigeria, schooling is mandatory . . . at least up to junior high school. It is also compulsory that every middle and high school student live in the dormitory, but the rules are changing.

When students reside at the boarding house, they are expected to abide by the school's regulations including codes of conduct. No student is allowed to leave the dormitory without permission. Holidays and visiting days fall on the first Saturday or the last Saturday of every month. Whether students live in the dormitory or at home, life is generally regulated. At home and school, students' activities are monitored and controlled by parents or by the school's authority.

Living in an African village is a treasured life experience—especially after a person has lived in cities for a while and reflects back to village lifestyle. For children and adults alike, the closeness to nature and the serenity of life generally are priceless. There are no traffic holdups (except in cities where traffic jams are horrible); there is not much noise from automobiles and no significant pollution. You can watch the shooting stars and birds flying in the open, blue skies. African rain comes at times without warning, and its mesmerizing, sleepy effect on people new to a tropical environment is a wonderful experience.

The close-knit family and other outlets are available to reduce stress. In terms of social gatherings, there is always one event or the other in which youths and adults in various groups and age grades can participate.

Village life is very interesting except that some of the basic amenities, such as good running water, roads, and electricity, are not 24 hours and 7 days in a week guaranteed. Homes have national or regional electricity grids with step-down transformers and connections to homes, but rarely do people have electricity regularly. Just as water pipes exist, but taps rarely run. In villages, these amenities are absolutely not reliable, if they are available. However, there are countries such as Nigeria, Ghana, and South Africa, among others, with rural electricity, water, and road projects primarily mapped out to benefit rural populations. Similarly in these countries, telephone services have equally received a huge boost in the last five to ten years. Wireless phones (for example, the satellite Global Mobile System) now connect villages, towns, and cities to the outside world. Villagers are having the taste of city life for those that can afford the luxury in Africa—things that are a necessity in the developed world. Things others in the U.S. and Western Europe take for granted. Any tourist to any African country will tell you that the serenity of "Nature-Watching" or being part of nature is one aspect of African life that is priceless. It is enriching and spiritually awakening.

STRONG FAMILY TIES

27. Question: What makes large African families living in the same compound possible? And what are the common problems associated with families living together on the same property?

Answer:

Previous questioners have asked almost similar questions, and my answers have addressed some of these issues. However, permit me to go further. As usual, I will answer from my experiences. I assume that using the closest example I have will always provide answers that you and other readers could relate to in understanding the positive and sometimes the negative side of African cultures.

The African traditional value system places children above other things in life. Since life is communal, the strength of the community rests on the strength of the family. An Ibo proverb says that, *"Nwa ka ego."* Children are priceless. In tribes such as the Ibos, the number of responsible children a family has, and is able to provide for, is admired. Africans by nature and culture love children. Like mother hens, they try to gather all together. But like mother hens that let grown chicks go at a certain time, African cultures enable grown birds to stay close to mother hens for a long time. That is why in almost every African culture, adult children (unlike their counterparts in Western culture that move out of family homes early) do live very close to their parents' home, even when they have their own homes or rented apartments elsewhere.

There are many advantages to families living together on family land. But in spite of the advantages of communal life, there are disadvantages. They include too much dependence on the family's head or a wealthy person in the family to solve every problem.

Individuals have different personalities. Too much closeness brings about sibling rivalries. No matter how one tries to manage these individual differences, there are always personality clashes and individual egos stumbling on each other. There are also moments of jealousy. There are cases of neighbors spying on one another—neighbors not minding their own business. Some of them do lead to conflicts when not handled well.

There are other forms of rivalries, including unnecessary and unwarranted competitions that often brew and lead to suspicions, hate, and crimes.

Capitalism, which is spreading globally, is encouraging extreme competition for scarce resources. Life is responding to environmental influences. These influences are readjusting and reshaping behaviors and values; taking a form once unimaginable in Africa. I am talking of the new generation's lifestyle of "cash is king." Life is defined by cash and carry. It has brought with it sometimes unnecessary competition, not just to contribute to national development but for neighbors to boost selfish egos. Some bad people have carried the attitude further by outwitting and outsmarting others through crook and unfair means to get rich quick.

"The ability to overlook certain things is the key to peaceful and harmonious coexistence." – Ibo proverb

LIFE AS AN AFRICAN TEENAGER

28. Question: At what age does an African adolescent leave home? That is, stop living with parents and become independent. How does the society prepare young people for the challenges ahead as responsible adults?

Answer:

Elders would always say that a "Strong tree is known immediately it shoots out its stem from the soil." In essence, a strong adult is known from childhood. Therefore, the society emphasizes counseling and coaching teenagers early through strong parenting and the engagement of teenagers very early in their lives in community tasks and activities that reinforce strong and responsible behaviors.

Responsible parenting is vital to bringing up strong, responsible adults for the family and the society in general. African societies recognize that there are roles mothers play better than fathers when it comes to raising up a child. Just as there are particular roles fathers play in the family better than mothers in bringing up a strong family. It takes both parents in African cultures to raise a strong family, and with uncles, nieces, grandparents, and neighbors in the same role of raising the child; it does not just take the father and mother but the whole village.

In the absence of a biological father in a family (which may be as a result of bereavement), there are father figures such as uncles, nephews, and grandparents on both sides, and of course neighbors, that ensure that a strong male child is raised for the good of the person and the society.

For the man, since he is really going to face lots of challenges, the closer the father is to a male child, the better. Teenage boys in particular need a role model, especially a father or a person he should look up to as a father figure.

Responsibility is important, and programs are designed to inculcate these behaviors as early as possible in a child. Some of them include participation in social activities, such as social and cultural groups like boy scouts, dancing groups, singing groups, and boys and girls clubs. Teenagers are groomed to live a life that is beneficial to themselves and the community.

There is no particular age that a teenager is absolutely free from parental guidance and counseling. As an adult, having a family of your own does not exempt parents from their roles as counselors. In essence, the culture spells that even with one's own family, a son or daughter must be respectful to parents and take their good advice as the truth. It is a taboo in some cultures for the first male child to live outside the main compound of his parents' house no matter how wealthy or independent he may be.

Overall, it all depends on what age a teenager leaves home to be "independent." But as I have explained earlier, most high schools operate boarding houses. Students in any grade that can afford the cost of boarding reside in boarding houses and others than cannot afford the cost go to school from their parents' homes. However, it is compulsory that students getting close to high school graduation must reside in the boarding house.

On completion of high school, with admission to college, life begins for the student as "an independent person." Parents or guardians still pay the bills, including school fees and boarding fees. This goes on until probably the young adult finds a footing in life; maybe a good job, trade, or business, or rents an apartment. These roles were, up till this time, performed by parents.

When a person is capable of taking a wife and taking care of a family without any financial support from his or her parents, that is partially when, in my culture, a person is regarded as independent. But, being able to marry, stay long in the relationship, and being fully involved in the daily lives of your children are some cultural values that prove that a man in particular is mature and independent.

29. Question: How do role models evolve in Africa? Are they the creation of the media or the society? Are they self-appointed or nominated by the media? Put it this way—what makes an African role model?

Answer:

Good character, exemplary lifestyle, devotion to alleviating human suffering, and most importantly helping others in need are some of the characteristics of a role model.

Former President Nelson Mandela is a classical example of Africa's role model. Other virtues such as honesty, simplicity, and devotion to causes that will promote love, peace, and human rights are some other qualities of a role model already witnessed in icon, former President Mandela.

The path to Mandela's success has not been a day's journey. Therefore, along the path to this success story, there are footprints he has left behind, and these are everlasting impressions that touch everybody—including parents that want young adolescents to observe and emulate him. Don't forget that African societies are close-knit, and the deed of a role model is always transparent for others to see and emulate, without the fanfare of television idolization.

There are many unsung heroes in African villages and towns, and they can be found across every tribe. Since everybody lives close to each other in the village, identifying role models is not difficult. Because there are sufficient evidences of good deeds that benefit the society, role models do not need the eyes of the camera, or to stand and speak on a pulpit, in order for them to be heard or identified. Their works speak louder than their words. Since every individual is different, there are some that are loud and want to be seen and heard. Majority, however are very simple philanthropists and very silent in their deeds in fulfilling the needs of the poor in the society. People always know that their charity is self-serving and not egoistic. They are real role models.

In spite of wars, diseases, and the hype of disasters, Africa has been blessed with many positive role models in all spheres of human endeavor—in politics, in commerce, and in industry. In rural villages, say for example in Ibo land, there are many role models for academic achievements. There are businessmen and entrepreneurs who, with no formal education, have overcome poverty on their own personal resourcefulness, and through their transparent efforts, they have built business empires. Their companies have performed financially well, and they employ many people. There are also educated corporate leaders, too, who have become role models by what they have achieved in the corporate world.

In villages where everybody comes together almost once or twice (or more depending on many situations) every year, young ones coming in contact with these role models do not need any protocol. They do not need appointments to visit him or her in the house—especially in the village. Some role models do see people almost every day of the week, especially young ones that want to be counseled by these role models.

In fact, in Africa, role models are not personalities and celebrities seen on television. In a society where television hardly operates twelve hours a day, seven days a week, and many households have television just as a necessity for news and information, role models are the people who you feel and touch and, in most cases, see everyday. They are individuals who have touched lives where they have lived and beyond. Their positive influences have been seen, and their good deeds have touched many lives. Television never crowns or robes any role model in Africa. Role models come to television because they have a message for the people, and when it is necessary, they use the medium to get it across.

Just as it takes a village to raise a child, it takes the same village to crown role models. Television cannot make or anoint a role model, rather the medium offers an opportunity for the role model to reach and touch more people.

A village starts with the family. The family is the first role model to a child. A family is a unique part of the village, and the village is a part of a community, and the community, an integral part of a larger society. An irresponsible child is a disgrace to his family because he is like a report card that the public sees first to evaluate how well parents have abided and enforced village-prescribed traditional values. In essence, a child not raised well is blamed on the family first, before the village takes its own blame, too. In Africa, where good name is valued and respected, no parents want a bad report card through the actions and behaviors of an irresponsible child in a family.

African families are close-knitted and life in general very communal. Families live close to each other in compounds, with uncles, aunts, nieces, parents, and grand parents for generations, everybody living very close to each other. Therefore any act of disgrace brings shame not just to the family, but also to the extended family and the community. For instance, stealing, robbery, killing are taboos. The news that any member of the community violated any of these offences or other taboos hits home hard. The disgrace violation of taboo brings spreads like a toxic gas inflicting its poison not just on the perpetrator, but also on the entire village. A child that does not live according to the morals and ethical standards set by the society may be seen as a child from an unstable and dysfunctional family. In creating a balance to fix what may be wrong, the village has various social activities that train and mold behaviors.

There are adults in every social organization, age group, and age grade that act as guides, and counselors, while a child passes through the rigors of behavior reinforcement. The process is not just a day's lesson but routinely followed coaching and counseling that last from childhood till the person becomes an adult. Now as an adult, the person is expected to belong to an age-grade where, in return, they may teach the lesson they leaned to others coming after them. The social organization he or she belongs to is expected to inculcate more responsibilities. Activities carried out by these age groups include emergency assistance, helping the elderly, road construction and rehabilitations, volunteer services, such as the reconstruction of a leaking roof, and construction of new homes for needy villagers. They also act in times of call to duty as vigilantes in the village.

Elders are seen as role models. They are the custodians of knowledge and therefore wise. Their wisdom is respected, and they have proven that they can be trusted. Their honest living, simple life, and achievements have granted them the powers of leadership. They are perceived as forthright and cannot mislead.

The rich and the poor do live as neighbors in the village. There is no Hollywood in African villages. The rich may build an expensive home with a walled compound next to the poor, but that does not make the poor living next to him flee or force the rich out of his property. Family land cannot easily be taken or given away. Once a neighbor, always neighbors, till kingdom come—unless one party decides to re-locate for reasons I have given before.

In spite of the disparity between the rich and the poor, traditional values drive behaviors. In fact, when a person is in a leadership position, there are more expectations from him or her of good behavior. Also, there are more expectations in terms of what the person does for the community and how he lives his life. There is nothing as motivating and empowering to a child or a teenager than to witness an unknown person in the village overcome poverty or other life struggles to become a successful person. Sharing that wealth with the villagers is altogether endearing and creates an everlasting memory for both youths and adults. As it takes a village to raise a child, so too, does it take a role model with very high moral and ethical values (among other assets) to motivate a child—and adults alike.

STATUS SYMBOL AND SUCCESS

30. Question: What are the ultimate status symbols in Africa?

Answer:

Yes, the answer may be money, big homes, a fleet of cars, and titles—including traditional and academic titles that some people want attached to their names. Africans are not materialistic, but there are societies where money is everything. In such societies or tribes, the quest for money has gradually eroded some traditional values such as honesty, spirituality, and philanthropy. Over all, the virtue that good name is priceless still holds strong as the most important value that people cherish and want to pass on to their children and grandchildren. There is rarely any society in Africa where doing "bad" elevates a person's status. Every society cherishes good people with good name, even though in materialistic societies, individuals of suspicious character may be "respected and worshiped" by people around them do so purposely for the sake of their wealth.

However, in spite of all that was said above, religion, customs, and cultures all combine to mold behaviors and determine what is and what is not important in a particular society.

New lifestyles of materialism in some cultures have eroded principles. In this subculture, what mattered to generations before no longer carries the same meaning to younger generations.

Taboos are still taboos, but violators do not get the same censor, or punishment, prescribed by tradition. The melt down is associated with the hybrid of cultures, which new generations are embracing, to the detriment of native cultures and values. However, others see the new attitudes as the end of time.

Irrespective of external influences on traditional value systems, the family still remains the most important part of life, and a strong family is by itself a status symbol. Philanthropy still matters. The number of people a person is able to feed, clothe, and provide shelter for matter. The number of people a person is able to send to school on grants and scholarships count to the society.

To the new generation, cars, land, acquiring titles, and other forms of material wealth are what determine who is and who is not successful. Because the society has shifted the paradigm of measuring wealth and status, some people have vowed to seek material wealth at all costs. The quest for exclusivity—to be counted as one of the rich in the society—has increased dishonesty, crimes, corruption, selfishness, and greed.

Traditional society still regards how well a family is raised as an important status symbol. How well members in a family are contributing to the society is still valued. Villages, like humans, have self-esteem . . . call it an image, especially how it is perceived by other neighboring communities. A son or daughter that contributes or supports efforts to boost the image of the community is respected, and the person enjoys elevated status in the society.

Capitalism (accumulation of wealth and investment) has taken root across previously socialist, communist, and traditionalist societies in Africa. The manifestation of these changes, both positively and negatively (of course), could be seen across Africa in the forms of modern lifestyles. The effects are manifested in terms of class structure, income, and wealth distribution; also in crimes that were previously unheard of in traditionalist societies.

Across the continent, capitalism has adopted new meaning. Capitalism is not new to Africa. What is new is, "Get rich quick at all costs." The mentality is seriously eroding values such as honesty, decency, and truthfulness, which once thrived and was preserved in traditional societies.

The middle-class has been left behind, and a weak economy has eaten deep into the pockets of a once thriving middle-class. Today, in most African countries, the new economic dispensations tend to box all people into two categories: an African is either extremely rich or poor. It is an anathema to Africa's future development, since no economy grows without money in the hands of the middle-class. Their purchasing power is what turns any economy around.

AFRICANS AND LIFESTYLES

31. Question: What impact does Africa's unstable and unpredictable economy have on people and their lifestyles?

Answer:

When we talk about lifestyles, many factors are always considered in defining and determining what lifestyles people have. Such features include an individual's income and how rich the country is; some countries are richer than others in terms of tangible and intangible wealth. Overall, better lifestyles in Africa entail being a businessperson, becoming close to government, or being a politician because a large percent of the wealth lies with the government. Unfortunately, the present democratic system is struggling to address this ugly phenomenon of wealth distribution, but much still needs to be done to get money into the hands of the people—the middle-class in particular. Recent privatization of state owned corporations and parastatals are geared towards what I have just described.

Overall, African societies are class-structured. There is the upper class; the extremely rich (wealthy) in Africa are estimated to be about 10 percent of the population controlling about 30 percent of the wealth in almost every country in the continent. There is the middle-class; they are the class that bears most of the brunt of unstable economies and wars—as long as they last. They have yet to be empowered to take control of their lives; instead, they have been intimidated by policies that infringe on their rights and freedom. They live the culture of watching and complaining, and yet little or nothing in terms of better social services comes to them.

There are a few countries, such as Botswana, Seychelles, and handful of others, where economic prosperity has impacted on the middle-class. Ghana, Nigeria, and South Africa have policies that, when managed, could yield similar results. But to say the least, lifestyles in Africa, except for the rich, are nowhere compared to their counterparts in the U.S., Western Europe, Japan, or even South Korea.

There is finally the "common people." They suffer the most, and they are the ones whose pain and suffering during recycled and re-occurring African crises hit most hard. They are the majority in almost every African nation, except for the few nations with fantastic economies that I have described earlier in the chapter.

The poor in Africa have no government subsidies. There is no welfare, no 401K, and their pains during hard times are often the family's responsibility, even when the policies of government are responsible for most of their problems.

With more than 4,000 ethnic tribes, different languages, religions, and political and social affiliations, it is very difficult to tell what determines the lifestyles of different nationalities and ethnic groups in the continent. For the lifestyles of the rich, life is as usual about luxury—extensive ownership of big homes, large acres of land, assorted automobiles, and money in the bank.

Africans are proud people. Even the poor do not want handouts. What they want are basic social services such as drinkable water, electricity, good roads, and incentives to enable them to have shelter over their heads. They want factories in which to work, no matter how menial the jobs are. They need seed money from lending institutions, banks in particular, to start small businesses—none of which is fully guaranteed in any country in Africa, and they infringe heavily on people's welfare.

Africans, including the poor—that the public is now used to seeing on almost every prime news channel in Western media—have dignity, and they don't want to be portrayed as being given handouts all the time. They want to be taught how to fish rather than the images we have made of them being fed a plate today, even as flies and roaches perched nearby. And they want their self worth intact, even amidst deprivation. The needy want to be counted, recognized, and not isolated.

TEENAGE SEX, DRUGS, ALCOHOL, AND BULLIES

32. Question: Growing up as a teenager, I encountered bullies at schools that I attended. There were also peer pressures. I guessed it might be different in Africa. What impact do these peer pressures have on teenagers and young adults? How do young people in Africa deal with problems such as drugs, smoking cigarettes or marijuana, sex, and other teenage pranks? How does the, "It takes a village" concept fit into the larger equation in abating these problems?

Answer:

There is no doubt that in a global village, young people have almost similar choices and preferences—even when we may think otherwise. I have also realized that teenagers share common problems of life when it comes to the impulse to have sex, smoke, drink alcohol, and abuse substances—including the use of cocaine or marijuana, cannabis, or herbal leaves, depending on the culture.

Of course, programs that countries implement to manage and control these social and health problems may differ. However, comparing what I witnessed living in African countries with Western culture, I could infer (if I am wrong, please correct me) that children born into Western culture, including African Diasporas, are definitely more likely to be exposed to a vulnerable environment that may lead them to have sex, do drugs, and abuse alcohol. Some say this is because of civilization, industrialization, and the powers of the media to influence behaviors—especially since Africa doesn't have the same number of televisions that operate 24 hours and openly disclose subjects such as sex and words regarded as taboos in African cultures, which of course are prohibited in any form of broadcast, advertising, or public display.

Even though human beings are physiologically the same, I observed that Western teenagers mature faster and age later than Africans or people from the developing world. But overall, I also observed that teenagers in Africa or South America feel pain, want

73

to belong and be accepted, and want to be loved. They want to be appreciated and motivated by parents and the society to do more. Of course, young people are more serious than older generations think they are.

It is also true that while others have nothing, some have almost everything in abundance. Some are measured by the size of the material wealth they possess, while others are measured by values other than money and material possessions. But underneath these differences are still the same universal teenage developmental problems that appear across the world.

I have also witnessed problems facing teenagers vary, and most of them are young people who are not equipped or educated enough to deal with the problems confronting them as they face them. And it is worse when there are inconsistencies in what adults say and do. These are the same adults with high expectations for the younger ones. It is, in fact, irony of providence that the young must deal with, along with the problems confronting him or her.

My experiences from traveling around the world show that the problems we have overcome, others elsewhere may be facing now. Just as problems others never imagined existed, we are defining, dealing with, and working very hard to manage.

Overall, our behaviors and attitudes seem to be moderated by our environment. How the society deals with these problems, and controls the attitudes and behaviors associated with them, may be different. It is what distinguishes or makes one society different from another.

In Africa, the family support system is strong and superb. The village concept of being a brother's keeper is routine and part of everyday life and culture. However, as I pointed out, some of the important elements of a traditional value system are gradually eroding.

Teenagers are always under the radar screen of parents and adult relatives alike. It is not just family members that are responsible for a child's upbringing but also the entire community. There are also uncles, nieces, and grandparents from both sides that keep track of children and young adults. It includes monitoring what goes on in their lives from childhood till they reach the age where society considers them as adults. There are also social systems that provide mentoring and monitoring. This does not suggest that these measures guarantee 100 percent success, nor does it promise complete protection against peer pressures to violate orders, rules, and regulations.

African adolescents don't express freedom, as Western culture allows young people do. Sex in Africa is talked about privately but not discussed openly. It is impossible, for instance, to see teenagers of the opposite sex holding hands while walking on the driveway. Kissing of the opposite sex (even husband and wife) must be internalized and expressed only behind the locked doors of the bedroom rather than in public—not even the sitting room. It is a socially incorrect to kiss openly. In short, rarely do I see Africans in my journey across the continent manifest as much of this behavior as I have in the West.

African cultures (and customs) have set roles that every teenager must follow, not just at home but also outside the home. Since life is communal, it is the community that dictates what is right and wrong. It is not the teenager.

At any stage of development, from childhood to adulthood, there are always social events, games, dancing, and nowadays, Christian activities that engage teenagers as they come of age. These activities shape their behaviors, and they also provide distractions so that teenagers and young adults do not stray or engage in devious thoughts. Teenagers, who are not enrolled in schools, pursue other careers. Some may enroll into technical schools and obtain apprenticeship to learn a trade or gain skills. Those not in school assist in the farms or at their parents' shops in the market.

Drugs such as heroin and cocaine are not as available to African teenagers as they are in developed countries. However, marijuana is a problem that I know city schools deal with occasionally. As I mentioned earlier, there are certain things that you don't hear of in African cultures. Some of these drugs fall into that category. It was not until the media exposed the ring of drug smugglers using Nigeria as transient route that it became public knowledge that drugs come close to Nigeria's borders, and people became aware that drugs existed in the country.

Underage drinking is rare, but as emphasized earlier, most teenagers are under the scrutiny of parents or elders in the house, and to some degree, that provides checks and balances. The presence of an elder often discourages young people from drinking alcohol at home. It is, however, very difficult to determine what happens when teenagers are on their own or with their peers. It is a social taboo for an underage teenager to drink. Doing so in the presence of his elders is strange and intolerable. The society frowns against these demeanors.

Underage drinking, smoking, and sex are against traditional values. Most teenage girls and boys that engage in smoking, drinking, and sex do so as a result of peer pressures. As many critics have expressed, the public distribution of condoms is an invitation for teenagers and young adults to engage in sex. Abstinence, they agree, is the only way of avoiding STDs and HIV/AIDS.

One thing unique about African schools is that bullies, and their victims, settle their differences by shoving, yelling, and bad-mouthing. Fist-fighting does rarely occur, but there was never a day in my twelve years in elementary and high school when you learned of a pupil or student drawing a gun on another student or using any instrument to attack fellow students.

African societies recognize parents not only as custodians, but active members of village vigilantes. The traditional value system is strong, and code of conducts strictly adhered, even when it is not perfectly followed. In the village concept, good conduct as well as bad behavior of a child are shared responsibilities.

33. Question: Is it true that children and women (the poor in particular) in Africa are still sold into slavery? I need all the answers (from a third opinion—outside the media and what our government tells us) that will enable me to better understand what is going on in Africa in the 21ˢᵗ century as far as slavery is concerned.

Answer:

Slavery is a global problem. It thrives in many cultures, and based on the reports of non-governmental monitoring agencies, including human rights groups, religious groups, and lay organizations, slavery, including the shipment of human cargoes for use to serve various purposes, still goes on around the world in the 21ˢᵗ century.

Child labor, another form of slavery (even as many disagree), exists particularly in plantation, mining, fisheries, quarrying, domestic service, and the commercial sex trade. It is not just the trafficking of slaves, women, and immigrants—recruitment of child soldiers as well are some of the human rights problems that we are facing around the world.

Also existing in subtle ways in some cultures are stereotypes and the discrimination faced by descendants of former slaves by some tribal communities in Africa, even when such prejudice is outlawed. By this, I mean biases such as not marrying out of the class, not taking some titles, and not participating fully in the political and social process in their communities.

Slavery in Sudan, as accounted by the media, is one of the sources that I know about of what goes on in the country. I have not been to Sudan, but my colleagues, reporters, have. I cannot, therefore, doubt these reports since they are based on eyewitness accounts. But my colleagues, who have been to Sudan and at war fronts, confirmed that captives from almost fifty years of civil war (the Sudan war started in 1955) were sometimes subjected to situations that were in violation of international laws on human rights regarding prisoners of war. They never told of any slavery or the selling and buying of humans as cargo; they told of war captives, including villages that are raided and treated inhumanly. Government soldiers then extort money from relatives and others to free some of the captives of war.

Slavery and the abuse of the rights of civilians and prisoners of war are crimes against humanity. However, one should understand that in protracted wars, such as Sudan has witnessed, many atrocities do occur—adoption, captivity, starvation (hunger as a weapon of war), and all kinds of abuses including "forced labor" or "slavery" do take place.

Eyewitness accounts disclosed that slavery is going on in Sudan, but it is not often highlighted in the media. Some compare atrocities going on in Sudan to ethnic cleansing.

Poverty breeds Africa's worst forms of child labor. Children of the poor become indentured servants in African societies. It is a common practice for poor parents to consent and give away their son or daughter as indentured servants and housemaids. In return, the child would be sent to school or learn a trade. There are no instances that I know of where parents would just "sell" a child to make money. It is a taboo, and in African villages where everybody knows everybody, and villagers are in close contact with each other, the whereabouts of a child is everybody's concern.

Selling a child is very possible, but it would be very difficult to conceal in a close-knit and open society. Of course, it could happen that parents may be told that their child is going to learn a trade, and he ends up in sweatshops or cocoa farms working as a child laborer. It is a possibility. But whether parents are aware that their child is mistreated or subjected to abuses as a slave, as we read in the media, is altogether another matter.

In Africa's servitude culture, poor parents do "invade" the homes of people they have "given out" their child to stay with because the child was denied a chance to visit home when the parents want the child home. A parent learning that their child is being abused is a matter most societies don't take as a joke.

Tanzania is among many African countries already addressing the problem of child labor. The International Labor Organization (ILO) is devising ways to support households whose children are at risk of joining the "worst forms of child labor." Called the Time-

Bound Program, it is framed in line with the ILO's International Program on the Elimination of Child Labor (IPEC), which has been implemented in eleven districts of Tanzania. The goal is to empower parents economically and to curb child labor. No child wants to be employed, and no parent wants to give out his or her child to be enslaved in sweatshops or cocoa plantations.

Primus Chukwuemelia Igboaka

PART III

SOCIETY: SOCIAL ISSUES, LIFE, AND CULTURE

AFRICAN MOTHERS & BIRTH CONTROL

34. Question: I've read about problems that various non-governmental agencies claim are related to Africa's over-population problems. Reports from such organizations as UNESCO, the World Health Organization, IMF, and the World Bank give the impression that the control of Africa's population is as crucial as her economic recovery and well being. Is population control realistically the solution to Africa's economic recovery problems, as some have suggested? However, if you don't mind (as a sideline), is it true that an average African woman has 9–11 children?

Answer:

The 2003 Nigeria Demographic and Health Survey (NDHS) indicated that Nigerian women ranked among the most fertile on Africa. The study sponsored by United States Agency for International Development (USAID) disclosed that an average Nigerian woman will give birth to 6 children before her lifetime. This is in comparison to her Ghanaian counterpart that will have between 4 – 5 children and South African woman an average of 3 children.

I do not know where you received the impression that an average African woman has 9–11 children. It is simply not true. However, in African cultures and religion, children are perceived as a gift from God, and as such, when a woman is blessed to have any, there should be no inhibitions whatsoever that should limit the number of children she and her husband are able to have. African culture still prohibit the use of condom or any form of birth control which the society is still struggling between new and old schools on matters of sexuality and birth control. Even as of today, the only church's recommended or approved birth control, the "Billings' Method" or the "Withdrawal method" of birth control is fraught by controversies between the church and state. Taking abortion pills was construed immoral and in our parents' generation, any attempt to do that brings about retribution from the society.

Recent reports from Africa, Nigeria to be specific, disclose that the preference for more children is high among first-time mothers. The reports said that an average woman with three to four children desires at least one more child, which is the average a Nigerian woman bears in her lifetime. For women with six or more children, they said that they don't want more. Total Fertility Report (TFR), according to the research, is 6.00, which means that an average Nigerian woman has six children. One must also take into consideration the fact that Nigeria is the most populous African nation. With Nigeria being the most populous country, it says much about the rate of birth in other countries, and with a population of between 2 million people and 25 million in those countries, there is no way, statistically, that Africa is overpopulated compared to its landmass, and resources.

The information and misinformation on Africa have often sidetracked many facts and figures, which would better educate people about Africa and her population. Africa's urban areas are what could be described in real sense densely populated, as a result of the migration of people from villages seeking work in the cities. Calculating Africa's land mass (see appendix) and population on inhabited lands shows that Africa is actually underpopulated. Of the top ten countries with less density of people per square mile, Africa counts for more than the top four countries on the list.

Christianity—in particular the Catholic church, with regards to family, abortion, and moral values—prohibits husband and wife from using any method of contraception (pills) to limit the number of children they could have. Most Africans are Christians and with any behavior tied to faith, conservative adherence is required. Christians follow the church values as long as they stretch. Parents never used any family planning methods of contraception, since it was prohibited. And since abortion is regarded as taboo, the result is that a spouse has as many children as possible or as is "destined" by God. That, on its own, has a tremendous influence on the number of children some Africans have.

Today, traditions and cultures still outlaw abortion as a taboo. However, that notwithstanding, more women are resorting to modern and traditional methods of contraception on their own, irre-spective of the church's bearing on the issue.

The love of children and an effective and strong family sup-port system are two of the motivations for a number of children in African families. However, before we allow the thought that Afri-cans always have large family sizes, it should be noted that there are growing numbers of families with one or two children. There are also African families without children, some by choice, even when it surprises others that a husband and wife can live together and do not want children of their own.

As I expressed earlier, many factors are responsible for large African families. There are economic, social, cultural, and personal reasons (such as a family that wants a boy or maybe an only child that wants to have a large family).

Bacteria and viruses once plagued the world (not just Afri-ca). About 40 million people died from Influenza in the 1900s. Dis-eases such as malaria, measles, tuberculosis, and chicken pox spread easily, fast, and killed people from one hamlet to another, spread-ing into other villages and towns. For a very long time, before there were vaccines and cures for these diseases, Africans and millions around the world also died in large numbers from these diseases and infections. Therefore, to reduce the number that may die from these diseases, having many children became a matter of survival, not of choice. In essence, the more children a family has, the lesser the chances that they will all die from diseases and infections.

Farming, fishing, and animal husbandry were the tradition-al occupations of Africans. The mechanical means of clearing the bush, plowing the land, planting, and harvesting needed a very large number of people in the farms. Historically, African economies were agrarian (and still are today). Cultivation and harvesting of the land depended strictly on manual labor, and since slave labor was never used traditionally on the farms, African subsistent farmers depended on human labor and children of their own to provide the necessary manpower to cultivate the land. Therefore, having many children became a necessity. It also served as an advantage to the farmer's interest and in determining the acres of land he could cultivate. In that era, when the number of acres and mouths one fed was a "status symbol," it was respected to have many children. Feeding many mouths at the same time and making money from the sales of his farm products placed the farmer as a role model and a person that must be respected in the community and in neighboring villages.

The other reason for the large number of children in African families may be as a result of culture. Culturally, there is always strength in numbers. A population of strong men that can provide defense in times of war and who can inherit the wealth left by the head of the family when he is gone is a guarantee for security and the continuity of a patriarchal family. Africa's social systems have no retirement programs for the elderly. There are no social security and retirement benefits, except for the working class. Therefore, a large family provides the social safety net necessary for survival and the sustenance of the elderly at late stages of life.

CLASS STRUCTURE AND AFRICAN SOCIETY

35. Question: How is the power structure distributed in African societies?

Answer:

Traditional African societies have powerful kingdoms where the chain of command flows from the people up to the leaders. In other words, the chief or king cannot make a decision without the overwhelming support or approval of the people. Members of the chief's council or the chief's cabinet nominated by the villagers (at times) represent the people. In this traditional setting, communal relations enabled neighbors assisting neighbors to navigate against the various obstacles of life. Also, villagers help one another to meet almost every need, including building wealth through co-operative unions. Some of the co-operatives operate like credit unions but are purposely designed and funded by members to help one another. In these societies, while a leader is respected, he is aware that respect is reciprocal, and the people must approve his position and actions.

Villagers take turns assisting one another, including clearing the farm, planting, and harvesting crops. Villagers also engage in what in Ibo tribe is called *"Isusu"*, where groups of villagers form social groups with the goal of contributing money and helping one another, each person taking his or her turn till the circle is completed; and it starts all over again as long as members agree to the agreement. Any member of the group could withdraw at any time. This, in essence, means providing others with money they could utilize in whatever purpose the individual wants.

The more money people have in their pockets, the more wealth they can build and invest. In traditional societies, the class gap was present, but not like what is currently observed happening in the same village. The extremes of the rich and the poor never existed in traditional society. Rather there was the rich class and many in the middle-class, with few that were in a position that we can describe as poor. As societies lean towards "capitalism" from village experience, instead of closing the gap between the rich and the poor, the middle-class is totally eliminated. So, what we have is the upper-class and the poor.

Africa's pre-colonial political system created leaders that listened to the people and carried out the will of the people. The Ibos of Nigeria practiced leadership by consensus building. Class never played a role in who could make a decision that affected the people. Anarchy was out of the question. The poor were guaranteed that the community would respond when in need.

African empires prospered, from Ghana, Mali, Songhai, and Egypt, and these societies were class-structured. The only good part of the social class was that all lived together in the village regardless of the roles people played or the classes to which they belonged. In African villages, the rich, the poor, and the powerful all lived close to one another in their respective family's land.

The colonization of Africa and its partition among Europeans brought about not just geo-political changes but also class restructuring that separated the ruling class from the masses. Class structure deepened and disintegrated more into the upper-class families, the middle-class, and the poor.

While the Europeans were in Africa, they ensured that new leaders, loyal to their interests, were in power. And the new leaders adopted the same bureaucratic leadership, status quo, and class structures that emphasized hierarchy from top to below in their new administrative set up. It was a system that encouraged caste-like structures, while it distributed power and wealth along the same line it created.

In business, in government, and in civil societies, class structures were remarkably enforced, and Africans occupying these positions were well laid to fit the various levels of authority some of their economic and political decisions made to maintain the class structures. The seriousness of the system was the class structure, which the system created, pitting each group against another for the benefit of the central authority.

36. Question: What are the symbols of success in African tribal villages?

Answer:

There is a generational shift on what measures and symbol-izes success in African societies today. There is no fixed answer to this question, but as usual, my answers are based from experiences that I have acquired from various cultures in the continent. For the older generation, the symbols of status were virtues of honesty, service to the community, and philanthropy. Even though these values are still respected, many of the new generation—young Africans—don't attach the same importance to them as generations before. Call this generation, the African "Baby Boomers." The shift in paradigm is responsible for crimes that were unheard of previously in the village. Also, the tide of capitalism is spreading across the continent fast amid decadence, and the quest for money at all costs are shifting what the present generation values from older generation. It would be wrong to say that money was not important during our parents' time, but there was not as much attachment to money as there is today. Life was once valued from the basis of what an individual could do for the common good of the society; it is now counted on "cash" and how many green notes a person is able to dole out.

One troubling problem with this mentality that "cash is king" is that otherwise good people are motivated to commit crimes and violate taboos just for the sake of making money and becoming rich. For the sake of clarity, this is not a generalized development, since old values are still intact and observed in most African cultures. What I am saying here is particular to just a few tribes, where the type of lifestyle I have descried is becoming a common culture.

African tribes such as the Ibos strive in "capitalism" before the Europeans first touched their feet in that part of Africa and amalgamated the Northern and Southern regions of Nigeria in 1906. However, the neo-capitalism, or new approach to capitalism, has made people recognize wealth as an end, no matter the means that is employed to acquire the wealth. In other words, money rules over society's strong values. In circumstances where the old values of our parents' generation were being tested, money rather than values (morality) has prevailed.

Like a whole basket spoiled by a few bad apples, the transformation of African societies in the name of development in the last decade or two, and the quest for money at all costs, is threatening the fabric of the traditional value system, the stronghold of African tribal cultures. They place little or no value on what matters in traditional systems—the truth and honesty that once reigned supreme. The source of wealth does not matter anymore as long as cash is on the table, even when the source is known and is questionable. That explains the increased rate of scams such as 419 electronic money transfer crimes, and other unusual crimes that were once only read in books but are now transparent in cities in some African countries. Authorities' efforts to stern the spread of the crime may be successful depending on how financially committed the government is to fighting wire fraud and Internet crimes.

In many African tribes, well-groomed and morally upright citizens are, and would always be, in the majority, but when any evil of any society—or related social problems such as armed robbery, ritual killings, and political assassinations—is not addressed, it sets off chain reactions that impede investment and development.

Overall, citizens who have excelled in the careers of their choice are still valued and respected irrespective of elements that may seem to shadow these traditional values. Philanthropy is appreciated and respected. The number of people, including relatives, one mentors or provides for, including financial assistance, counts as a measure of success and status in African societies.

FEMALE CIRCUMCISION

37. Question: I have read and heard so much about female circumcision in Africa. Is circumcision done, as suggested, to reduce female libido or for any other cultural reason that, in the West, we are not aware of?

Answer:

Female circumcision is a global phenomenon practiced in other cultures, such as in Asia, South America, and the Middle East. However, in the last decade or two, Africa in particular has come under serious scrutiny, stopping the practice only in Africa will eliminate it around the world where the practice goes undercover, in very remote villages. This lack of focus elsewhere by feminists, human rights activists, and women advocacy groups has irked African traditionalists that claim that attempts by some groups in the West to single out African culture for automatic change suggest that Africa is a target for other hidden agendas that may be different from the reason given for the campaign. Some Africans disagree.

It is true that anything that has to do with culture is difficult to change. The scrutiny of the old custom by "outsiders," as natives consider these advocates of Africa's culture change, still received resentment from villagers and rural villages where the practice is still going on, and may not be changing soon.

No doubt, the news media has played a major role in this campaign but not with too positive reviews by many in Africa. As a journalist who strongly refuses to take sides on issues other than to inform the public, I believe that there is a complete misinformation and miseducation of the public in regards to female circumcision, now called Female Genital Mutilation (FGM).

For example, the idea that every woman in Africa is circumcised is totally false. The idea that women are dragged to the "Mutilation chambers," where they are strapped down to have crude instruments dipped into their private parts, where the intrusion leaves a wound that never heals, is outrageous.

Established medical facts indicate that there are complications and obstetrical risks witnessed from excised women, especially those that are crudely performed. I belong to the school that believes that, like some old customs (which the majority of people still hold to strongly), the present efforts to stop female circumcision may eventually succeed. But it is still a long way from happening. Apart from some tribal villages where female circumcision occurs, there are other villages where the practice never takes place. In Nigeria, there are cultures where circumcision is observed, but the practice does not appeal to majority of mothers as before.

Just as some cultures and religions abhor male circumcision, so too do some cultures in rural villages stigmatize women who are not circumcised. The attitude I am describing here transcends class, education, and religion.

In the same parts of the world where critics argue that it may be unnecessary to circumcise a man, there are people within the subculture that still have a strong opinion that a man must be circumcised. In both sides, you could find a number of tribes in Africa that don't circumcise men.

The reasons for female circumcision have not been well established; however, critics claim that it serves no purpose other than to limit a woman's sexual pleasure and reduce the libido or high sexual drive. But, there were women that were circumcised, yet had high libidos.

Female circumcision, in many parts of Africa, is seen as a set of values, norms, attitudes, and a symbol that cultures believe (where female circumcision still exists) shape their perception of a woman, her place in that particular society, and what behavior is expected of her. Without her performing the rituals of circumcision, she is perceived as "incomplete" and "unprepared" to perform some roles expected of her as a woman in her society.

The journey has to start somewhere, and it has already begun with reforms. Federal and state laws are being implemented across African countries to "reduce" the practice in some cultures in Africa. In Sudan for example, the government has banned certain forms of female circumcision, but still women engage in them and even hide medical complications (if any) for fear of legal repercussions. There are cases of young women that request (even when their mothers oppose them) to be circumcised because among their peers, it carries a stigma that they are not ready to face.

SOCIETY AND THE STATUS OF WOMEN

38. Question: What is the status of women in Africa?

Answer:

The roles women play in traditional African societies are not limited to those roles that have traditionally been assigned to them. To say that African women are overruled or controlled by men is a stereotype that never holds any ground from the tribe I came from. This may not be true in other societies, but women have been prominent in the society and play roles that men at times stand beside and observe in wonder. From evidences documented by historians testify to the valor of African women soldiers at battlefields. In Dahomey for example, kings and kingdoms were at a point in that country's history guarded and protected by mostly women because women were strong and did a better job in protecting the palace than the men. There are no limits in the roles women play in these societies.

The symbiotic relationships between African men and women are such that none could exist and function well without the other. Behind any claim of success by men in whatever endeavor, there are women who have worked so hard behind the scenes to make the success where men often take all the credit.

In Ibo culture, even when the roles men play (such as providing financially for the family) seem to get all the attention, there is no denying that the roles women play to make that happen do not get the same attention.

In most African cultures, women are involved in all aspects of life—farming, merchandizing, trading, small business ownership, manufacturing, and politics. Women have performed diligently in spite of interferences by men for a very long time. There is no denying that a "male-dominated" world seems to undermine these roles, but the successes women have made in African society are enormous.

In fairness to men and women in Africa, there are responsibilities that men perform well and better than women, just as there are roles women perform better than men. The respect for each other's roles has made African societies (the ones we don't see on the media) very successful. Divorce and suicide rates are very low, and in some cultures, non-existent. Violence and homicide by husband against wife or vice visa is also extremely low.

I traveled to Togo, Cote d'Ivoire, Sierra Leone in 1983 and again in 1990. I witnessed the diverse roles African women play at home and in boosting the economy of their countries. I realized that these roles were not just peculiar to Nigerian women, but were also prominent across these African cultures. In Ghana for example, where there is a matrilineal based social system, a man's wife and children belong to their own matrilineage. The women have somehow "influential powers" in marriages. Though men marry women they love, the culture gives the women the right to exercise the freedom to live in her father's house and visit their husbands, if they choose. But it is woman's obligation to cook for her husband and play other roles, as assigned by the culture to women in that society. The woman can build a house in her father's compound and enjoy all the privileges that the society confers for achievement on men.

When I was in Cote d' Ivoire and Togo, I witnessed the same pattern of hard working women in these West African countries as I observed in Nigeria. I also realized that behind any successful business entity, be it family-owned, entrepreneurial, or corporate business, there is a successful, strong woman either as owner or as adviser. In retail shops, women are at the front counters in small, family-owned businesses, as well as receiving customers and performing account-balancing duties on a daily basis. Overall, the roles women in Africa play in their economies cannot be underestimated. Their influences weigh heavily, openly and privately, on every decision their spouses make.

There were African women that took over the throne as an inheritance. Queen Jinga of Ngola for example, and in 21st century Africa, the installation of Botswana's first female paramount chief, Kgosi Mosadi Seboko following the death of her brother, Chief Kgosi Seboko II. She is not only the queen but also the head of the Botswana House of Chiefs, a well-educated woman, and a single mother of four. There were also African monarchs that ascended the throne by their valor, strength, and leadership qualities. Another example was the vibrant and famous Queen Aminatu of Hausa land.

Growing up in the village and in my culture, I witnessed that some mothers wore long, ivory bangles on their legs. I learned from my grandmother that these were titled women—well-respected women in the society who can carry on duties that in peace and in crisis were ranking in importance as the elders of the village. They were counselors, motivational speakers, organizers, and could mediate in a crisis, especially on women's issues.

The ivory bangles were badges of honor and a symbol of status in Ibo society. Women who wore them were a respected class of women. They had power and influence in African cultures, to say the least. In short, by tradition, some women wearing these rings on their ankles could participate as "jurors" in elderly council meetings. Where they did not, they were informed first of any decision on issues of importance, such as deliberations on village matters, community projects, death announcements, and organizing women for almost every social, political, and health issue that related to the community. They could head or appoint mediation panels to listen to allegations of theft and other misdemeanors in the village.

Women also performed roles as priestesses in traditional religion. They were also musicians in local shrines. In most situations, women performed the roles and duties arising from that of their husbands as chief priests.

The Baales were queens that reigned in the Yoruba land of Western Nigeria. They were known to be very powerful and very strong leaders during their reigns—so powerful that neighboring kingdoms with men on the throne never dared them during their reigns.

The struggle for African independence from the British occupiers was, at some political fronts, fought by strong African women such as Mrs. Ransome Kuti, Mrs. Onyekwulu (Nigeria), and others. There were Makeda, Queen Sheba (Ethiopia), and Ann Zingha (Angola), who won battle after battle in her war against colonialism when her brother was King of Angola. Also not to be forgotten is Winnie Mandela in apartheid South Africa.

AFRICAN MOTHERS AND BREASTFEEDING

39. Question: Mother and Child: Do African mothers breast-feed their babies publicly? I learned that it is culturally compulsory that women feed babies with breast milk rather than artificial milk. At what age do mothers stop breastfeeding their babies?

Answer:

The advantages of breast milk to the well being of a child cannot be overemphasized. Current studies have indicated that breastfeeding is nutritious for the baby and reduces the chances of the mother having breast cancer. In cultural myth, even before scientific proofs, Africans knew that breast milk increased the immunity of a child against infections diseases. Africa's life lessons are at times learned through folklores. There is a belief that children fed with artificial milk or cow milk end up behaving like cows themselves and do not have common sense.

Certain obligations are dictated by traditions, and some of them are very beneficial to the society. Breastfeeding happens to be one of them. In short, it is an "obligatory duty a mother owes to her child" and to the society where it takes a village to raise a child. In fact, the mother is fulfilling an obligation to the society, herself, and to her child. She is also benefiting the community that sees children as an asset that must be protected always, and it starts from the womb.

The age a mother stops her child from breastfeeding depends on the choice of the mother, how long she is able to produce breast milk, and how tolerant the baby is to breast milk. When a baby has an appetite to feed on breast milk, in traditional society, the baby can be breastfed for six months to one year. There are babies fed by their mothers till they are two years old. There is an urban myth that says that breastfeeding reduces the chance of a mother being pregnant, and in tribal societies, that entails extending the breastfeeding, especially where (birth control is a taboo), and such beliefs were held as the truth.

Scenes of mothers breastfeeding their little babies in public places are rare. However, it is not unusual to witness market women breastfeeding in the privacy of their stores. For the working class mother, some private and public companies have a long maternity leave for mothers. Therefore, by the time a mother resumes work, the baby may have grown to be able to accept regulated feeding.

If you could review some of my previous answers about Africa, and the "servitude culture," getting nannies or housemaids to assist in family duties and chores is not as expensive or difficult as it is in Western cultures. Grandmothers living with their daughters for months after delivery are an African culture that is alive and well intact. It reduces the burden from the new mother's shoulders and reduces the emotional problems that may affect breastfeeding. In other scenarios, nursing mothers may resolve to allow the nanny to bring the baby to her work place to feed during break periods. A working mother may choose to drive home during breaks to feed her baby. This is assuming she lives close to her work place. Many offices have flexible regulations when it comes to nursing mothers and the breastfeeding of their newborn babies.

It is an important moral, cultural, and health concern that the traditional value system defines and reinforces. No matter the level of a woman's education, position, or social class, this particular obligation from mother to a child must be fulfilled.

Privately, the majority of mothers do feed their babies in the comfort of their homes. Working mothers have tight schedules, and these roles do affect the duration mothers' breastfeed their babies. More educated women tend to limit the duration they feed their babies. They are more likely to stop breastfeeding earlier than any other group of women.

With global attention focused on women's issues such as mothers and breastfeeding, and the debates over private versus public breastfeeding, African women are not left out in these debates. On the other hand, the controversy over whether women should breastfeed publicly versus whether it should be privately done still goes on. However, the decision and choice of where to breastfeed a baby is in the hands of women. The choice is that of the mothers to make, not the government. And in conservative African societies, the choice of mothers about where to feed their babies is always in the privacy of their homes, or in rare cases, at secluded areas of choice.

AFRICAN ETIQUETTE

40. Question: Is it true that women do all the housework in Africa, while men provide financially for the family?

Answer:

The answer to this is yes and no. In fact, it is defined by tradition that men take care of and play the role of financial providers to the family. But in my travels across the continent, I found no culture where women don't work in the farms, trade in the markets, and work in government offices or the private sector. Therefore, these roles don't work as dictated by customs and tradition.

Africa is not a monolithic society. Therefore, what holds in one place may not hold in others, but there are few tribes (which I have not yet witnessed) where women just sit in the house and take care of the children and cook for her husband and the family.

We should also realize that women, apart from providing the environment for men to work and provide financially to the family, perform both roles of being financial providers as well as home takers, yet these roles are not much talked about or recognized. In essence, there are many societies where women play both roles jointly with their husbands. Some men do realize that taking care of the home, as most women do, is more difficult than it is to make money.

From my travels and experiences of the cultures I have observed and lived within, the roles women play in different societies have been redefined in many ways. In other words, it is wrong to draw a line, or paint a brush, over the roles women play in these societies because they vary. In an era when agriculture was the main sources of income, and men were defined by the acres of land they owed and the food they were able to produce, women toiled days with their men in the farm, yet it seemed as critics express, all the attributes went to the men.

Women hardly stayed at home in the sense of just being a homemaker and not doing anything else. It is rare that you find a woman in Africa that fits that category as has been described of African women. Even in rural African villages, men are exempted from taking care of children, but women perform the role efficiently and still work in the farms. They are the ones that harvest vegetables and fruits and other farm produce and sell it in local markets to make money for the upkeep of the family. They are the ones that will come back from work with the husband and run straight to the kitchen to fix the dinner, and the list goes on and on.

From observing these roles, both from the monetary aspect of the family life and the parenting roles women play, it could be summed up that societies where the men actually leave home early in the morning and return in the evening with cash on the table for their wives are not too common. I say this because women still work and share responsibilities with the men in these societies, even as it may appear on the surface that men leave money on the table for their wives to take care of the family.

African women were known to be better farmers, traders, retailers, middlemen, and wholesalers. A trip to any African local market shows the resilience of African women in retail business. They open the shop in the morning, do customer services, and perform the role of managers and accountants. Women can also mobilize and organize the labor force more effectively on short notice and efficiently, too.

Lifestyles continue to evolve, with women taking the lead even when these roles are not adequately recognized and, in some cultures, not well rewarded. Stereotypes still relegate these roles to the background.

In almost all spheres of human endeavor, including politics, women play significant roles in Africa—often serving as political "mobilizers." Today, more women are elected into political leadership positions than before. Still, hurdles remain to be crossed. In Nigeria for example, in Ibo Tribe and in schools in South Eastern Nigeria, girls (students) far outnumber boys in both elementary, high schools, and colleges.

Africans respect the fine, old tradition that a gentleman should always respect and adore the women in his life—his mother and his wife. When a man respects these two women in his life, it is assumed that the man will respect other women. It is also defined by culture that the man should always protect the wife and family from danger at any time and in every circumstance.

RAPE - A CULTURAL TABOO

41. Question: How big a problem is rape in Africa? Compared to the United States and Europe, do you think there is a correlation between rape and sexual exposures on television, magazines, and in advertising that explore our mentality about sex and sexuality?

Answer:

I am always skeptical when it comes to comparing data. First of all, there is no data from Africa to compare statistics with elsewhere just as there is no "continental data base" on other problems by African governments and their agencies. Secondly, victims of rape in Africa hardly report to the police, and where they do, they don't want to be identified because of the stigma it carries when a woman has been a victim of rape.

Answering your question is very difficult, but what I know is that media images of sex, pornography, and billboards that exhibit almost nude images of models do not exist in Africa. But all I can say is that the probability of rape occurring in these environments as a result of media sexual exposure is low when compared to an environment where these experiences exist.

By tradition, African societies are conservative, private, and "secretive." The fact that it is a very private society makes it even more difficult for victims of rape to come forward because they are scared of the repercussions and stigmatization by the society.

Africa is not like the West when it comes to transparency over matters that are considered private and hidden from public. In essence, people are scared to come forward with problems because the society, rather than sympathize with the victim, would rather isolate, stereotype, and ostracize the victim—including the person's family at times.

To commit rape is to breach a taboo, and like any violator of African taboos, the penalty for a rape crime is huge when the perpetrator is caught. Perpetrators may be forced into exile and jailed Traditional courts in Africa handle crimes or misdemeanors such as rape, divorce, stealing, and burglary. Overall, the powers to prosecute villains are extended to higher courts from the state civil court up to the Supreme Court.

In traditional societies, the first reaction to any incident of rape is for the elders to intervene. Depending on whether the villagers want the case to proceed further (in most cases, they don't because of privacy and to avoid the stigma it carries when a victim is known or goes public), the next arbiter is the traditional court.

There are tribes in rural villages that see rape as a spell that a society must deal with drastically and immediately, or else the crime may bring "bad luck" to the village.

The worst incidents of rape occur during wars. Soldiers in uniform perpetrate rapes as a vengeance against women on the opponent's side. They perceive the rape of women as an expression of intimidation, humiliation, and victory for the defeated. It is not committed in an organized pattern per se, or with the knowledge of the commanders; but rag-tagged soldiers most of the time commit these crimes against women on the enemy side.

Feminists and human rights activists have long been very active in many parts of Africa, making it possible for victims to speak out without losing face or being stigmatized. While a lot remains to be achieved, the campaign has enabled states to impose stricter laws and punishments for offences against women, such as domestic violence, not just rape. It is a wonderful development in African societies where secrecy is the culture. Or families from either the husband's side or from both sides often resolved matters involving domestic violence

Women's groups in countries such as Namibia fought hard to get their country's parliament to take drastic measures against rape. They won their battle when the parliament adopted a motion that imposed incarceration (including a maximum of 45 years imprisonment) for rape.

AFRICA'S HOMELESS

42. Question: How does society treat its homeless people—I mean, victims of society's social and political injustices—the poor that we always see in the news?

Answer:

Poverty breeds the worst type of homelessness. Wars bring about their own homeless people, especially women and children that never imagined in their lives they would be homeless—people displaced from their homes and farms in some of these deadly and recycled wars. The destruction wars bring not only affects the country where the wars originated but also the life, and economies in neighboring states. As we have seen from experiences of protracted wars, the chain reaction economically, politically, and in terms of diseases, too, is enormous. As these wars erupt, the number of refugees they create grows and spreads across from the country at war to neighboring states and beyond.

Refugees that end up living for years in crowded camps stray into neighboring countries where they find themselves in "no-man's" villages and cities. Most times, authorities are not prepared to deal with the refugee situation until they became overwhelmed by the problem. Such reactive approaches, just like most African problems, continue to affect the number of people that would have been accommodated at camps and what they needed during the time these wars are going on. Also, the unpredictability of the political environment does not help matters either.

The disadvantages of refugee problems are numerous, apart from stretching the meager budgets of the governments that host these refugees. There is always the possibility that some refugees may engage in illegal activities out of desperation in places they were quarantined, thus undermining internal security of host nation.

Men and women stricken by poverty are another group of homeless people. Often the option available to most of the men in this category is to make the street their homes.

There are also men and women with untreated psychological and psychiatric problems who end up on the streets. In most of this group, their families or villages may have exhausted their resources, and in societies where mental health problems are left to spiritualists or faith healers, the government does not provide the medical care that these men and women require to function as normal citizens. The reality is that so-called "mad" people in Africa can function well with proper medication. It is unfortunate that in Africa, mental patients are treated worse than HIV/AIDS patients.

Regrettably, there has yet to be any sustained campaign to educate people about tolerance and caring for the mentally disadvantaged in African societies. And Africans have yet to 'advance' to the level of accepting their mentally troubled brothers and sisters as men and women that need medical attention and could be healed; rather, they see them as people that should be forgotten or abandoned.

Mental health awareness in Africa is at a lower level than elsewhere in the world. Yes, there are mental hospitals and institutions, but little attention is given to these institutions, which in the developed world attracts huge government and philanthropic budgets and donations annually.

There are also other groups of Africans that could be classified as "homeless." They are the nomads. Their lifestyle entails moving with their cattle, all year round, from one part of any country or the continent to the other. They move with their cattle looking for pastures to feed their animals. These nomads, at times traveling thousand of miles on their journey, sell their cattle as they move from place to place.

African cultures encourage hospitality. Because family members are in close contact most often and in good relationships, it is often seen as shameful if a family, or an entire village, allows one of their own to roam on the streets or be homeless.

Rural-urban migration and high costs of living in cities have created a new class of homeless people. They are artisans and laborers—people that have migrated to cities looking for jobs but ended up living in shanties or in ghettoes. Some even end up sleeping under bridges and on the streets. It is strictly an urban problem and does not occur in rural villages.

AFRICAN PRIESTS, THE CATHOLIC CHURCH, AND

CELIBACY

43. Question: I'm a Catholic, and I followed Bishop Malingo's controversial marriage (that he later denounced). However, I learned that as the Catholic Church in the United States was struggling with problems of child abuse, the African Catholic Church had problems of married priests and priests who are still in the church but have children of their own.

I could recall that when Bishop Malingo was asked in one of his interviews on the cable television whether he would stay in Europe or return to Africa, he said he would still remain a Catholic priest (even though he was married then) and hoped to finally settle in Africa.

I have not been to Africa, but his statement did suggest that African Catholics accept married priests. Is my observation right? If it is, do they still celebrate mass like their orthodox counterparts in Europe? If not, could you please give me more insight into the matter from an African perspective? Do you have statistics of African priests that have left the priesthood or married in Africa?

(Archbishop Malingo has since denounced the marriage and returned to the Catholic Church. This question was addressed before this development.)

Answer:

Your question is more than triple-barreled. First of all, as I stated earlier in my previous responses to questions about African statistics, there is no data bank that I am aware of that is available on the number of married priests, those that have children while still priests, or those that have left the church. But from the vows of their sacrament of ordinance, "Once a priest of God in Catholic Church, always a priest forever." It is a vow that is permanent, even after the priest may have left the church. But as the situation is in Africa, they cannot celebrate Mass, consecrate the Holy Eucharist, or distribute the communion.

But the irony of Catholic priests that have left the church in Africa, and including what I have witnessed in the United States, is that a large number of former priests do not attend mass service anymore. It is not because they don't want to as my inquiry indicated, but because of the stigma attached to the decision and social ostracism that emanates from their social cultures. African cultures perceive deviant priests as persons to be isolated and not embraced.

The Catholic Church is a powerful, conservative religious institution. It is even more conservative in Africa than elsewhere that I know. African cultures being conservative in shaping behaviors add to the strictness of the church's laws and order. Therefore, when it comes to supporting the Vatican or its doctrine, and abiding by what the church teaches, Africans are strongly behind the church in all its conservative philosophies. The Catholic Church is very universal in terms of its rules and orders, the same as in its doctrine on celibacy. Africa may be the last place on earth to deviate from the church's policies; rules and regulations, even as few members of the clergy prove otherwise.

Bishop Malingo is, no doubt, one of the most respected (African) priests in the world. His popularity and influence in Africa and Europe would have plunged had he married. Secondly, there would be no Catholic Church to host him when he touches feet on African soil. The bishop starting his own church is out of the question because it would be very difficult to attract the following he already enjoyed as clergy of a very popular church in that part of Africa.

Archbishop Malingo's incident came at the wrong time in the Catholic Church's history in Africa. Already the church is facing serious threat from Catholics leaving the church for faith healing churches and coupled with the attraction of Africans to Islam; it was not a situation that the church was ready to deal with at the time.

The Catholic Church scored high in Africa when Malingo denounced his marriage. The church was not prepared to lose one of its own leaders at this time in the history of the church. There are over 360 million Christians in Africa, of which Catholics account for about 123 million. It is not surprising that the Catholic Church has a very strong hold and influence on the life of people in general.

Bishop Emmanuel Malingo has since returned to priesthood and remained a clergy.

WOMEN, PRIESTHOOD, AND CULTURE

44. Question: I was in Africa, and I witnessed that Christian denominations—the Catholic Church in particular—are dug into the controversy of women and whether they should be ordained priests. Do you think that the church's policy on female priests may change with time? What is the position of African churches, not just Catholic and Anglican, on women and priesthood?

Answer:

The subject is a very delicate one in particular, more so for the Catholic Church than it is for the Anglican Church. The African Episcopal Church, a branch of the 77 million worldwide Anglican denominations, has ordained women priests. The ripples it sent, and the controversy the ordination generated in Nigeria for instance (in the 90s), have yet to settle. It was healing before the issue of gay bishops came up. Still, the church is doing a great job in convincing conservatives that it made the right decisions on these delicate and dividing policies.

As events from Africa have repeatedly shown, including the refusal of African clergy to accept the bishop, or people associated with him (for the time being), the division brought about by the last episode of the gay bishop investiture may take longer for the church to heal.

African bishops, especially in Nigeria, with more than 17 million members of the church, the second largest membership in the world after Britain and the home base of the church, were quick to react against the nomination of the first openly gay bishop of the Church in England, which failed, unlike the bid in the United States.

The issue of female priest seems largely unresolved, especially in the Catholic Church where Pope John II has remained steadfast to the dictates of Vatican II. The church has not reversed its position on celibacy and the ordination of female priests. It seems it will not change for a very long time (at least speaking from an African perspective).

The subject of female priests and ordination is not as controversial in Africa as it is in the United States, and for now, the compromise is accepted. Africa's Catholic Church's tie with the Vatican is strong, and Africans never disappoint when it comes to loyalty based on principles that the church upholds, and the religious and ethical morals that it preaches and inculcates into followers through its institutions. Any changes (if any in the future) that may apply to Africa as far as female priests and married priests must come from the Vatican. For now, the Vatican II council rules and regulations of the church have not changed position on these issues.

A look at the traditional African religion long before Christianity came to the shores of the continent; African women played different roles in assisting traditional priests. Women participated in worship ceremonies, offerings, and exorcisms. Their roles also included assisting the chief priests in delivering offerings. They also transported offerings and items of sacrifices made to gods to near and far away "altars" or shrines where they might be needed. In some rural villages in Africa, Africans of traditional beliefs still practice their traditional religion, and women still serve as priestesses and spiritualists.

On the subject of female priests, opinions on the subject still remain divided. Advocates for female priests, who still feel that their voices are not heard, want immediate changes, and to their regrets, no such changes will be coming soon.

CHILD LABOR

45. Question: Child labor is a global problem. Somehow, Africa's child labor seems to be portrayed in the news as the worst case. What motivates a parent or parents to send his or her child to labor camps' bondage? What initiatives are being made to reduce these human tragic problems?

Answer:

The efforts of developing and industrialized nations to fight the problem of poverty have not succeeded for reasons that would be the subject of another book. Some critics have claimed that the world, not just industrialized nations, is not doing enough, but as some have agreed, like fighting terrorism, the same effort should be made to eradicate poverty. Of course, the results of any of these wars take time, and only time would tell whether our determination to eliminate these problems would be successful. But whether we accept or deny it, both wars need the efforts of all, including the poor nations themselves, to succeed.

It is often a wish that the world would be a more secure and peaceful place if we were putting the same zeal and energy into fighting poverty that warlords place into causing or igniting wars. Regrettably, as long as there is inequitable distribution of wealth, and the majority remains in poverty, child labor will not go away.

As long as the wide disparity of income exists (as is witnessed in almost every African county), the poor will continue to be marginalized. Since they are not privileged to gain from the state, and neither are they privileged to programs that alleviate their subsistence living, parents of these poor children see their children hawking items on the street, working long hours in sweatshops, or in coffee and cocoa plantations as a means of their child contributing to the desperate financial need of their families. Unfortunately, children in these types of families are at high risk of joining the "worst forms of child labor" to make that happen.

Child labor will unfortunately continue to exist in Africa and the rest of the world unless the global community, not only African governments, does something to improve the standards of living for the majority of Africa's poor. And it seems from government policies, global trends and statistics, that we are not close in any way to closing the gap between the rich and the poor. When governments continue to frame policies to alleviate the deplorable situation of the poor, it would practically be impossible to reduce or eliminate the practice of child labor by legislation alone.

Most poor African children sell or labor daily amidst economic deprivations and hardship, working endless hours in cocoa or coffee plantations with little or nothing in wages, just to support their families financially. While we condemn child labor, and we should, this reality is what we often don't want to face. It is not a matter of choice and options. This is the mental picture of reality as far as child labor is concerned in some situations in Africa.

When a child toils all day for pennies or nothing, it is an abuse and a crime against the child and humanity. It is a matter of concern to everyone, not just child safety advocates or human rights groups. It is an evil of society that exposes the most vulnerable, the poor, to the environment society has created.

Across the continent, 30 percent of the wealth is controlled by just 10 percent of the population. The poor, the majority, is left to scramble for the crumbs on the "master's" table (the minority rich). With no basic amenities, inadequate health care, and few social services, life is at the mercy of hope, which does not feed a family. What the family provides is therefore what they depend upon for their survival.

Under these pitiable circumstances, it becomes folly therefore for the poor to anticipate that the government would come to their rescue. The alternative is to do what is legitimate and necessary, and that is earning money to survive, even when it entails sending a teenage son or daughter to work in cocoa plantations for a nickel a day to avoid starvation.

AFRICA'S NEW SLAVERY

46. Question: I have traveled several times to some African countries, and I have also lived in many countries in Africa. When I first heard the news about slavery in Africa, I wondered in what part of Africa the slavery being highlighted in the media was taking place—because to be honest with you, I never witnessed or heard people talk about slavery taking place in all the countries in which I have lived. I have lived in Ghana, Nigeria, and Angola. However, I have not been to Sudan, but from what I see and read from the media about slave raids, and the payment of ransom to free some "slaves," I wonder whether these images are real or part of propaganda to bring the issue of what was going on in Sudan at the time to center stage of global politics.

As an African (yourself), do you see any role politics played on the whole publicity about slavery in Africa? I know there are places in Africa where legacies (past) still exists among natives or indigenous Africans that are not much talked about. Please, could you shed more light to these comments, and is my observation right?

Answer:

I am not aware of any slave raids that were staged, but I watched the television documentary on CBS 60 Minutes that you were talking about. There have been media claims and disclaims over whether the pay-off scenarios on the documentary were staged and captured on camera to support the campaign against atrocity that was then going on in war-ravaged Sudan.

However, as I have said in my response earlier, I have not been to Sudan; but reliable sources in that country, including well-respected bishops, priests, and other leaders, have told the world that slavery was going on in Sudan. Since these men and women are credible people, the public believes they were telling the truth. There are also eyewitness accounts from some Sudanese living in the United States, with relatives still in their country that gave credence to the claim that slavery was allegedly going on in Sudan.

Sudan has been embroiled in war for more than fifty years, which is unprecedented in Africa, and under such circumstance anything could happen. It is possible that abuses take place. The world celebrated when the peace agreement was reached between Northern and Southern factions in the prolonged war, but there are doubts as to whether the parties are living up to the terms of the cease-fire agreement. The international community has, for now, been made to understand that the war is over. However, the transparency of the central government will tell the United Nations investigations whether slavery actually took place in Sudan.

As to the second part of your question about slavery and the presence of a caste system, there are parts of Africa where stereotypes, and subtle discrimination exist which trample on the rights of the descendants of former slaves to marry from non-caste families. In Ibo land, any discrimination of the descendants of Africa's house slaves is outlawed and punishable by fine or imprisonment

The caste system in Ibo land was banned by legislative order and put into law in Eastern Nigeria on March 20, 1956. Before the law was introduced, the system fostered an environment where it was very difficult for children from caste families to marry outside their own subgroup.

The caste system does not discriminate regarding employment or the level of education a member of the caste can attain. But the psychological impact for one to know that he is stereotyped or classified into a box (just as racism does) is very discomforting, nauseating, and emotionally traumatic. It remains an ugly chapter in history that is still very difficult to close especially with older than new generation.

TRIBALISM, RACISM, AND HATE CRIMES

47. Question: What patterns do hate crimes and racism take in Africa? On a scale of 1 to 10, how do you rate these social problems when comparing the rate at which these crimes occur in Africa to Europe and the United States in particular?

Answer:

Let me say again that it is practically impossible to measure and compare the statistics regarding these crimes. There is no matrix to measure these phenomena on a comparative basis. African problems are also impossible to compare with other African nations, with the exception of the information and data that we have from the United Nations and other agencies that gather reports internally on each country.

In making a comparison, we often try to relate the experiences of the continent to those elsewhere around the world; we should realize that Africa is not a co-federation, and since every country in Africa is independent, statistics on every problem (when available) are purely, and purposefully, for internal or domestic use. There is, therefore, no data bank on African problems, with the exception of the data provided by the United Nations and its agencies. Even at that, this data, according to some critics, is still questionable.

There is racism in places where there are racial mixtures of blacks and whites and other minorities in such countries as South Africa, Angola, and Zimbabwe. Also, in work places such as Nigeria and Kenya, where local Africans have often expressed disappointment with the manner in which the multi-national companies recruit middle and upper management staff from abroad, neglecting to promote qualified Africans to take over the vacancies. Their complaints were that they have stayed with these companies for too long and have the right experience and training; therefore, they deserved the positions that are being filled with young managers who are headquartered in Europe and the United States. Also, they are worried that these companies are using Africa's domestic natural resources as their main source of revenue and neglecting domestic employees that would invest their wealth locally, which is not good for the local economy.

As a reporter, I found that most of the companies that received these types of complaints from African employees were petroleum and manufacturing companies. Now as a business school graduate myself, I realize that it may, after all, not be racism but a very important aspect of a multi-national company's strategic management policies to match competition from companies on the global market. However, many Africans see such overseas hiring as "racism."

For hate crimes, there are uncountable violent clashes between tribes, some of which lead to the destruction of entire villages and deaths. This is in addition to tribalism, which is rife and alive in almost every country in Africa.

Tribalism is contempt for other tribes. The political marginalization of people not from one's tribe, especially coming from the leader of a country, is the worst scenario of the evils of tribalism in Africa. Many Africans will tell you that tribalism is responsible for the uneven development of villages, towns, and cities across countries in the continent. Tribalism is also the purposeful discrimination of other tribes, keeping them from getting government appointments and employment to key decision making positions.

The belief by one tribe of being superior triggers discord. One tribe stereotyping the other as lazy, foolish, or lacking in morals in most cases translates to bigotry, hatred, and spite of one tribe against the other.

The Ibos of South Eastern Nigeria are called, "The Jews of Africa." Taken on its positive connotation, Ibos are admired for their industry, strength, and hard work. Ibo men in Africa are astute and very ingenious. An average Ibo person is very industrious and resilient, like the Japanese; very creative, like the Israelis; and very prudent, like the Chinese. On the negative side, they are admonished for being too clever, independent, selfish, and money-conscious, or too capitalistic. In essence, these are positive stereotypes that never come with admiration, only jealousy, despair, and contempt.

I tell my questioners that racism, hatred, and tribalism cut across every race and ever social and political boundary, at least from personal experience. They prevail in different forms and shape opinions about us to others and vice versa. They also unconsciously shape political, economic, and social policies, and at times leaders apply the "isms" in decisions they make, even when they are in denial.

It may be difficult to face, but one of Africa's most troubling problems is "religion in politics." Religion in politics is divided across ethnic lines, which makes it difficult to separate the three—religion, politics, and ethnicism. Today, in almost every nook and corner of Africa, the devastating consequences in terms of political instability, religious intolerance, and religious clashes cannot be overemphasized. Most worrisome is the infiltration of "distractors," fundamentalists into the country to fan disunity through religion by whatever means possible. The effect of religion in politics is not just that it distracts governments from pursuing most economic problems; it also wastes resources. The cost to lives cannot be measured in both short and long runs.

Looking at the interplay of these elements in Africa's politics, and the devastating consequences, would make critics appreciate why the clamor for separation of the church and the state is necessary for peace and security, and the key elements in the development of any nation. The irony of African tribalism is that like all negative "isms," politicians fan the flames of bigotry for their own personal gains. They influence or capitalize on these sentiments to gain votes and tribal "support" from their tribal men and women. All these developments are at the detriment of national interests, peace, and tranquility.

The picture of certain wars in Africa could also be described partly as a consequence of balkanized tribal rivalries, often based on tribal and ethnic identities that date back to the eras of colonialism. Politicians play tribalism to keep tribes fighting each other, while the tribe in control of authority at the center maintains power and the status quo. While the people are fighting among themselves, the central government distracts the competing tribes—at least disorganizes the threatening tribes (especially the powerful ones)—from being orderly enough to challenge the government at the center.

When all these influencing factors mix together, coupled with the frustrations brought about by poverty and ignited with fanaticism, the situation becomes chaotic, as we witness in most African conflicts.

The Hutus and Tutsis are the same people and even the same majority Christians, but tribalism was responsible for the mayhem that claimed thousands of lives. The Elendu and Etundu tribes of Congo are the same people, but tribalism led to killings in the mineral-rich villages in the Democratic Republic of Congo. The warring factions of the Warri people in Nigeria are the same villagers, but "hate," not race, causes the same recycling of old problems that often lead to the destruction of property and innocent lives.

In small African villages, unreported tribal (community) clashes do occur. Villagers fighting over the rights to pieces of land inherited from their forebears for no reason. People do resort to violent approaches to solving problems rather than following the usual process of negotiating and resolving the conflict. Some of these conflicts are confusing and baffling—as parties resort to fighting when peace has not even been given a chance. The irony of the whole situation remains that the land that caused the conflict is usually empty, never before used for any human activities.

Of course, the apartheid system in South Africa was the extreme of both tribalism and racism.

However, caste systems in Asia and parts of Africa could be placed on the same pedestal as social injustices that do no good to civilization and economic prosperity. There is tribalism in

Africa, but it takes different faces and shapes; at times happening at the watch of an outsider who assumes all is well, but internally there are implosions that citizens know too well.

PART IV

POLITICS: LEADERSHIP AND DEMOCRACY

AFRICA - THE POLITICS OF GENETICALLY MODIFIED FOOD

48. Question: I was surprised that millions of Africans are dying from draught-caused famine, while tons of U.S. donated grains are being rejected. Why did Africa reject food sent to help the poor and the needy . . . when millions are dying from starvation?

Answer:

I am often disappointed at the way some issues, which impact not just the United States' relationship with Africa but also our relationship with the rest of the world, are played in some sections of the media. Regrettably, most of these issues or problems are just scratched on the surface or are portrayed in a simpler context of sound bites, news flashes without thorough analysis. The consequence is that when these messages are repeated over and over, people base their opinions on them. The irony is that the other side was never heard. Don't get me wrong, the media has been helpful—especially the powerful media in the West, with all the resources at their disposal to help bring some Africa's predicaments to the attention of the world. But some of the issues as they relate to Africa are not given an in-depth or objective enough analysis to make the audience pick and choose sides.

A typical example of the issue that I am talking about is the media blitz on "Africa and the rejection of U.S. donated foods. Africa never rejected genetically modified food (known as GMOs), but three countries—Malawi, Zambia, and Zimbabwe—rejected the donated food because of the form in which the grains were shipped. First, among other strong reasons why the countries concerned here wanted the corn meal rather than grains was to protect their future export trade with European countries, who claimed at the time that GMO foods were not yet certified for human consumption. What was at stake was indeed in what form the food would be allowed to enter ports. It was therefore not an outright rejection of donated food, as most media reports suggested. These countries wanted donated food in cornmeal (powdered form) rather than grains, the way the United States shipped the food aid.

Of course, Zambia, Gambia, and Zimbabwe knew well that accepting the corn seed would not benefit their countries in the long run, especially their export trading with the European Union. The United States is out of the picture as far as food imports from African countries are concerned. Therefore, for purely economic and commercial (trade) reasons, these African countries do not want to jeopardize trade relations with the EU than banned GMO food products at the period from entering their respective countries. In fact, from the economic sense, listening to their long-term customers (since the EU is a major importer of their products—not just corn but other food products) will pave the way for better future trade relationships.

Protecting African corn from being overrun by genetically modified crops was the strongest reason why the donation was not accepted. For Zimbabwe, the political relationship at the time with the United States and President Mugabe created suspicions that defiled the intent of the donation, from the country's viewpoint.

Every independent nation in the continent makes decisions it finds appropriate and suitable to her national interests and economic prosperity. Prior to the controversy over the donated GMOs, some African nations have collaborated in the past with the United States Department of Agriculture in improving agricultural development in their respective countries. This relationship dated back to more than three decades and has had tremendous benefits for African farmers long before the controversy on rejected GMO food came into the picture. In selected African countries, for example, pest resistant crops are not new to farmers. Therefore, the link and impression created by the media that Africa's "rejection" of GMO donated food is political is untrue. It is more of an economic decision based on national interest of respective nations rather than a political one that influenced their decisions.

Very few African nations export agricultural products to Europe. European nations have opposed and restricted any importation of genetically modified products entering EU countries (lately the opposition has mellowed down, and the lifting of the ban provides a clause, provided GMOs are labeled). Since Africa is their important source of supplies, including corn, there is the fear that raw products from the GMO's donated corn seeds may be planted in rural villages and, as a result of cross-fertilization, overrun native crops. Europeans have a preference for African corn because of its quality, taste, and value, and it has a very strong demand in Europe; therefore, Europeans don't want GMOs ending up at their dinner tables.

While the politics and the saga of GMO foods and the rejection of donated food played well in the media, there seems to be an aspect of African culture and tradition that people from the West do not yet understand. An average African has ears for local and international news from sources other than the radio or TV. Face-to-face communication thrives, and since the news began to spread that the donated food was genetically modified—and that it was another attempt by the "West to feed Africans with Cat Foods," even when it is not true—it created fears, and people began to question the intent of the donation.

This is true of African culture. Suspicion, like superstition, is flu-like. It is ready to spread and die down immediately if there is an event that seems to prove the rumor or suspicion to be true or untrue. The European Union's outright rejection of imported, genetically modified food gave credence to the beliefs of some Africans that GMOs are not safe (even when the opposite may be the case). Therefore, under these circumstances, there was already apathy among natives as to whether there were genuine intentions actually behind the donated food.

Africans, including the poor have dignity, which they want preserved, even amidst crisis and deprivation. Talking down to the poor as if they are lazy and responsible for the fate that befalls them is critically frowned at in African culture. It is part of human nature, as well as simple decency, to be treated respectfully when being given a hand out.

African cultures also frown at giving and telling. It's psychologically depressing to Africans when such "give and tell" is associated with innuendoes and controversial statements that demean the intention of the giver.

Cultures are deep rooted in Africa and define every aspect of life, both for the poor and the rich. Cultures play in different tunes, and people expect that their culture will be respected irrespective of assistance or help coming their way. A show of respect for people's cultures inspires confidence regarding the motives of the donors. In fact, without observing the sentiments of African cultures, communication between donors and receivers will continue to lead to misinterpretation of good intentions, which may increase or damage diplomacy and good relationships. Such is the predicament of Africa and the United States and Europe, in some situations, as far as interpretation of motives are concerned. The end result is that the problem ends up hurting the poor because the African wealthy class has no need for assistance.

AFRICAN KINGDOMS AND INSTITUTIONS

49. Question: What is the status of past African kingdoms? Does Africa still have kings, queens, princes, and princesses? If they do, what roles do they play in modern tribal societies?

Answer:

African kingdoms are sketchy in books and literatures. I am talking of other great empires of Africa other than the Egyptian Empire. Other great African empires of Ghana, Songhai, Benin, and Mali have historical perspectives and have contributed immensely to the strong cultures, traditions, and to the development of a global civil society and modern civilization. These were great dynasties, with strong and powerful kings that had international reputations and respect. Even early European explorers described life in some of these empires, Ghana in particular, as "superb." The Ghana Empire, with its abundant gold, was a kingdom that travelers, explorers from far, migrated to in order to trade—especially gold and spices.

The Ashanti dynasty functioned well and was politically and economically relevant. Some of the African "forgotten" empires, for example the Mali Empire, recently started receiving attention following excavations and the archeological discoveries that unfolded, revealing unknown history and the importance of the Mali Empire to modern civilization.

In present Africa, there are many modern towns and cities located where these powerful kingdoms once stood. Far from African kingdoms, some African tribes trace their origins to powerful kingdoms outside the continent. For example, the history of the Kanem-Bornu tribes of Northern Nigeria can be traced to Yemen and Babylon—the Tigris and Mesopotamia, the Islamic enclave of modern Iraq—the birthplace of modern civilization that we sparingly recall as we do of the Egyptian or Greek empires.

There is rarely any village in Africa without an institution that is represented by kings, chiefs, or paramount rulers, as the case may be. In fact, these leaders today play several functions, including roles as advisors to governments and parliament in modern democracy, especially on issues relating to customs and tradition.

Kings, queens, and chiefs today are identified by different names and titles, depending on the part of Africa in which they reside and what the tribes choose to call the institution and person(s) representing the establishment. Chiefs play several functions, as earlier disclosed, including roles as counselors, mediators, and judges in customary courts, where more than 90 percent of civil and criminal cases are handled.

The status of these leaders varies in their societies. It depends on the tribe, the roles they play, and the size of the kingdom. Some are more powerful than others, and some are actually involved in political decision-making at state and local government levels—the same as their prominence in national policies, even when it is not openly manifested.

There are different classes of chiefs in the Ibo dynasty. When the British colonized some African states, part of their bounty in the partition of the continent—in Ibo land of Eastern Nigeria, for example—was to alter dynasties and introduce the title of warrant chiefs. Unlike the traditional rulers selected by the people, the colonial government-appointed warrants chiefs who were titular heads. It was a policy aimed at reducing the power of these powerful men and women. It enabled the administrators of colonies to consolidate power to civilians that are committed to British authorities.

The institution the king or queen represents commands great respect from his or her people, which in turn transforms into the individual holding the office. The office is by heritage or by appointment—or by other selection processes that may be approved by the community's elders' council, traditional laws, and today, by the government.

50. Question: How are kings or queens chosen in Africa?

Answer:

The people select or nominate a king or a queen. But in most cultures, the person to be chosen must be a descendant (immediate or second generation) of the royal family. It is the prime consideration for selection of who to crown the king or queen. In some cultures, the selection of the person could be by appointment or by order of inheritance, as outlined by family history or the village's history. Africa, as I have explained in an earlier chapter, is not a monolithic society. It all depends on how customs stipulate the process in a particular culture. There are no hard and fast rules on the matter. There are cultures where the records of achievement or bravery influence the choice a candidate to be nominated as the king or the queen.

The village and town the king or the queen represents in Africa's democratic process have needs. The most important needs are social services—electricity, good drinking water, and roads. As I pointed out earlier, since influence counts in some ways in making a community benefit from the location of these amenities, the person nominated to fill this important position is important. Traditionally, the choice or nomination of a king or a queen has been simply by inheritance.

The nomination and crowning of an eligible candidate to the throne must meet all stringent traditional and cultural conditions and follow the necessary guidelines as specified by the elders' council, clan heads, and people. Petitions against the selection of a particular candidate may result in controversy. Such disagreement, when it occurs, may delay the coronation of a king to the office. Any petition rejecting or challenging the selection process of a king may be heard in traditional court, and in the case of an appeal, it may drag from civil court to the Supreme Court.

Ibo tribe is a highly democratic society, and the system has sanctions against autocracy and dictatorship. The appointment and crowning of a king is a tedious process and takes a fairly long period of time depending on how quickly villagers can resolve political differences and controversy surrounding the selection of a candidate for the throne. When the decision is finally made, the community can go the distance in defending their nomination and why "A" rather than "B" is crowned the king.

When the king is alive, there is no succession to the throne. Although royalty is beclouded in secrecy, next of kin may succeed and take over the role in terms of emergency or sudden death. That is upon notification and approval of people and the royal council representing all the clans in the community.

In some cultures, a search and selection process for successor to the throne starts early, even when the king or queen is alive, especially when ill health hampers his ability to perform his duties.

A child protégé may be nominated to the throne in some cultures. In societies where this tradition holds, the teenager is first of all groomed, and when he is ready to assume the responsibilities as the king, he is officially crowned. During the grooming period, the elders' council and the head nominated by the ruling body (most of the time, one of the chiefs) perform his roles. He may finally assume full responsibility at 21, depending on the age that tradition specifies that he be crowned the king.

DICTATORS AND THE DEARTH OF

AUTHORITARIANISM

51. Question: We have heard and read so much about African dictators and life-presidents. Are there African leaders that have left office and transferred power (willingly) to a democratic elected successor in free and fair elections?

Answer:

At the beginning of the 21st century, more African nations are democratic than in the last three to four decades after their independence. Dictatorship, which swept across Africa during the cold war era, reached its peak in the 80s. In early and mid-90s, it was alive but not without resistance from the people. In the democratic process evolving in many African nations, what we witness now, as internal, political disturbances by oppositions in the past would have motivated a military take over. In the absence of vibrant economic prospects, anger and frustrations—the same vulnerable environment that created dictators that sweep themselves to power—exist today, but the will of the people to resist such an uprising is the reason why it has not taken place in some countries. Of course, people must voice their opinions and disappointments.

But, let us not forget that the political after-shocks witnessed during the cold war era are still reverberating, and like everything that is Africa, there is never an end, except after a long devastation, including the loss of lives and property. Tribal rivalries and clashes, which are mostly small but lead to several deaths in rural villages, are attributes of the frustrations and hopelessness among the people.

The changing political landscape in Africa, on a positive side, can also be attributed to new global order as well as the impeccable style of leadership that Africa has witnessed in handful of positive leaders in the continent.

President Houphouet-Boigny of the Ivory Coast, West Africa was one of Africa's longest-served leaders, but his impeccable record while in office speaks of a man with a vision and mission that improved the economy and the lives of his people while he was in office. Opposition to his government disagrees, but I am writing based on what I witnessed on several assignments to Cote d'Ivoire and compared to many African nations. Boigny's achievements were responsible for his long term in office.

Presidents Kwame Nkrumah of Ghana and Lumumba of Zambia, at the time they were in office, had impeccable records that would have made the electorates vote to keep them long enough in office. Evidences of their legacies speak for themselves even when their lives were cut short during Africa's most important moments in history.

General Murtala Mohammed of Nigeria was a Muslim and a military leader, and his accomplishments during his short tenure gave hope to Nigerians of a leader that actually came to redeem the people and reinvigorate the economy. General Murtala Mohammed would have been elected a democratic leader (had he sought nomination as a civilian president) had he not been assassinated in a military coup d' etat. President Obasanjo is another African leader that was a military general who rebounded back to office as a democratically elected leader of his people. President Obasanjo voluntarily relinquished power to a democratically elected government in 1979. He came back, and he was re-elected the democratic president of Nigeria and served second term.

Africans can tell good leaders from bad rulers. Unfortunately, most African nations have not been endowed with many good leaders that love their own people and inspire the people to rise and raise the standard of living. Most successful nations in the world have one thing in common – good leaders ready to sacrifice for the love of his people and ready to empower and motivate people even in most difficult times or situations.

President Mandela is not the only known African leader that retired and voluntarily handed over the mantle of leadership to a new breed or generation of African successors. In Kenya, Arap Moi's leadership came to an end after an election in December 2002 that witnessed the election of a successor at the end of his twenty-four years in office and the defeat of a candidate he had handpicked to succeed him.

52. Question: Why haven't Africans taken on the responsibility of removing dictators and sit-tight presidents from office and insisting on elected leaders for their nations at any costs?
Africans can see that economies around the world that have fared well have democracy and stability—including institutions that make development happen intact.

Why is it that Africans don't think that what is good for the goose, as far as global economic prosperity is concerned, is good for the gander? (That, amidst her huge wealth, it should put its house in order to start gaining from the huge wealth with which it [the majority of African countries] is endowed?)

Answer:

In an interview with one of Nigeria's fathers of independence, Dr Nnamdi Azikiwe, known as Zik of Africa, he remarked (while responding to questions filed by journalist, including myself) that, "It is a mad man that fights a man with a gun." The question and answer by Africa's great father of Nigeria's independence tells why it was difficult at particular times in Africa's history to resist or remove dictators from office. Today, in some countries in Africa, as in the last five years, several dictators, or coup plotters, have failed in the bid to grab power or to destabilize the elected democratic government.

As a young man in college—and like many of my colleagues who wanted to express freedom of speech and draw attention to social, health, and economic policies that concerned the people but were never addressed or were dismissed by elected officials or the government—parents always warned that, "You are sent to college not to demonstrate, petition, or manifest any opposition to authority." As many students know, parental opposition means a lot—else you may be deprived of allowances or your school fees. In effect, students' lack of interest to participate in social justice is dampened early from home. The result is that the few that dare demonstrate are regarded as "rebels" when in many developed nations, what shaped their democracies are such demonstrations and opposition to what we see in the developing world. I tell people that great countries, such as the United States, as we see its strength and global might, are where they are today because of the sacrifices made by millions of people who fought for freedom of human rights and freedom of expression, both internally and internationally. This, unfortunately, is not the case yet in most developing nations. That is changing somewhat but not at a rate that will bring instantaneous results or show non-performing leaders and dictators that power belongs to people and not the minority in power, or that power diminishes when the leaders are out of touch with the people and not delivering on promises or implementing policies that would improve the life of the middle-class and the poor.

Why don't Africans often take to the streets to demonstrate or protest what seemed to be a routine military take-over of government? Well, Africans do. Take Nigerians for example—the people did protest, and it was very intensive and violent as a result of clashes by protesters and law enforcement agents. It was during the nullification of election results in which Chief Abiola was denied the rights to take over office.

Africans are also very resilient people. Protests and opposition to occupation and bad administration dated back to pre-colonial eras when people revolted against bad rulers. Kingdoms have rulers toppled and replaced.

Of course, the longevity and acceptance (so it appears) of any African leader to whatever position the leader finds himself, whether as a dictator or life president, would not have been possible without the support or recognition of some politically powerful establishments made up of individuals both inside and outside the country. Succinctly put, these brutal dictators and sit-tight presidents are in office because they have a "stamp of approval" from this clique of power brokers. As a reporter, I realized that the same power brokers that dine at night with coupists or dictators are the same people that criticize them during the day.

In fact, Dr. Azikiwe, this doyen of Africa's independence, was echoing the fears that Nigerians have and the helplessness of Nigerians at the time (not now) to withstand military interventions in government. However, during the draconic regime of Abacha, the media, respected for the fearlessness and determination by crops of men and women behind the media, did mobilize the people to resist the government, which in the end resulted in the election of Chief M.K.O. Abiola, who later was jailed and he paid for freedom with his own life.

Many African nations have witnessed and gone through the same watershed in their political history. The era of dictatorship and life-term presidents in most African countries is fast phasing away. The African Union, through new thinking and vibrant leadership in key countries, is working hard to avoid having African democracies interrupted, setting back the hands of the clock in terms of regional and continental stability. Time is running out for leaders that don't perform as well as dictators. The global economy and the gap between rich and poor nations is becoming a concern to African governments and a wake-up call to turn around the economies of their nations with the huge human and material resources available in almost every African nation.

Consider a country such as Nigeria, with only three elected presidents in four decades of history, and compare her stability to countries such as Taiwan, South Korea, and Singapore. There is no need to search for answers as to why Nigeria is running far behind time, while these nations once placed in the same developmental category as Nigeria, and with the potential to become industrialized nations, are doing well.

The simple conclusion is that free market democracy, even though it is not full-proof, when adopted well and practiced according to its principles, no doubt will yield the right results—of course, with a strong foundation and institutions in place to make it happen. Dictatorships never allowed freedom of people to thrive; it never promoted freedom of people to initiate and participate in brainstorming for the betterment of the country. Dictatorships never loosened the grip on the means of production. Therefore, in the absence of freedom, fears thrived, including the fear of resistance. Tribes were played against each other, as the early colonialists did, and the consequence was ethnic hatred—tribes tearing each other apart while the man in control of power at the center stays on. And by the time the people fighting knew it, he had already been in office for almost a decade.

It may be wrong to sweep all military leadership in Africa under one carpet, but bad leadership is, to some extent, responsib.e for the majority of the economic disarray that Africa of the 21st century is facing. In essence, looking to the past without developing strategies for the future leads to a lack of development.

Togo's Gnassingbe Eyadema and Gabon's Omar Bongo have been in office since 1967. The only longest serving African military leader is Libya's Muammar Gadhafi, who has been in power since 1977. But one should not forget the success stories of Africa's long-served leaders, such as President Boigny of Cote d'Ivoire. He transformed his country with revenue from just one cash crop—cocoa—and later expanded into coffee and palm oil exports to build an economically viable state, unrivalled in the Western coast of Africa. His leadership placed Cote d'Ivoire on the global map and gave Africa a development model never thought of—a well-developed agricultural sector that could sustain a nation's economy, not just mineral resources such as gold, diamonds, and petroleum.

AFRICA'S DEMOCRACY VERSUS DICTATORSHIP

53. Question: How many nations in Africa are democratic . . . because the impression I have is that one out of three African nations is ruled by military men and life presidents that extend their tenure in office and do not want to leave office voluntarily. How true is this observation?

Answer:

It is not true that military men and life presidents rule one out of three African countries. As I discussed earlier in this section, Africa was another stage for a cold war, which unfortunately was underreported. The use of military henchmen to remove democratically elected governments were events orchestrated in the past for interest other than the countries where these coup d'états took place. From Angola and Namibia to the Congo, to name just a few countries, the confrontation between communist ideologies and their supporters versus Western democratic ideologies were at collision course in Africa. These clashes were partially responsible for some African conflicts.

In spite of all the military coups that have taken place in Africa—according to fact books, 80 out of 100 in the world took place in the continent. However, Africa still has more democratic states and leaders chosen through elections than regions such as the Middle East and Central Asia.

Africa's Western-styled democracy is young and, unfortunately, the infrastructure necessary to build a complete secure and functional democracy, as is in the West, is absolutely not yet present. It is not a presumption to disclose that Africa's democracies were founded on porous foundations of staggering and severe economic environment, the fragility of the system is highly unpredictable. Growing unemployment, economies dependent on only one source of export for revenue for foreign exchange, huge debts, and high interests rates on loans; closed the Western markets to African goods and services as a result of subsidies, tariffs, and the under-pricing of African goods—all are a threat to Western-styled democracy in Africa.

The survival of the democratic process in Africa hinges on many factors, including the ones listed. Meanwhile, administrations with leaders who have the zeal and fire in their bellies to overcome these problems are still unable to reduce the hardship of the people, even as their terms in office are running out. Since the masses are unwilling to endure, the consequences are massive protests, the distraction of government (occasionally), tribal clashes, and other forms of instability that threaten democracy, which the same democracy and free market economy are supposed to protect.

These situations make it difficult to predict what will happen next in some countries in the continent with such a shaky democratic foundation. From records of successful stories, so far, some new African leaders have proved that they are equal to the task of ensuring stability in the continent no matter what the situation is on the ground. The leadership peer-review initiative under the new African Union charter is working well—such as the plan that led the Liberian crisis to advance towards peaceful settlement, with former President Charles Taylor agreeing to leave his country on exile to Nigeria. The initiative also helped resolve the coup d'état in Cote d'Ivoire, Sao Tome and Principe, and Guinea Bissau. It gives hope that peace and stability could be possible when parties are ready to heed to mediation and negotiations. It also demonstrated that African leaders could influence and persuade fellow leaders (suspects of dictatorship and otherwise sources of confusion in their states) to concede power for the common good.

I was near to completing this section of this project when a military coup took place in a very small island of Sao Tome and Principe. President Menezes was overthrown in a coup d'état as he was attending the Leon Sullivan Summit in Abuja at the same period that President Bush was in Nigeria. Through mediation and working in concert with the African Union, the President of Gabon, Congo Brazzaville and Angola President Obasanjo was able to go back home with President Menezes after negotiating with the leader of the coup, Major Fernando Pereira.

There were about 11 nations in late 2002, out of 53 countries in Africa that were undemocratic. By this, I mean nations without elected leaders, even where the leaders are not military. These figures are uncertain as events that unfold after this book may have gone to press may change the statistics—positively or negatively. But the African Union's efforts in settling disputes point positively to a peaceful direction.

Like the political problem in Cote d'Ivoire, and the coup in the former Central African Republic (CAR) in 2003, the intervention of African leaders such as President Thabo Mbeki of South Africa and President Olusegun Obasanjo, along with regional presidents, reduced the mayhem and bloodshed that often accompany conflicts of those magnitudes.

In the CAR, Chief Francois Bozize, with support from the military, took over the government. President Ange-Felix Potasse has been the democratically elected president of his country since 1993. However, in spite of these shortcomings, human rights and democratic pressures never ceased to mount for political and economic reforms by governments in the continent that do not want to be democratic. Ensuring that democracy is not derailed is an important initiative in the new African Union charter.

AFRICAN LEADERSHIP:

APPROACHES TO SOCIAL AND HEALTH PROBLEMS

54. Question: About African statistics in the media: why is it that we never read about statistics collated and analyzed by African researchers and agencies? Why is it that collated data and the analysis of Africa's accounts of events and problems are told from Western perspectives rather than from Africa's viewpoints?

Answer:

Whenever I am asked this question, my first reaction is how many African experts and professionals do you see on Western television talking about African problems, whether positive or negative? When Africa's side of events is not presented, it seems to show that nobody cares whether Africa is heard or not.

There is no place on the face of the earth as overwhelmed, some call it "infatuated," with statistics as the United States. It is a very positive stereotype because it shows a nation that is concerned with every aspect of its growth and ensures that it monitors all aspects of its environment to gauge strength and weaknesses. Most importantly, the statistics help it to know its strength, weaknesses and where threats are coming from. No doubt, statistics provide monitoring tools and predict future trends. All these are positive steps when the statistics are accurate and scientifically gathered and analyzed. But the reverse is the case when the same data are falsified with an outcome meant to suit agendas or objectives, which we have repeatedly seen in studies on almost every subject, including history, medicine, science, and technology. It is also wrong when statistics are gathered or acquired for the sake of immediacy and political convenience (to make a statement, stereotype, or to criticize).

The concern for accurate statistics and analysis is important to African governments, but it has not been a priority. Governments have not invested enough in this important sector of monitoring, evaluating, and forecasting future growth and development. In

African countries today, there are government agencies and ministries responsible for gathering statistical data and making analysis; however, their scope is limited by costs to domestic matters and themes.

In fact, the Office of Budgets and Statistics, depending on other appropriate names they are called in respective African countries, are restricted in the information they can gather and the data they can provide. More so, the analysis of data is restricted to domestic use and application.

No African nation gathers statistics for comparative analysis of regional problems, not to mention the continent or comparing them with the rest of the world. Statistical data are not gathered to reflect on how problems impact domestic policies at the present or for any future actions to fast forward or slow trends.

Investment in data gathering and analysis is limited or, in most countries, non-existent. With Africa's lack of investment in data gathering, coupled with limited budgets, the void left over as a result is filled by non-government agencies such as the United Nations or private research organizations and institutions that "urgently" needed data for their various analyses and decisions on global matters. And the irony is that these agencies or organizations interpret their results to address their research questions. Of course, they do not have to wait for Africa to provide them with the data they wanted. These are the institutions and organizations that also have the budget to undertake such large-scale data gathering exercises. What we are not often told (at least the public) are the limitations, including logistical problems that often confront individuals, organizations and agencies gathering these data on African problems. These problems, those of us that have gathered information on any part of the continent, know very well they are multi-dimensional and do affect results.

Many critics say that statistics on the ground are not always in harmony with data reported to the public. In other words, there are beliefs that propaganda and the lived experience are different. When the two are merged, it could create the potential to undermine the credibility of information sources and the data accompanying such messages.

It is often difficult to estimate, for example, war victims that in some instances span over years and criss-cross countries and battle fields for the mere fact that it is politically and militarily incorrect for both sides to give their actual figures (just as we witnessed in the recent Gulf and Iraq Wars). It is therefore extremely difficult to put figures to what we don't know. Yes, estimates are right, but when we give the estimates such value and over-play it in the media as if they are absolute truth, that is where the problem lies for critics from Africa that doubt any figures placed on most African problems that one views or reads in the media. Unfortunately, it brings about mistrust and makes people doubtful of the objective of the agencies or organizations gathering and releasing these data results. Of course, don't get my wrong, there are reliable data collected over years by organizations such as United Nations and its affiliate organizations that are indisputably reliable, but not all have measured to the level of objectivity as far as measuring Africa's problems and situations on the ground were concerned.

Awarding figures for political correctness and expediency is what I am stressing here. It is not only dangerous but also undermines the reasons and essence of such data gathering. For Africa, data on victims of wars, especially the dead, are difficult to calculate.

As a journalist, I have reported events where statistics are repeatedly involved. Uneasy and chaotic moments do not provide good environments for getting accurate data. Similarly, the success rates in analyzing problems and coming out with the right results in such circumstances are very limited.

55. Question: With reported cases of many Africans dying from infectious diseases, I was expecting that African governments should have contingency plans and react proactively towards tackling these re-occurring health problems, including using herbal medicines to control diseases. I learned that the poor cannot afford the cost of regular medicines. Why were Africa's leaders very complacent in tackling the spread of diseases, such as malaria, influenza, typhoid fever, and meningitis, with natural or herbal medicines?

(This was one of the most frequently asked questions. They were asked in different ways. It has been my decision to tie them together.)

Answer:

It would be wrong to assume that because there is no media publicity or attention on Africa's efforts to find a cure for most of the diseases threatening lives that Africans are not doing enough to find a cure for these diseases—especially the ones that you have listed.

In the words of my colleagues in the media, African leaders are not doing enough considering that health care annual budget is below 5 percent of annual budgets every year across the board—in almost every African country. These figures are frightening compared to the huge budgets allotted to military and sports; figures that are far below the World Health Organization's projected health care budget for developing nations.

To date, health care remains the most under-funded (in budgetary allocations) across the continent. Health professionals remain the most underpaid, of course taking after teachers.

The majority of the African population still depends on herbal medicines. It was not long ago that a rekindled interest in natural medicines as an integral part of its healthcare program began to gain government interest. Before, it used to be African governments that led the campaign against alternative medicines for Africa's poor. Herbalists were targeted in orchestrated warfare, but that has drastically changed, especially with the emergence of the HIV/AIDS epidemic and the high cost of medicines and treatment for the deadly disease and others such as malaria, dysentery, and diarrhea.

Since the 80s and early 90s, the efforts to combine natural and modern medicine as an integral part of health care have gained momentum. With HIV/AIDS, it was not a matter of convenience but a necessity that such collaboration be sustained. So far, modern medicine accounts for less than 30 percent of the health care needs of the people, while majority still relies on herbal medicines for everyday medical care.

The majority of herbalists practice African religions, and in places where the majority are Christians, such visits to an herbalist used to carry a stigma. But that has changed in the last decade or so. However, dominantly Christian-populated villages and towns still have the attitude that visiting an herbalist is "unchristian." In the face of the rising costs of modern medicines, the poor suffers most in this kind of environment. In essence, since the government and church recognize only modern medicine, which is unaffordable to the majority of the poor and working families, the restrictions on alternative medicines only add to their health care problems.

Presently, the question is how far merging modern medicine with traditional medicine can go. It is not a matter of neglecting it anymore. As a medical doctor trained in England summarized the new scenario during a conference I attended, when the debate was heating up as to whether African traditional medicines should be merged with modern medicine in treatment and healing in the late 80s and early part of the 90s, he said, "What is the trouble with that traditional medicine) . . . after all, most tablets are derived from herbs, and African natural medicine is all about herbs."

There is huge quantity of adulterated drugs floating particularly in markets in developing countries. It is estimated that as much as 70 percent of medicines are adulterated in some African countries. Many deaths from what we label "diseases" could be attributed to fake medicines, especially as their cheap prices tend to attract those that cannot afford the cost of going to clinics and hospitals. With fake drugs in circulation and freely obtained over the counter, the reliability of modern medicines comes into serious scrutiny by the cross section of the population. People that have all along doubted whether modern medicines provide the "actual cure," as have been publicized by manufacturers and health experts, found a loophole. They capitalized on this weakness to support the opponents' notion that Africa is overdue for accepting traditional medicines to meet the primary health care needs of the majority of the population. Nigeria and a few other countries have risen up strongly to curtail the circulation of fake drugs and imposed strict laws and penalties to stop the menace.

Underneath the mind of these customers, there is also this indifference persisting among Africans that most generic drugs made overseas and shipped to Africa do not come close to the quality and standards of the ones manufactured in other countries.

In fact, the majority of Africans agree that imported medicines distributed in Africa do not go through the same scrutiny or testing process during manufacturing as those made for European or American consumers.

Another popular approach to the African health problems is Faith Healing. In Ghana, faith healing has a large following, such as people like Ester Aalakailey Akuetteh from Libadi, who died at the age of ninety, and Rev Afutu, the founder of the Charter Healing Church, with the aim of healing sickness and disability through gospel music and prayer. Similar churches are springing up and gaining huge fellowship by men and women who claimed they were inspired by God to heal the spirit and exorcise evil spirits. Faith healing sects within the Catholic and Anglican churches have witnessed tremendous growth in the last five years.

No doubt, African leaders should have contingency plans and react proactively in cases of emergency, say for example there is an outbreak and spread of a new disease. Recent efforts witnessed by department of health monitoring groups by some African countries during the outbreak of SARS showed that there has been an improvement in the timing response and policies to control the spread of infectious diseases. Sustaining the effort is another question that only African leaders should be able to answer, since finance remains serious handicap that restricts budgets to departments that are in charge of some of these problems.

Africa also has a very high mobile population (frequent movements in and out of cities at any time, including huge numbers of immigrants—most of them unscreened). With such a highly mobile population, tracking patients with health problems, such as infectious diseases, is a very difficult task. Monitoring the spread and responding quickly to such an outbreak would no doubt make a huge difference, at least on infection rates and death tolls that may arise from the disease. Nigeria's quick reaction to the outbreak of SARS in the manner of quarantining and observing passengers coming into the country would serve Africa well in the future.

56. Question: What is Africa's population?

Answer:

The United Nations' current statistics based on estimation is 841 million people. It is projected that Africa's population will grow to 856 million by 2020. However, the latest reports from the Population Reference Bureau in a report authored by Carl Haub indicates that Africa's population could soar to more than 1 billion over the next half century. The latest edition of the "World Population data sheet" estimates that the global population will grow by 46 percent between now and 2050 to about 9 billion. Africa is supposed to grow to more than double in population, to 1.9 billion, by mid-century.

China and India remain the most populated nations on Earth. Africa, with 53 countries, still has a landmass as big as China, the United States, Europe, India, New Zealand, and Argentina combined. **While the six zones have a total area of 29 million square kilometers, Africa has 30 million square kilometers**. So, Africa is not a small continent, as is often projected on maps, drawings, and aerial pictures.

With the world's population at approximately 5.6 billion people, Asia, according to the United Nations' Population statistics, has 59 percent of the world's population; Africa, 12 percent; and Latin America, 9 percent.

AFRICA'S DIASPORA

57. Question: How many Africans reside abroad or overseas?

Answer:

The migration patterns of Africans over the centuries have made such a count impossible. Africans continue to migrate from one part of the world to another. There is a new migration pattern of the 21st century through visa lottery. The visa lottery is a kind of ballot for choosing among millions of qualified applicants from countries under-represented in previous U.S. ethnic immigration. Based on ballot selection, ever year, lucky winners are automatically granted green cards, or permanent resident permits, to live in the United States. There are also immigrations as a result of brain drain—professionals leaving their home countries to seek employment, or to care for their family, in a new land.

The last United States Bureau of Census data available indicated a population of more than half a million Africans in the United States. Based on regions, statistics show the following: North Africa, 99,044; South Africa, 34,707; West Africa; 111,566; Africa (not elsewhere classified), 37,402, Eastern Africa, 72,300; "Middle Africa," including Angola, Cameroon, and Zaire (Congo) as classified in the data, 8,800. Not included as Africans but as foreign-born population are Caribbean, Dominican Republic, 347,858; Haitians, 235,393; Jamaicans, 334,140; and Trinidadians and Tobagonians, 115,710. Many agree that the above statistics are an underestimation, since reliable sources disclose that Nigerians alone in the United States count between 2 and 5 million.

Statistical projections, as we are already aware, are just representations, not actual fact. In addition to 13 percent of African-Americans that have already traced their roots to Africa, about 5 million Africans, or the Neo-Diaspora, have migrated to the U.S. recently.

African people have been migrating and emigrating in and out of the continent for more than 8,000 years. The Bantu people of West Africa, about 3,000 years ago, began to move into what are today South Africa, Tanzania, and Namibia. Certain unaccounted populations of Africans reside in Asia and South America.

AFRICA'S REGIONAL ORGANIZATIONS

58. Question: To what regional and continental organizations do African nations belong? How effective are they? What roles (if any) do they play in resolving African conflicts? How do these organizations measure their successes considering that Africa still has political unrest, tribal clashes, the protracted wounds of present and past wars, and the continent still shelters countries that still count as the most unstable places on Earth? Take Sudan for example: for 50 years, it has been embroiled in war; Liberia, another example that has, for the past 14 years, been at war, and peace seems not to be near, even with the exit of Charles Taylor. Does it make sense that Africa has these organizations with member countries that have standing armies and military, yet Africa wants the United States in Liberia (experience of Mogadishu not withstanding)?

Answer:

It takes more than just having an organization or organizations to stop war from happening. But the role organizations such as the United Nations and the African Union, among other sub-regional groups, play in reducing conflict situations that would have escalated to more wars (had they not mediated) cannot be overemphasized.

Realistically, times are changing in Africa. Yes, most of the regional wars (in pockets of countries in the continent) have lasted as they did because of unresolved differences and a lack of compromise between warring parties in spite of regional, continental, as well as global negotiations and mediations. No two parties conflicting would end violence unless they both agree to do so. Therefore, in such circumstances, the mediator may do what is possible to resolve the standoff, and an agreement may be reached, but as soon as the mediator turns his back, the choice to continue or end the conflict rests on both parties. Such is the situation in many of Africa's conflicts and "settlements" that often become more difficult because of politics, past grudges, and the huge divide of tribes stretching back to colonization. Also, religious differences that are intertwined with politics have not helped conflict resolutions.

However, irrespective of past experiences, Sudan and Liberia's conflicts may be finally coming to be over, if parties could keep to the peace agreement reached on these conflicts. Without the mediation of the African Union and the global community through the United Nations, these peace accords would not have been possible. The African Union's success story so far at peace mediation and making sure those dictators don't return to power is its greatest achievement. Unlike the former Organization of African Unity (OAU), described by critics as a "Toothless Bulldog," the new African Union and new crops of African leaders are giving clout to the new "Bulldog" in the house, which so far has better management approach and control on problems confronting African nations and the people.

Yes, Africa has regional and continental organizations to which member states belong. These organizations bond the regions and member nations together. They have resolved conflicts, and they have "caused some," as critics alleged. But overall, they have been a strong, unifying force in almost every regional conflict in the continent and beyond. From diplomacy to the contribution of soldiers to United Nations peacekeeping missions, Africa has contributed to peace around the world—from Bosnia to East Timor to name just a few places.

The Organization of African Unity, now the African Union (AU), is the organization that binds all the 53 nations in Africa together. Apart from AU political roles, it establishes educational exchange programs; trade; and air, land, and sea agreements between nations in the continent. It has enabled Africa to steer different opinions and come out with one voice on matters requiring Africa's stamp of approval on international policies that impact African people and countries in the continent.

The Organization of African Unity (OAU), the symbol of the dreams of Africa's independence leaders, was born in 1963 in Ethiopian's capital of Addis Ababa.

The founding fathers of the organization were President Julius Nyerere of Tanzania (now deceased), King Hassan of Morocco, and Ahmed Ben Bella of Algeria. The African Union (AU) is described by critics of the former OAU as a more vibrant union. It was inaugurated in Durban, South Africa in July 2002, and it replaced the OAU. The idea for the African Union was bred in July 2000 when African leaders signed an agreement in Togo.

In spite of its accomplishments, critics are quick to point out that the failure of the OAU was because it lacked the willpower and financial muscles to make the drastic changes necessary to stop Africa's conflicts. Also lacking was the clout to bargain or develop economic relationships with willing allies without sacrificing Africa's sovereignty and the internal security of individual states in the continent. The OAU also lacked the will to follow through on its decisions and their implementations as far as many reforms were concerned, including stopping wars and coup d'états. These weaknesses, including finding an economic roadmap for Africa, are what the African Union was formed to address. So far, many critics of the OAU have given the new AU thumbs way up.

On the regional level, organizations that foster cooperation within their respective regions have performed creditably well compared to the bigger umbrella organization.

Since the birth of the African Union, observers of the old OAU and now the new AU have expressed their opinion that there has been more cohesiveness and cooperation between these regional organizations and the AU in addressing African problems and coming out with one voice.

Some African nations are also members of The Commonwealth of Nations, comprising 54-member states once under British rule. In December 2003, the member states' presidents were hosted by Nigeria. Members include Britain, Canada, Australia, Nigeria, Ghana, Zimbabwe, and others. Nigeria's career diplomat, Emeka Anyoku, was the Secretary General of the organization for three terms until he left the office in 1999.

In the Democratic Republic of Congo, a cease-fire agreement was negotiated and truce was reached because of African Union mediation. The same mediation has taken place in Sao Tome and Principe, Mauritius, and Cote d'Ivoire, where civilian governments were overthrown but were reinstalled through mediation by regional organizations and the African Union. In Sudan, the AU was responsible for the cease-fire agreement and peace agreement that may finally bring to an end conflict in the war-ravaged nation. The roles of ECOWAS and the African Union in stopping wars in Sierra Leone and the failed peace in Liberia cannot be underestimated.

The reason why global peace is not a burden that one nation alone can handle is exemplified with peace missions in Bosnia, Kosovo, East Timor, Columbia, Philippines, and the Middle East. Africa has her huge economic, political, and health care problems. The AU is requesting assistance from the international community just as member states work to contribute peacekeepers elsewhere around the world. We witnessed the horrific outcome of neglect in Rwanda and the genocide that took place.

STATISTICS AND AFRICA IN THE MEDIA

59. Question: Since Africans and African governments express doubts, and claim that most statistical information on most African issues and problems don't reflect the reality of the problems and situations on the grounds, are there efforts being made by African governments to correct this problem by providing accurate data to agencies, institutions and others like journalists that might need these information or data on timely and current manner?

Answer:

As any reporter on various beats, gathering information through any governmental agency to do analysis on almost any story will tell, it is very difficult to get information or data from government sources. I have disclosed some of the reasons in my earlier responses, but the reality is that most information when available are being protected because of 'national security.' When a reporter tries to generate data to back up a story, it is often very difficult on the field to get the information required. When it is long-term research, a reporter is confronted with problems, such as logistics and a culture of secrecy as far as respondents opening up to freely answer questions on a survey.

Huge surveys and statistical analysis take a lot of money, which many African governments have other 'pressing' priorities and less to invest in this area. In the presence of a vacuum due to the lack of information on African issues, different agencies such as the United Nations and other non-governmental agencies come in to fill in the dots, even though they have their own reasons for conducting the studies.

Of course, African countries are gradually responding to the need to provide current and accurate statistical data, but with funding still at very low level in terms of budget allocations, there are limitations to the extent these departments would go with collating and updating these crucial statistical information

PART V

MYTHS, STEREOTYPES, AND MISCONCEPTIONS

THE JUNGLE THEORY – MYTH OR REALITY

60. Question: African images in the news and in documentaries tend to show deplorable mud huts inhabited by tribal people. I see red-earth, unpaved roads, jungles, and empty plots of lands with trees and shrubs. Do these images tell of the real Africa, or is it just the selective camera eye view of reporters, producers, and cameramen?

Answer:

You are right. I was surprised when I migrated to the United States about ten years ago and saw these images of Africa on television. As a reporter, I cannot believe that these are images of the Africa that I know, at least having had the experience of traveling around the continent on assignments and leisure trips. This is the 21st century, but the images I witness being portrayed of Africa depicts the "Out of Africa," 40s image that still plays once in a while in the media with any story that has an African theme.

The United States still remains one of the nations with the greatest wealth in the world, and often I see the media trying to make comparisons as unrealistic. Repeatedly showing Africa's weakness irrespective of her major problems is, in fact, not the reality of what the continent and the people are. I am not in any way saying that the pictures or images are not genuine (some of them are), but being human, there are images that send different messages, even when we have not said much. I perceive such exhibitions as subjective, selective and unrealistic of the true Africa that I know. I often tell my questioners that negative images of Africa are like going to poor ghettoes (every nation has at least some) and telling the world that this is what the whole country looks like.

The expectation that the media should act as a public relations outfit for Africa would be an overstatement; however, there are responsibilities that practitioners owe to the public, not just their readers in their places of operation, but the global village. Of course, the freedom of expression has a wild area that it covers, guaranteeing the press broader freedom and opportunities in the U.S. than elsewhere, but images that demoralize, sensationalize, and put fear into people repeatedly, to many critics of the media, are irresponsible. Some people go beyond that and compare the media's use of the airwaves to produce images and comments that scare investors out of Africa as the equivalent of a "media war" against Africa. I may not agree with the last assertion because Africans, including African leaders, are responsible for Africa's fate. However, by the media not reflecting on the positive sides of Africa, it has shown that it is not fair, objective, or balanced in regards to reporting Africa in the news and in documentaries.

There is an African adage that says, "The eyes see what you want them to see." In essence, African images that do not show the reality of Africa's rich cultures, traditions, and people, I have observed, is an integral part of western media culture, not just United States. Life in the cities, villages, and the hard working middle-class people are rarely shown in the media. Like any city or people, Africa has its good sides, bad sides, and Africa's ugly side is the least threatening to global peace and tranquility.

The image of Africa in the Western media not only carries a negative evaluation but also some degree of fear and anxiety. Honestly, I was overwhelmed by this question about Africa's image in the media, since it was one of the most frequently asked questions. First, it tells of the sincerity of questioners about their perception of Africa from what they see in the news, films, and other sources. Secondly, it tells of the weakness of African leadership in confronting this image problem with greater zeal. What a bad image does to any institution (country this time) that is targeted is that it reduces the country to rubble without any weapon of mass destruction. And unlike rebuilding structures that take just money and will power, a country with a damaged image is not that easy to rebuild.

Nations are like big corporations. They need to advertise when it is important. They need to create new images for Africa. Corporations need lobbyists, effective ones for that matter. African leaders on their part have not reached out to the rest of the world in terms of advertising, promotion, and selling Africa and her potentials to the rest of the world. Africa needs to harness this crucial aspect of strategic communications management, among other options, to be able to attract investors.

The most striking consequence of the negative images of wars, diseases, and disasters is that investors are scared away, and African nations and people are deprived of billions of dollars floating around the world (stock markets) in the hands of investors willing to seek places where they could get good returns from their investments. No investor wants to invest in a place where wars, starvation, and diseases seem to be replayed on and on (even when these images don't tell all the truth). Overall, negative images hurt Africa, and they are dangerously anti-development.

As a travel and tourism correspondent driving long distances on the road or flying in the air over major cities in the continent, I have witnessed that Africa's skylines are not much different from what a visitor would see in capital cities such as Europe or elsewhere. But we cannot use the U.S. superpower as a point of comparison in terms of infrastructures and technology. Doing so, especially with African countries, is a mismatch. As I said, there are many things African countries have that are indeed lacking elsewhere around the world.

Since your question touched on the African mud huts shown on television—as if all African houses and homes are represented by this image—I will say that there is no denying that such huts still exist in some villages or that the people that live in them find them as comfortable and affordable as we find living in brick houses. Huts, however, can mostly be seen in rural villages, where at least for now, the preservation of old traditions and cultures is facing the struggle of a lifetime. Huts are very adaptable to African weather, especially in warm temperatures. Cost is another reason; the raw materials used in building the huts can be sourced locally. In my village, there are no houses as at present with thatched roofs. The majority of the villagers still miss their mud walled and thatched-roof huts, unlike the cement walls and shining zinc roofs that now cap every house in the village. Many villagers still feel that, like most symbols of African cultures and traditions that are gradually phasing away, if time is not taken, it won't be long before this beautiful African tradition goes away.

SHOW ME A TRUE AFRICAN

61. Question: Is it true that African-Americans, as well as Africans born to parents that have lived too long in the West (Europe and the United States, in particular) are not considered "true Africans?" How do our African brothers or sisters see us (African-Americans)? What responses will I get as an African-American going to the motherland for the first time?

Answer:

First of all, let me tell you that the reception you will get when you visit Africa will be warm and deeply heart-felt. One characteristic (behavior) that I discovered while traveling around the continent, and it is deeply rooted in African cultures, is the "openness" of Africans to visitors or immigrants—not to mention a son or daughter that they have not seen for a very long time. Experiences do vary, but the majority of African-Americans (the number continues to rise) that have lived or visited the continent will tell you their experiences. It might be difficult to adapt to the cultures of the motherland, which are mostly conservative. Secondly, don't expect everybody to treat you like a prince or princess when you come to visit or to live. The more you act like a foreigner knowing you are black, the more a person may dispose himself or herself to un-welcoming treatment.

I was confronted many times with this question, but I have yet to see an African that expresses the opinion by words or deeds publicly or privately to suggest that African-Americans and Africans born overseas or raised outside African cultures are not "true Africans."

"What is a true African?" I recall a guest asking me. "After all, we were once all Africans." And I cannot disagree with her, except that people have traditions, cultural norms, and values that they want observed and preserved. These minor differences enable us to appreciate our diversity. On that ground, I say we are different, but our differences are less than what we have in common.

Not having been born in Africa should not be an obstacle to a person celebrating his or her African heritage. However, there is an African proverb that says, "Where you are born and live is your home, and you must protect it." When you look at the whole scenario from the context of the proverb, you will understand the migration patterns of Africans over centuries and the settlement of people from across regions in the continent. Also, it tells why Africans are open to immigrants and visitors that decide to live permanently in the continent. Africa's open arms, warmth, and wonderful reception can only be witnessed in few cultures and places in the world. Any visitor, immigrant, or resident in Africa could relate well to what I am saying.

Practical experience shows that an African can easily take a "foreigner" into confidence, first without any restrictions until maybe the trust is betrayed.

African cultures are interestingly simple—and at times complicated and intriguing. To some in the West, including reporters, still find them very difficult to understand and accept. Take for instance a child born in Ibo land outside the culture—even when both parents are from Ibo land, he is said to be "Born in the Bush." A child therefore born in New York or Chicago is regarded as a child begotten in the "Bush." It does not in any way suggest that he is not an African child, nor does it mean that the child was actually born in the bush. It is not derogatory, but it shows that any child that is born and does not hold strong to the cultural identity of his African parents is not fully integrated in the society and should not lay claims to being truly a son or daughter of the land.

The reality of being an African to many traditionalists is not a matter of identity when it is convenient to the person. It is not a matter of being black only. It entails understanding and speaking at least one native language. It does also entail coming from a tribe and being brought up in a particular tradition and culture, where the tribal values are observed and lived everyday. Knowledge of African values and living according to the tenets of these cultural values are key requirements for a person to be identified as "a true" or "real" African.

The expectations and constraints of traditions and cultures notwithstanding, African people do have big hearts. They always leave their doors open for a person that does not meet these requirements earlier disclosed to learn, and be a true son or daughter of Africa. They are volunteers ready to assist or help. But I tell you that no matter what anybody thinks and says, you are an African, not by the color of your skin, or where you live, but by the color and depth of your heart—your conscience. But as long as you are of the human race, you have a link to Africa. After all, we were once all Africans.

The ways in which Africans see and receive Africa's Diaspora, I have already talked about in my earlier response to similar questions. I tell you that anybody black, white, or yellow coming to Africa for the first time will receive more attention than me, who is a native coming home after a long time residing overseas. Africans are very hospitable people, and they will stretch their benevolence to the limits to accommodate you, being an African-Americans. It does not mean that everybody welcomes you with a red carpet, but the instances in which a person would not be well received are few. Many African Diasporas are already living in the motherland, and one of the surprises any visitor coming to Africa expresses is the number of blacks from Brazil, the Caribbean, the Virgin Islands, and the United States now living in Africa. The number is growing, and it is expected to grow further by the middle of the 21st century. In fact, one of the surprises of President Bush's trip to Africa, just like others have witnessed also, was the number of African-Americans living in different countries in Africa, especially South Africa, Nigeria, Ghana, and Senegal to name just a few countries.

62. Question: My sister is married to an African, and there are Africans I have met that disclosed to me that blacks, especially African-Americans' claim to the motherland is a matter of political convenience rather than a genuine connection to her problems, aspirations, and development. Could you please explain to me what this brother meant by this, and tell me if other Africans share his opinion?

Answer:

I recall a professor in an African history class talking about the origin of humans—how we all are descendants of Africa. Scientific proofs also point to the same conclusion about our common heritage. In essence, since our ancestors were taken out of the continent, and we all trace our heritage to Africa that alone justifies any claim to the motherland as legitimate, as a birth rite. It also removes the notion entirely for any suspicion that we are laying the claim as a matter of political convenience and not committed to her development.

Talking about commitment, there are organizations that are based in United States and known to be made up of African Americans that their commitment to African problems have helped give direction to positive development in African continent. Trans Africa, for an example – the Washington lobbying group with former leader, Randal Robinson have been involved with African problems and alleviation of African bondage and liberation from apartheid, poverty and colonialism more than any other known groups in recent memories. African – Americans in the U.S. Congress have sponsored and pressed for approval of bills that was purported to foster development in Africa. Former United States U.N Ambassador Andy Young is devoted to African plight as no other former senior U.S. government officials. Talk show host Oprah Winfrey are among black philanthropists involved in building and improving lives for South African poor. So I dismiss the notion that African-Americans claim to motherland is purposely as matter of political convenience when race-ancestry politics and identity comes up in United States political arenas.

Although cultural differences exist among Africans in the Diaspora, including children born of both African parents, nothing anyone says or misconstrues will prevent this connection to the motherland, especially when we are black. As an American-Italian or Irish-American doesn't have to be born and live in Italy or Ireland to celebrate his or her Irish or Italian heritage, neither should an African-American have to wait and confirm his or her DNA as coming from a particular tribe in Africa to celebrate his or her rich African heritage.

But don't forget, we must love the place we now call home. An African proverb says that a person who does not know his or her history is bound to repeat the same mistake (of history). The same adage says that a person, who does not know where he or she is coming from, may not know where he or she is going next. When a person is ignorant of where he or she comes from, the person is like chaff. He or she could be blown by the wind to any direction.

However, while we recall where we came from, we must recognize that we live in a global village, too, where understanding of our own culture will endear us to understanding other cultures and through the process, create a diverse world where everybody has a say.

There is no doubt that a cultural divide exists between Africans born in the United States or Europe and Africans born in the native motherland, including African-Americans. The differences do not deny or exclude one's history, heritage, or claim to African roots. There is also belief among traditionalists that suggest that Africa's Diasporas no longer observe "motherland cultures" in their new lands, and that automatically denies the person the right to his or her claim as a "real" or "true" African. It is an opinion that they may be entitled to, but whether they are right or wrong is not a yes or no answer.

AFRICA'S TOURISM AND WILDLIFE

63. Question: Outside Serengeti wildlife (the one I regularly watch on television and in documentaries), are there locations in other African countries where I can see animals in their natural habitat, such as in the Serengeti? Is it also true that wild animals live and roam about among Africans in their villages?

Answer:

It is not true that wild animals roam about in villages with villagers in Africa. Villages that are close to the parks that we are used to seeing on television are rare and very isolated farming hamlets. Honestly speaking, it is rare that one sees humans live close to the parks as films and movies do portray.

In Tanzania, there are other wildlife parks, not just the Serengeti. There are Kigoma, Lake Manyara, Mikumi, and Mt. Kilimanjaro parks. In Kenya, there are the Maasai Mara and Amboseli Parks; in Uganda, the Semuliki National Park; in Zimbabwe, the Hwange and Chimanimani; in South Africa, the Tsitsikamma; in Cote D'Ivoire, the Parc National De Tai; and in Nigeria, the Yankari and Kainji Lake Resort, just to name a few countries with wild parks and animal conservation programs.

Yankari wildlife is about 225 miles north of Jos, and it is a very beautiful park for observing the wildlife in Nigeria. This is also the case with the Etosha National Park in Namibia. These parks accommodate a large population of animals roaming on their natural habitat.

Apart from these reserved forests, domestic animals such as dogs, cats, goats, and chickens are common animals that roam in the villages. Goats and sheep cause damage to food crops and therefore are kept in their pens most of the time.

Africans don't keep snakes, turtles, spiders, scorpions, and roaches, as pets that I observed are the case in Europe and United States. Lions, hippos, crocodiles, elephants, antelopes, zebras, giraffes, leopards, bushbucks, and waterbucks all live in the wild, and none that I am aware of live in residential homes.

To reduce the high rate of animals killed by poachers, and displacement as a result of urban development, authorities and animal rights groups have joined forces in creating buffer zones for wildlife conservation.

The worst threat to wildlife is the demand for the body parts of some endangered species of African wildlife in international markets. Other developments not favorable to the preservation of animal species are human activities—construction and the felling of trees for firewood and timber.

Remote farming villages close to parks or reserve forests do sometimes receive "unwanted guests" in the name of animals that encroach on farms. Of course not without confrontation by villagers whose crops and property these animals endanger.

Wildlife is not evenly located across states in the continent. Africa's top wildlife countries are Botswana, Kenya, Namibia, South Africa, Tanzania, Uganda, Zambia, Zimbabwe, Burundi, the Congo, Lesotho, Malawi, Rwanda, Swaziland, and Mauritius and Seychelles Islands.

VOODOO - AFRICAN RELIGION OR MAGIC?

64. Question: Is Voodoo religion, myth, or just part of the mainstream misunderstanding of African cultures and beliefs, perceived as "bad, darkness, and evil?"

Answer:

Christian evangelism swept across Africa in the 60s like a blizzard. Its effects on the traditions and cultures of African people were beyond imagination, both on the positive and on the negative sides. On the positive front, the education missionary schools provided is responsible for the huge and untapped human resources that abound in every field in the continent. Some traditions and customs, such as the killing of twins and sacrifices, were discarded because of Christianity. On the negative side, like when one is stripped of his identity, the inability of Christianity to identify values that are traditional and incorporate those values to African culture was a battle too late won from the part of Africa where I came from. Nobody disputes that people should welcome other religion such as Christianity (as my family and my entire village have), but the way traditional religion was abandoned in some tribes left some people wondering if any society survives long enough through history by turning against its own religion.

Traditions and cultures define people. Owning one's culture as well as religion helps build self-identity, self-esteem, pride, and respect from others; the opposite is the case when the same tradition and culture are trampled upon or allowed fade away. It consciously or unconsciously wipes away people's pride, self-identity, and even self-worth.

One of the conditions in my part of Africa for a convert to be trusted as a true Christian was to denounce traditional beliefs and religions. And since African religions have rituals included into the worship, these rites were considered "idol worshiping." Converts were persuaded to destroy or give away their statuettes, figurines, amulets, and other "charms" associated with traditional religion.

Therefore, it became an abomination for one to identify him or herself as a Christian, and at the same time have these symbols in his or her possession.

Traditional worshipers were addressed as "pagans" or idol worshipers. "Fetish" practices, some of them magical and extremely difficult to understand, became evil practices, too, and that is where the perception of voodoo as idol worshiping or evil originated.

In fact, voodoo religion as it is practiced in Togo and Dahomey is a synthesis of many religions. Voodoo involves shared rites and offerings to deities and gods. Many of these voodoo rites and traditional values are preached against by Christianity. The situation does not help in bridging the deep gully that separates the two religions either. From the perception of early missionaries, the word "paganism" conjures all things superstitious and evil, including voodoo. It is to Christians an evil with which no true faithful should be identified.

Exorcism and spiritual healing are a part of African traditional worship, and in performing rituals and certain practices, sometimes acts that are beyond human imagination were involved, and those "mysteries" that appear "magical" and unexplainable turn into being "evil" by the definition of skeptics that may not understand the rituals. Some call these rites and mysteries voodoo; others say it is idol or "devil" worshiping.

The big question therefore that still remains unanswered, even among Africans, is what is voodoo? Is it religion or magic? Is it the so-called animist religion that goes together with black magic? Meanwhile, the answers vary—even among African Christians and traditionalists.

Voodoo is still identified as a religion that started in the Benin Republic and Togo. It has since grown and is now practiced across the globe—from Brazil, Guatemala, Haiti, and Cuba to the West Indies. Voodoo was recently recognized as a religion in Haiti. Former President Aristide, a former Roman Catholic Priest, signed an edict recognizing the religion into law. Meanwhile, the world's voodoo day was celebrated in Benin in West Africa in 2003.

BACK TO ROOTS

65. Question: I am very familiar with the story of Alex Harley. Were there other prominent African-Americans that have traced, or are in the process of tracing, their roots back to Africa?

Answer:

Alex Haley was not the only descendant of African slaves to trace his roots back to Africa. From Brazil to the Caribbean, Trinidad, Tobago, and Cuba, many blacks have been tracing their roots back to Africa.

Statistics are not available on the number of African Diasporas that have traced their roots to Africa. The number continues to grow since the 70s when the fever caught African Diasporas, especially after the First World Black Festival of Arts and Culture held in Lagos in 1977. As mentioned earlier, people are always surprised at the number of African-Americans and blacks in general from Brazil, the United States, the Caribbean, Cuba, Haiti, and the Virgin Islands and Europe that now live in different countries in Africa.

DNA, genetic science, is making it possible for people to trace their roots back to Africa. Presently, there are two companies (and more are on their way) that are involved in the genetics business. They assist interested African Diasporas in tracking their genes and narrowing it to a particular region or tribe in Africa.

African tribal characteristics are physical and, at times, transparent, too. In essence, a person can identify and distinguish the physical features of a man or woman from West Africa from an East African. It is not always very difficult to tell an Ethiopian from a Ugandan, and the same goes in distinguishing a Kenyan from a Sudanese or a Somali. A Fulani could easily be distinguishable from a Yoruba or an Ibo person. Facial and physical attributes are like DNA, without the details of genetic lab work and processing. The only difference, however, is that physical identification is by a guess.

In Africa, Nigeria for example, there are many African Diasporas who have traced their roots to tribes in Nigeria. They have resettled in the society as part of the business and intellectual community contributing to Africa's development. Some of them have sought, and been elected and nominated to, government positions at state and federal levels in countries they now call home.

Let us, however, not forget that Liberia was the first independent nation in Africa founded by freed slaves from the United States in 1822 and proclaimed a republic in 1847.

The story of Olaudah Equino is an interesting "back to African roots" story that addresses your question. In 1756, Olaudah Equino and his sister were snatched from their village in Nigeria. He was just eleven years old when he was kidnapped and separated from his sister, who herself was taken as a slave.

Olaudah Equino, before finally coming to Virginia in the U.S.A., passed through Barbados in the Caribbean. After buying his freedom as a tobacco plantation slave, he moved to England. There he became one of the opponents of the Slave Trade. He became a writer and wrote an autobiography titled, *The Interesting Narrative of the Life of Olaudah Equino or Gustavus Vassa the African,* where he described the evils of the slave trade and slavery. The book has an abridged edition titled *Equino's Travels.*

In 1998, Equino's origin was traced to the Edeke village, Isseke in Ihiala Local Government Area of Anambra State, Nigeria. Dr Catherine Acholonu of the British Council Library, Enugu, Nigeria disclosed that Olaudah Equino was an Isseke man sold into slavery in the 17th century. Her discovery was unraveling history, and it was made possible by modern forensic technology after several years of research and travels across Europe and Africa. Equino's mother was also traced to a neighboring town of Uli, Ihiala Local Government Area in the same Anambra State in Nigeria.

AFRICA AND REFUGEE PROBLEMS

66. Question: The images or media footage showing long lines of refugees, mostly women and children, walking long distances are constant reminders of the suffering and deplorable conditions war brings to Africa. These images have become constant props for the media blitz of a "troubled continent" always in desperate need. What initiatives (if any) do African leaders take to arrest these troubling (war, diseases, and disasters) situations before they become the huge problems that we see on the television?

Answer:

The global political environment is often very unpredictable. Take a look at hot spots on the globe and the number of conflicts, government changes, assassinations, religious and ethnic turmoil that have taken place in different countries in the last two years. This alone tells of a world that is full of uncertainties. The count, unfortunately, continues to grow with the events in Afghanistan, the Middle East, the Philippines, and remote villages in parts of South America, such as Cambodia, Nicaragua, and Columbia.

No one would have predicted that the war in Afghanistan and Iraq would occur less than two years apart. The same political uncertainty is transparent in some African countries. The difference is that rarely are African wars waged to benefit the majority of the people, since most wars are factions against factions, and they are internal and have never benefited the people. Neither have any of the conflicts in Africa brought wealth to Africa, rather they drain Africa's wealth—including human lives.

Less than six months after the wars in the Republic of Congo, the Central African Republic, Sierra Leone, Liberia, and Sudan were being slowed down, and a cease-fire agreement was being negotiated, a coup d'état occurred in Cote d'Ivoire (of all places in the West African region). It was very shocking to international observers because the country has been, for a very long time, a beacon of real and true African democracy. It was without doubt the most stable democracy in Africa before the unrest. There was a coup d'état in Sao Tome and Principe, a small island nation of about 170,000 people. However, it took strong leadership in Nigeria to settle the political disturbances and restore democracy to the small Island Republic.

As if these events were not yet enough, a new military leader in Guinea-Bissau, General Verissimo Correla Seabra, overthrew the democratically elected government of former President Kumba Yala. Even though it was reported that the new military government was cheered and welcomed by political leaders and a cross section of 1.3 million people in that small country, the same Nigerian leadership was there to restore peace and order. While it is true that these African situations have been partly resolved, it remains to be seen how they hold when the African leaders that initiated these peaceful mediations are gone out of office.

But on a more positive side, Africans have been involved in finding solutions to crises around the world, not just in the continent. Africans participated in World War II at various fronts on both sides. African soldiers participated in wars in Europe, the Congo in Africa, and in Central Asia. African soldiers were some of the most respected and most enduring and admired warriors on war fronts, on the French side during World War II.

African soldiers still take duties as assigned under the United Nations Peace Keeping Mission around the globe. Africa's involvement is not just in Africa but also in such places as Burma, France, India, and Cambodia.

With resources in short supply, Nigeria alone spent over $5 billion on peacekeeping under the military wing of the Economic Community of West African States, known as ECOMOG, in the first phase of the Liberian crisis between a span of five to ten years before the U.S. became involved in 2003. More than 1,000 Nigerian soldiers lost their lives in peacekeeping missions in Sierra Leone and in the first phase of peace-missions to Liberia.

Africa's peacekeepers operating under the command of "UN Soldiers for Peace" participated in many missions including Somalia. In March 1993, following the withdrawal of U.S. Marines, Nigeria, Zimbabwe, Botswana, and Moroccan forces moved in to the countryside of Mogadishu to replace other forces that were confined to the city.

Other peace missions were in the Republic of Congo (Zaire), Namibia, Angola, Western Sahara, Somalia, Mozambique, Uganda, Rwanda, Liberia and the 2003 African-brokered negotiation and settlement of disputes, wars, and coup d'états in Sudan, Angola, Sao Tome and Principe, Cote d'Ivoire, Burundi, the Congo Republic, Central African Republic, Namibia, and Mozambique. Nigeria has always provided safe-havens to refugees and millions of Africans displaced by war, draught, and economic emergencies. When the Liberian crisis started in 1990, an estimated 3 million Liberian refugees fled to Nigeria, Ghana, Benin, and neighboring West African states.

From the liberation of Angola, Zimbabwe, and South Africa, African governments were fully involved with providing financial, as well as tactical, support in addition to global efforts to eliminate imperialism and apartheid.

PART VI

STEREOTYPES, MISINFORMATION, AND

MISEDUCATION

AFRICA AND POLYGAMY

67. Question: Is it true that men still marry many wives in Africa?

Answer:

It is true that some African (traditionalists) men marry more than one wife. However, drawing a definitive conclusion because of a minority of tribes where this culture still exists does not tell the whole story. In fact, in my Ibo tribe, the population of polygamists has dropped drastically since the 70s and with the spread of Christianity. Polygamy is now viewed as a social "aggrandizement" rather than something to be embraced. However, in spots of the continent where the custom is still intact, tribal men still marry more than one spouse, and they are proud to be polygamists.

The impression in the West, and it is confirmed by most of my questioners, is that most Africans are polygamists. This perception is not true. The truth is that the majority of Africans have only one spouse. African men that are polygamist maintain this culture for various reasons. It depends on the situation and circumstances to which the polygamist is exposed or his beliefs that justify his marrying more than one spouse. My account from talking to both parties in polygamous relationships revealed that marriages in most instances are by the choice of a man and the women engaged in such relationship. Rarely are people forced into polygamous relationships. There were instances where women, especially those at a very young age, were forced or persuaded to marry men they didn't want as partners because of the imposition of customs and cultures, but some of these women managed to run away from their husbands.

In the rural villages as well as in cities, most polygamists are Africans of traditional beliefs; the few that wanted to keep their traditional beliefs and still be Christians were ex-communicated, since the church never approved polygamous relationships. These "traditionalists" still believe that it is part of "African culture" that they marry more than one wife. They are not ready to give it up or to bow to any outside pressure. But their beliefs notwithstanding, African cultures strongly emphasize that children are from God. Having as many children as possible, and raising them, is the main reason for such interest by polygamist for that kind of relationship.

Because Africa is so diverse, polygamy is however not frowned at in some cultures, while in others, it may be very unpopular. In a society where the "culture" is unpopular, the practice carries a stigma, especially in places where Christians are in majority.

In pre-colonial Africa, they were other factors responsible for men going into polygamous relationships. Some of them are economic, personal (egomaniacs), political, as well as social and environmental considerations. Some lump these elements together and describe them as cultural factors. Other Africans disagree.

However, while growing up in the village, one explainable reason given as to why some men marry more than one spouse was because polygamy provided the head of the household in an agrarian society with more hands to work on the farm. Since labor is manual, having many children provided the family more hands that could assist with clearing the forest, planting, and harvesting crops. Many hands on the farm therefore provided more harvests and food to sustain the family, as well as wealth from the revenues derived from the sold harvest. In fact, a boisterous harvest in that era symbolized wealth, which attracted the respect of neighbors and villages far and near. It also elevated the status of the man (as industrious and hardworking—virtues admired in African societies).

Socially, there is pride in the number of children a couple has and is able to provide for. There is pride in increasing the family's strength through numbers. With increased numbers, it is assumed that they become powerful strength. Force, defined in terms of having or raising well-disciplined and industrious children who are able to continue the family's heritage, traditions, and cultures. These elements are still as important in African cultures today as they were centuries ago. The village looked forward to (respected) men and daughters to expand the family tree, especially as older generations aged and passed on.

The emphasis on male children still remains as consistent with African cultures as it was in the 60s, even though many Africans may disagree with me that it is relevant. Some men marry more than one spouse because the first wife or the second is unable to provide a male (perceived as heirs to the family's throne, its name, image, and what it stood for). Others marry a second wife due to fertility problems; in very rare situations, with the approval from the first wife.

Wars, diseases, infant mortality (health), ego, and "selfishness" are other reasons why men marry more than one spouse. Africa still suffers high infant mortality, and in essence, the ability to reproduce reduces the risk of children dying from infectious diseases. Modern health care has improved longevity, unlike in the 40s and 50s. However, much remains to be achieved to reduce the mortality rates to bearable levels, particularly infant mortality rates.

No society is exempt from provocation, and the need to have standing "foot soldiers" or armies to fight and win a war cannot be overemphasized. African tribes have fought several wars and at different fronts—including among themselves and in resisting external threats and invasions, for example the offensive of early Europeans. Tribal wars, the unpredictable take-over of tribal lands, and the consequent community clashes are some of the unexpected events which villages must have men to defend against.

When wars were fought with bows and arrows, or on horseback, the number of soldiers that were physically mobilized and sent to war fronts was important in determining the outcome of those wars. Therefore, the chances of winning a war were higher with a large number of foot soldiers or warriors, as was the case in those eras. As we have seen in today's warfare, too, advancement in technology, aircraft, military tanks, and radar guided missiles are still not enough of a deterrent compared to sending men and women to fight at war fronts.

The "Social Net" is another important African culture that accounts for some of the reasons why men take more than one wife. An African proverb says that, "When parents take good care of their children, their children would reciprocate, and in turn take care of their parents at their old age." Culturally, it is the duty of the child to take care of his ailing or aging parents. In a society where there is no social security, no 401K, and no social welfare programs or retirement benefits for the uneducated, the investment in having many children helps in alleviating the problems of elderly care and hospice care.

Culturally, children must provide for their parents at old age. That circle must be maintained. And the larger the number of children in the family, the less the burden on adults who take turns to care and provide financially for ailing or aging parents.

Society changes over time. African society, as far as polygamy is concerned, has changed drastically from what it used to be in the 20s, 60s, and now. In present Ibo tribe of Nigeria, being a polygamist is not socially correct because before Christianity, the majority of Ibo men had just one spouse. It carries "social stigma" in my culture now for men to be married to many wives. Of course, the polygamist may have different beliefs and a different perception of this lifestyle.

Some men marry to boost their egos and self-esteem. They marry many wives to induce competition among their wives. They marry so as not to be "slaves" to one woman, especially the ones that can use "food" and "sex" as weapons to punish the man during marital disagreements.

Economically, it is not convenient for polygamists these days that believe that it is a "culture" that must be embraced and preserved. The cost of keeping a monogamous relationship is escalating. When it is not cheap to feed a family with one spouse, keeping two wives or two families is expensive. It also takes an emotional toll and financial stability to manage a large polygamous family.

The present economic downturn in some African countries is spiraling down to villages. Deflation, inflation, and the high cost of living in most African countries have contributed in no small measures to reducing polygamy and the number of children a family could have.

In African societies today, women, especially educated ones who marry into a polygamous family, have their own reasons; some critics say that these reasons differ from the reasons women in previous generations had for marrying polygamists in traditional societies.

68. Question: If men marry many wives are women equally allowed to marry many husbands or to share husbands?

Answer:

African women are by custom and tradition prohibited from marrying more than one husband. It is a taboo and, culturally, an abomination. There is no history of any woman in my culture that has violated the taboo.

Women marry just one husband because the essence of marriage in traditional customs is to have children, and it is important that the paternity of a child (or children) remain easy to establish. Especially as children (men in particular) remain in their father's house to continue the lineage.

Also, since a woman bears that fruit of love—that special bond between a man and woman based on love and trust—it is important for the man to establish that he is really the father of the child. And as such, a woman having many husbands would not serve this important purpose.

Married men from the ancient accounts in Egypt had affairs—sexual relationships with other women other than their wives—and married women were not supposed to have affairs with other men. In modern times, just as some men clandestinely flirt with other women when married, some women also cheat on their husbands. It is a taboo in African culture, but it does happen secretly in extremely limited cases and numbers.

In African villages, a neighbor's affairs are another neighbor's business. People interact face-to-face on a daily basis, and as such, rumors of infidelity can easily spread. There is nothing so shameful, devastating, and damaging to reputation and self esteem as rumors of infidelity or reckless sexual escapades by a husband or his wife circulating in Africa close knitted village. And when it is true that the woman is found cheating, the mere rumor alone brings about isolation and, at times, social ostracism. Of course, there is no public forum or talk show where people can freely express their opinion on issues that are private and confidential (sexual in nature, including cheating wives or husbands) and emotionally disturbing. In the absence of these forums, people snoop on neighbors to know what is happening, and that "Snooping culture," in part, explains why rumor mills are "common cultures" of villages as well as city lifestyles.

Rumors of infidelity, when supported by evidence of a cheating wife, account for one of the worst African taboos in the sacrament of marriage.

Atonement for any breach of cultural taboo takes a lot of healing, more than seeing a counselor (elders, clergy, and mediators in the village). Any act of infidelity, especially from a woman's side, could lead to divorce. Some consider this to be male chauvinism or a double standard.

Among Catholics, one of the sacred vows that the church approves for reason for divorce is infidelity or a spouse committing adulatory. In Africa, the stigma of infidelity by a female spouse, unlike the husband, remains with the woman for a very long time—maybe for the rest of her life.

69. Question: I would like to visit Africa and enjoy the serenity of nature; I love nature watching. I want to see the rainforest and feel the stillness of virgin forests and wildlife. Is it true that tourists can watch animals from the windows of their living shelters or hotel rooms in Africa?

Answer:

I know that in parks, there are resorts or camps with rented rooms owned and operated by Africans and international business-es. Some of these camps are close to the parks, but not too close that animals could just walk in. Tourists usually board specially de-signed vehicles or trucks to take a view of wildlife.

On a broader scope, Africa is endowed by nature with a huge landmass of virgin forests, plains, landscapes, waterfalls, and long, navigable and winding rivers. Far from these natural gifts, Africa's treasures, unique tribes, abundant wildlife, and beautiful blue skies, along with her traditions and cultures, continue to attract curious tourists from across the globe.

The media impression of Africa will be less influential on our perception of Africa when we can rely on first-hand experi-ence. On that experience, the impression that you have of visiting Africa—be it Kenya, Namibia, Botswana, Angola Ghana, Nigeria, Tanzania, or South Africa—and observing animals living and min-gling with Africans is totally false. Images I have seen on television, cable, and documentaries depicting these scenes of Africans living close to wild forests are rare.

It is a stereotype to think, at this age and time, that Africans share their compounds with animals. On a very serious note, when I tell questioners that Africans do not keep snakes, spiders, and other creepy animals as pets, some of my questioners doubted me. But it is a fact that only domestic animals such as goats, sheep, cattle, and roosters are animals that you could find near homes. Africans do not keep pets such as lizards, snakes, spiders, turtles, pigs, rats, and roaches, as I have observed in homes in Europe and the United

States. Other pets that are common that can be found in most homes are dogs, cats, and rabbits.

Animals are seen as creatures that were created for various purposes—such as dogs that are friendly, guard, and protect the owner. Goats and cattle are meant to provide meat for food. Goats and sheep are domestically bred and sold for additional income when the need arises by some families in the village. Other domestic animals are sheep, pigs, geese, and cattle.

Depending on the region of Africa, there are remote farming villages where animals may, once in a while, stray into homes. That does not in any way suggest that Africans live with animals.

The impression that when you go to Africa you will see animals roaming everywhere could be summarized by the experience of this first-time American teenager who moved with his parents to live in Togo, West Africa. Part of his first letter to his friends in the United States read, "So . . . no, I haven't been bitten by a lion . . . almost by a dog . . .. I hope at some point when I am here that I will take a trip to some places where I can see lions, giraffes, elephants, and gorillas."

The common truth is that for an average African to see animals as we see them on U.S. cable and satellite television channels, such a tourist may have to travel long distances and spend lots of time and money to see animals in the wild as seem on television. It is, however, not yet a pastime of Africans to be too deeply involved in animal watching. Campaigns to make that happen are gradually picking up.

AFRICAN HISTORY TODAY AND TOMORROW

70. Question: Our High School educational curriculum here in the United States was very silent on Africa—her history, tribes, traditions, cultures, and peoples—including black experiences such as African-American ancestors' journey out of Africa. Even at the college level, the same history books are still silent on Africa's empires, except for Egyptian civilizations.
I want to know if Africa's educational curriculum was written from a European's perspective as well, and if so, did they maintain the same code of silence in regards to Africa's history—slavery, colonization, great empires, and kingdoms ... and about the great men and women that lived at those times?

Answer:

African history was taught at schools in Africa but was missing certain details. It was not until the 70s that a new curriculum on African history—some written from African experiences and perspectives—gradually began to replace the once dominant European history books. By this, I mean that history was concentrated on a particular country where the history was being taught. Pick up a history book and it tells of the early "discoveries" of Christopher Columbus and voyages by Magellan but nothing whatsoever about the people living in these places before Columbus or Magellan "discovered" them. There were never history books about African history in the 70s when I was in high school. My first class on African history was at college in the mid-80s.

The history of West Africa, for instance, was not taught in East African or South African schools, and the history of West Africa was never in the curriculum of schools in East Africa. The history of countries in the continent was restricted to just schools in that particular country or maybe in the region. No South African history was allowed into West and East African academic curricula. These great divides are still there, and after more than 20 years, programs to close the gaps were launched, these gaps still exist.

In elementary schools, history was taught as part of lessons on "Civics." Before a new curriculum emerged, lessons about early European voyagers and their discoveries on their travels to African countries, towns, and villages were the dominant themes in most history books. Literature was not spared the European flavored accounts either. Topics such as great Europeans and Shakespearean books—*Macbeth* and *As You Like It*—were not just taught but acted in plays. *Oliver Twist* and *Gulliver's Travels* dominated literature curriculum. The very few African-Americans in Civics books were Booker T. Washington and Dr. Martin Luther King, the founder of the Protestant sect of the Anglican religion. The stories of Martin Luther King Jr. were never told from civil rights perspectives.

Growing up as a child, I observed that geography textbooks were also written and taught from a European perspective. All pictures and illustrations of geographical features and landscapes in texts were European or of the United States. The geographical features of Arizona and the Great Ohio Valleys and Lakes were some of them.

I read about the Cuyahoga River and Lake Erie when I was about twelve years old. However, in the latter part of the 70s, geographical features of Africa began to replace textbooks with European perspectives. In fact, it was not until the middle 80s that finally, African curriculum in various subjects, not just geography, began to reflect more African themes and illustrations than European.

As of today, textbooks by Western authors, and written from Western experiences, are still available. However, African authors have made great strides in the direction of providing African-themed books to students in the classroom. There is no doubt that a lot remains to be done to achieve full independence as far as completely African-themed books in classrooms are concerned. Universities and colleges are still caught in the web of relying on completely Western books now, especially from the United States, for classroom instructions, than from African authors writing on subjects from local perspectives.

Talking about African empires, little attention was paid to Africa's great empires other than Egypt. Not much of history is written about other great African empires such as the Songhai, Mali,

Benin, and Ghana Empires. The Ghana Empire, for example, was described by early Europeans to be developed by all standards based on what these explorers had witnessed in other empires they visited including Egypt and Greece.

Similarly, the silence about booming international trade at that time between Africans, Arabs, and the Chinese before the Europeans came into the scene was unraveled in later books. Agriculture and mineral wealth (excluding oil) were the foundation of most African economies. African historians are emboldened enough now by the lack of African accounts of history to tell their own history.

71. Question: My husband turned down a group trip to Africa—the vacation would have taken us to Tanzania, Kenya, and Senegal. The reason why he turned the trip down was because he was not sure about the measures taken by African governments to prevent the spread of infectious and deadly diseases, such as Ebola, HIV, and AIDS in Africa.

(This question was asked six months before the Severe Acute Respiratory Syndrome [SARS] outbreak.)

Answer:

I am telling you that your husband should have sought more information from many sources available now (including government sources, embassies, and the Internet) before deciding to cancel his African trip. Ebola affected a smaller village in the Congo Republic, and it has since been brought under control. There are efforts to produce Ebola vaccines. The first laboratory test on the effectiveness of the vaccines was successfully carried out.

Canceling a vacation that comes up only once in a while just because of a phobia for diseases or a suspicion of contracting a disease sounds unbelievable to me in the 21st century global village. Because you read that certain diseases are "prevalent" in some parts of Africa or anywhere in the world is not a justifiable reason for you to call off a vacation. You never disclosed whether your husband did his research first before making his decision. However, all I can say is that he missed a wonderful opportunity. I would recommend that he take advantage next time around to see the beautiful African landscape, warm climate, its people, traditions, and cultures.

I do not know the feedback your husband got from other members in his group that never looked back and went on the trip. What were their experiences after their vacation? Don't forget that other than American tourists, million of Europeans and Asians travel to Africa annually, especially to the countries you mentioned. Had there been any new outbreak of diseases, the world would have heard about it. Don't forget that we live in a global village, and as far as information dissemination is concerned, news comes at unprecedented speed and spreads to every nook and corner on the face of the Earth. Had there been any outbreak, no doubt the world would have read or heard the news.

Like any travel overseas, be it to Asia or South America, the chances of being infected by a dangerous disease are small as long as one receives the necessary vaccines and other precautions are taken. Finding out what immunizations a tourist needs to receive is the first step.

We witnessed how the global alert went out during the outbreak of Severe Acute Respiratory Syndrome (SARS). The world community reacted quickly to the outbreak. When the news went out about the outbreak of SARS, for example, suspected travelers with the virus were placed under observation, while others were quarantined. There is no disease that is limited to one part of the world anymore, especially with the fast mass transit of people from one part of the world to another. Much like you were afraid of traveling to these African countries, people on the other side are also worried about the diseases that may be brought to them from traveling through different parts of the world and then returning to Africa.

Modern medicines and improved technology have provided the quick identification of most viruses when they first emerge. While the cure for some diseases have been found, HIV/AIDS and SARS remain challenges, and science and medical communities are rigorously working to find answers to their cure in order to stop the spread of these deadly diseases. Of course, research efforts have increased over decades, but much still remains to be achieved—especially in the areas of research to discover vaccines or medicines that will finally eradicate these diseases.

Faster transportation and the mobility of knowledge have improved the development and distribution of drugs. Drugs that are available could be easily formulated and mass-produced. Most major U.S. and European drug and pharmaceutical companies are among some of the multi-national businesses operating in Africa. Therefore, easy access to medicines is not a problem for those that can afford the cost.

The United States and African embassies have a list of precautionary measures published regularly on pamphlets and flyers informing tourists of what they must know and do when visiting countries around the world. Some of their contents include information on immunizations, security precautions, travel requirements, customs, and do's and don'ts in cultures. This is information that is very important for successful trips to Africa or elsewhere in the world.

There is no guarantee that any trip in any part of the world will be risk-free. When we observe all precautions, listen well, and read and follow thoroughly all instructions from experts about materials on the list of our travel kits and health guide brochures, there is no doubt that our fears can be conquered. With all these precautions, we are bound to make and enjoy a successful trip.

Africa is a land full of traditions, cultures, people, and many tourist sites and landmarks. I will not discourage any tourist from experiencing the African never mentioned in the media.

I have these words of advice for a savvy traveler: no matter where you are going in any part of the world, get your immunizations; always know as much as you can about where you are going; and always ask questions if you don't know certain things. Other than that, always enjoy the wonderful experience of traveling to Africa and the great opportunity she offers to tourists to relax and explore. Africa is not just a place of war, diseases, and disasters.

AFRICAN MARATHON GOLD MEDALISTS:

MYTHS AND STEREOTYPES

72. Question: I have listened to some television commentaries and news analysis on the performances of African marathon athletes. From the words I heard on the radio and television from some commentators, I gathered that Africans do well in marathons because the athletes were exposed, at their very young ages, to tough and rough conditions from their childhood. I was told these included such things as, "walking to school and running the hills." I gathered too that these conditions do prepare the athletes for the challenges of running and winning long distance races. How true is this, and what is the African magic for winning these long distance races?

Answer:

It is true that East Africans do well in world marathon competitions around the world, but I strongly disagree that it is simply because of the environment these athletes were born into in their villages. I have personally heard over and over some commentators say exactly what you are asking me over the airwaves. I am not just shocked by these comments but also surprised by the invention of "geographical factors" rather than hard work, stamina, and endurance, which are factors responsible for any win in games or sports like marathon races. Climbing hills (which is not true) or walking to school on foot has nothing to do with an athlete training well and winning a gold medal, (later as an adult) as a result.

Kenyans do not win marathons because of the so-called high hills and mountains in their part of the world. The condition of an athlete's preparation, rather than the geographical features of his or her birthplace, is what influences great athletes. Winners are known by strenuously training, building stamina, and of course, team and competitive spirit.

It is not just Kenyans that win marathons. The success stories of Ethiopians, Moroccans, Tunisians, Russians, and the Italians in winning marathon races have nothing to do with the landscapes where these extraordinary men and women were born. The diversity of winners shows that any athlete, no matter where he or she comes from, that has the strength to endure rigorous training and that has a disciplined mind and body can be a winner.

Training and building good physical strength are roads to success in long distance running. Commentators that fail to compliment the hard work, training, endurance, and determination that lead to these successes are escapists, attempting to downplay success and renounce giving credit to whom it is due.

If being born and raised up in mountainous countryside is responsible for an athlete winning gold medals in long distance races, then we can assume that people in other African countries or elsewhere with similar geographical features and elevations as Kenyans would have their own share of marathon champions. That is so far not the case. If geographical factors were responsible for Kenyans winning in marathon championship medals, then Greenlanders would have been winning all the winter Olympic medals in ice-skating and other open races on ice. But that has not been the case.

The marathon, like any other long-distance race, is one of the ultimate sports for testing endurance and stamina. To be a participant, you must of course be in good physical and health conditions. Preparing oneself to be in good shape requires a lot of exercise, training, and good eating habits, among other measures.

Most marathon athletes from Africa migrate to Europe and the United States because of better training facilities. They do this because the environment will enable them to train well and build their strength and stamina—elements that determine who will become a champion.

IMAGE IS EVERYTHING:

AFRICA'S NEGATIVE IMAGE IN THE MEDIA

73. Question: Why is it that I don't read much news about Africa's economy, social, and technology news, unlike news about violence, diseases, and disasters? Do you think it has something to do with news selectivity by correspondents or editors that determine what is African news in the media? Or is it because Africa has nothing to offer the world in fields such as science and technology that is newsworthy or that will count in today's global economy and development?

Answer:

There are more than 160 U.S. companies, including multi-national corporations that make up the Corporate Council of Africa (CCA). The council has been in existence since 1993, and its goal was to strengthen the commercial relationship between the United States and Africa. In areas of science and technology, not only are United States companies and major universities involved in training but they are also harnessing African talents through research and development in almost every field of science and technology. To give the impression that Africa has nothing to offer to the world in the fields of science and technology is an academic arrogance that should be avoided. The problem is that African scientists are not encouraged or empowered; they are not motivated and financially supported like their colleagues in industrialized nations to face the challenges in these areas.

Nigeria recently went into the space technology program. It took the administration of President Obasanjo, after more than 43 years and more than ten heads of state, to make the feat possible. Also, not to be overshadowed was the role-played by Nigeria's new space agency and the young talents that executed the task of sending Nigeria's first satellite to space. They add to the hope that young talents in Nigeria will not be wasted, as has been the case in the past.

"Dog bites a man" does not make news, but "A man bites a dog," will. That same traditional principle about what makes news in reporting is very much the order in 21st century news reporting. I guess it is the same principle that guides news reporters and editors in selecting what is news about Africa.

Africans, like any other people on the face of the planet, have life; they are people that live like the rest of us, conduct their daily activities, and make news in all aspects of human endeavors, not just bad and depressing news. There are also economic activities going on in every country in Africa's fifty-three independent nations. There are sporting activities of national and international significance going on, and in terms of content in news in radio, newspapers, and television, little or nothing about them is reported. This is the same pattern of reporting businesses in Africa. Business as usual goes on daily in every African country and almost every sector—not just gold, diamonds, petroleum, and gas trading but in other areas. These activities are estimated to bring in billions of dollars annually.

Africa has its share of global economic activities. African products are still exported to Europe and Asian markets. African exports include cocoa, yams, peanuts, cotton, tea, coffee, animal skins, and hides, just to list a few products. Mineral exports, not just uranium mined in Niger, Namibia, Gabon, and South Africa, include gold, diamonds, zinc, bauxite, aluminum, and precious stones. Other exports are textiles, rubber products, and furniture.

Africa's leadership shares most of the blame for how the people and the continent have been reported and presented to the world for more than 40 years since most African countries gained their independence. In the 21st century, the same "jungle, destitute, savages, disease-infested " mentality is still playing in the news, even though in recent years there has been decline on the frequency these images air or are printed as headlines in the media. What may be responsible is partly our century-old style of doing things and Africa's negligent of how her image is played around the world. Hardly do our leaders study and evaluate the global environment and proactively react to changes in the environment. Rather Africans wait too long, and when the world seems to be very much ahead, we then play catch-up games. By the time you know it, it is too late.

African leadership approaches to managing people and Africa's resources need a total re-assessment. No nation in the continent should be "economically poor" at the level most countries are today—especially with abundant human and natural resources. Africa is due for an overhaul. Good leaders that are known to foster their country's growth and development must be retained in office. For now, limiting the terms of such leaders is not good for Africa. However, non-performing leaders should be allowed to serve their full terms. Democracy is good when defined by the people, as we have seen with leaders that were shoved out because of their non-performance. Africa needs leaders with a strong knowledge of human resources management and development, motivation, empowerment, and inter-play of global politics with growing economies, especially African economies.

The launching of a $1.5 billion satellite by Nigeria in September 2003, executed by Cosmos Launcher in Plesetsk, a district of Moscow in the Russian Republic with a base mission in Abuja, may be a sign or a step towards better communications with the rest of the world. Africa is overdue for satellite television that is as powerful as Arab satellite television networks. There is nowhere else in the world where a nation depends on others to boost the country's image. It is therefore incomprehensible for African nations to depend on the international media to do so.

Africans, both at home and in the Diaspora, have excelled in arts, sciences, and technology. The latest of Africa's wonder kids is not just in computer sciences but also in architecture. African-born British Architect David Adjaye (a Ghanaian) is "the young wonder of [the] London design world." His architectural ideas of using mud—traditional African building materials (used in making African huts)—are transforming and changing the face of global architecture. He is working on projects both in Britain as well as in the United States.

Take the Middle East for example. News from the region used to be from one source, CNN. In a span of five to ten years, the region has established more than three satellite television stations, all beaming news 24/7 across the globe. Just as Africa waits for technology to be transferred on a platter of gold upon the huge human and abundant material resources she has, it also waits for the rest of the world to build or improve its image. From my experiences in the media and from living overseas, that is wishful thinking.

African stories I have read in the media, from the Olympics coverage to wars, natural disasters, and diseases in Africa, are all slanted to give the impression of a continent in the vicinity of poverty—a ghetto. They all have twists of stereotypes, innuendoes, and ridiculous meanings.

GIVING A DOG A BAD NAME . . .

74. Question: Why you don't have to wait anymore for the media to know the truth about Africa—her beauty, her traditions, her people, and cultures.

I have traveled across Africa and many parts of the world; I never realized how beautiful Africa is until I completed this awakening journey. Initially I thought that the continent began and ended with Nigeria, my home country. But the more I traveled, the more I discovered that there are many things that one village lacks that others have in abundance.

Considering Africa's size and dispersed population, exploring the continent is a huge exercise in terms of money, time, and the choice of images to record.

The beautiful weather during different seasons, good climatic conditions—tropical and temperate—beautiful, glowing rainforests, terrain, images, and geographical landscapes are the dots that merge to show Africa's beauty. Temperatures during rainy seasons reach probably the 60s or 70s and as low as the 50s at night. Tropical rains bring life to a halt, and of course, there is the rhythmic sound of African rainwater on zinc roofs, with its mesmerizing, sleepy effects.

I made my first trip to the Ivory Coast (Cote d'Ivoire) in 1982 and repeated the trip in 1990 as a member of team of journalists - aviation and tourism writers from Africa. I suddenly came to the realization (which many Nigerians and Ivorians still have not taken notice or advantage) that their countries are very close to each other, just about 1,000 miles from Lagos to Abidjan, two former capital cities of both countries. Citizens of both countries not yet realized the potentials of each other to tap into them, and share these prospects. The reason I was told by officials in Cote d'Ivoire that this occurred was because the French and English colonizers never wanted the two economies linked. Therefore, economic cooperation, trade, travel, and tourism were not recognized or promoted.

Cote d'Ivoire, the French colony, was during colonial occupation and afterwards structured to be disconnected from English speaking African nations. Phone lines, telecommunication exchanges, and other forms of communications were routed to originate from France. It was not until the 80s that direct dial from Nigeria was installed without going through Paris—the French capital. These creations of the past, and circumstances that surrounded these colonies, have remained difficult to untangle, even with the progress that has been made.

The same colonial bridges that have separated Portuguese-speaking Africans from the Spanish, English from the French, and the Arabic African from one another in all aspects of economic, political, and social activities still remain intact.

The Internet and satellite communication systems, telephone services, and global mobile systems have exposed Africa to opportunities never before imagined. Africa cannot wait for the media to do that anymore. African states are still struggling to close the colonial past; overcome the limitations of transportation, trading barriers and improve relationship with neighbors both regional and continental dimensions. They have realized how these gaps impeded Africa's interstate relationships and economic development.

Tourists or future immigrants could travel to see for themselves without relying on what they read or hear from the media. Also, we can pass lots of information by word of mouth through friends and relatives who are living in or who have visited Africa before. Pictures, art works, and other gift items could also make an impact. Cheap vacation cruises abound, unlike before. People should travel to witness rather pass judgment based on stereotypes and images that don't tell the entire story right. We don't have the media to blame anymore, rather ourselves for not reaching out to resources that are available and would give us balanced and objective information about the African continent, her people, traditions and cultures.

African nations like Ghana, Nigeria, South Africa, and Senegal have been and still are creating "homes" for Africans in the Diaspora, and a visit by you, with friends or relatives, would be an overwhelming experience. It is one of the best gifts anyone could give to the self or to someone they love.

I always recommend Africans taking one or two African-Americans or their neighbors—color or race notwithstanding—

while vacationing in Africa. Some have started the program individually and voluntarily. Africans are very hospitable people, and you will not encounter any cost of accommodation or feeding as long es the visitor is a guest to an African. Of course, there are group-discounted tickets and vacation tickets with hotel reservations avai_able through some airlines during off-peak seasons.

ALL IN ONE BIG FAMILY

75. Question: I have interacted with many Africans and being an African-American married to a Cameroonian, I have observed (please, correct me if I am wrong) that Africans have their biases and stereotypes of African-Americans. Is it true, and what are these biases and stereotypes? How do you think it could be overcome?

Answer:

As a seven-year old boy, I was not surprised that my son came back from school and narrated to me what his classmate asked him about Africa. They have already started forming stereotypes of Africa (from school) as a 'jungle', (not even as a tropical forest) about the continent, the people and where his classmate posing the question knows that we migrated to United States. My son till date continues to query me about the impression he had of Africa from his friends regardless of all the positive things—pictures, films, homemade traditional and church weddings, anniversaries, books, and educational tools—we have in the house and have continuously exposed to him and the stories behind them.

The height of his query to me about Africa came to climax when he told me that his second-grade classmate asked him to "Ask Dad, if it is true that "Africans suck blood." The child was referring probably I guessed to repeated documentaries that often air on television channels depicting the Massais and their 'old or ancient rituals' of sucking blood from their cattle. A person wonders why a child should be exposed to such gory images at that age and as it is, that was what sparked the curiosity of the seven-year-old classmate of my son to ask the question. I was now worried because never in my house have we exposed our children to images of Africa that can be seen on the television news or in "Out of Africa" documentaries and films including those ones in popular 'geographic explorations' and documentaries they produce from them. Also, I felt that the curious child that asked the question should not be blamed either. What we as parents and teachers teach them, along with the images we expose them to at home, are what shape their impression of others including Africa as these children's curiosity and exchange of ideas tell.

Without too much diversion from your questions, I have observed in the cultures where I have lived and studied that there is always a stereotype of one group of people against the other. In families, too, there are stereotypes of behavior some of us—even brothers or sisters—exhibit in our homes, even when we are of the same parents.

Overall, there is always a positive and negative stereotype But whether they are often the truth or not is not the scope of this project.

In short, in every group, both on a local level and on a national level, groups stereotype each other. Yes, there are positive stereotypes and there are negative stereotypes. Stereotypes are not the truth, but most times, there are elements of stereotypes that are true. There are stereotypes that are exhibited by a minority of the population, which we often use to define others in the group. Regrettably, the minority is not the true representative of the majority of the population, but we generalize their attitudes or behaviors to mean that they apply to everyone in the group. Since one person or a few in the population cannot be a representative of all, that is where stereotyping is wrong, and labeling people does not improve relationships and the diversity of the human race.

It is still possible that people can look around and see that even in our tribes, where we are of the same color, we have more in common but still have stereotypes.

When you review my response to the last questioner, you may understand that from West African sides for example, nations colonized in the region by the British, the French, and the Portuguese were separated for so long. A nations' proximity to another nation was never intended for people to know themselves. Therefore, the potentials of each nation never benefited one another.

As Africans, we are taught nothing about the African-American's experience in the United States except sketches of history about a few heroes such as Booker T. Washington and Martin Luther King.

Migrating to the U.S., I witnessed that African-Americans do not know much about Africa either, and the majority of Africa-Americans see the motherland from the unimaginable images of poverty, diseases, and disasters, so the stereotype exists of Africa from the standpoint of what the media relays to blacks about their motherland. Taking Black Studies classes at University, I realized that there are many things that Africans do not know of African-Americans, and history books don't talk about Africa.

In the 21st century, the images still presented to the public depict the same "stereotypes" of Africans in the media. There are deep misconceptions on both sides about issues that we should know in order to help educate others, which most of the time, we don't.

Again, as a reminder, this is the 21st century, and with the Internet and the best communications network ever, we can no longer rely on only one source of information to tell us stories about Africa and African-Americans in the United States. It is our duty to bridge the gap and to eliminate the stereotypes. Some of them have been projected for so long that it will take a tough stance to change.

In whatever circumstances, the duty is on our shoulders to correct misrepresentations and stereotypes through interaction and communication. Absolute communication gaps foster stereotypes, and with reinforced publicity, these stereotypes become cemented in the minds of people that want to believe in them. When we do bridge the gap, not only between whites and blacks but also between blacks in the Diaspora and blacks in Africa, these stereotypes will be minimized and eliminated in the long run. We may realize that we are all of the human race, and in a global village, we must see each other as brothers and sisters, whether black, white, or yellow.

COLOR AND AFRICAN IDENTITY

- NOT AS CLEAR AS BLACK AND WHITE

76.   Question: I am a brown-skin, full–sized African-American woman. I tell you this from personal experience that black brothers seem to fall over their heels for lighter skin and slim women. Do African brothers in the motherland have the same preference for slim and light skin women as they do here in the United States?

Answer:

I talked about stereotypes in my previous responses, and in fact, it would be falling into the same trap of stereotyping to assume that because few men choose light skin women over dark skin women that it is a common behavior. Africans come in rainbow colors, similar to what an observer witnesses on the streets in any U.S. city. And in most families—including extended families—there may be one member or another that has light skin as well as dark skin.

Young men and adults don't pay too much attention to color anymore except for a few, where it may make sense to date based on the color of skin. I am not talking of places like South Africa, Namibia where the color of white and black still divide people. But in my tribe, it is true that there are men that admire and have a preference for fair or light skin women. It is not so manifest or such a problem that one should devote time to thinking about it. It is a matter of personal preference and choice. And African cultures do respect people having such choice.

What I know as a social concern (not a problem) is that it is not fashionable to date thin or overly slender women in African culture. Overall, any woman, whether thin or not, is accepted for who she is inside rather than for her size or shape. Big or large-sized women do not at all attract any stares, neglect, and stereotypes, as some cultures do unconsciously. Being too thin gives more room for suspicion that the woman is suffering from genetic abnormalities (anorexia) or dying of an incurable disease.

Good health and shape are important to African woman, and since most daily activities involve manual labor, the need for fitness center-type aerobics is unnecessary. Fitness centers exist but are mainly popular in cities.

A "typical" African woman is not thin, or fat, but she is endowed with beautiful curves—some call it a figure 8—or 'the idealistic' anatomy of a real woman. That means a lady with moderately curved hips and a moderately sized chest, not big or fat, but not too slim either. My description is not a rubber stamp of beauty in its entirety because beauty is in the eyes of the beholder. It also takes more than just body fat and skin to measure beauty. In my culture, where slim and "large-sized" women run indiscriminately in families, there is not much attention paid to the size or shape of a woman's body.

COLOR AND AFRICAN IDENTITY

77. Question: Is it true that in Africa a person is identified as white once he or she has a drop of white blood in him or her?

Answer:

The reason why some people share this opinion is very difficult to explain. However, critics attribute the mindset or belief to colonialism and images that have been presented over the media for a very long time. These negative images tended to reinforce the "Out of Africa" syndrome that plagued the airwaves and television for centuries. And this was played with the image of the whites on more positive sides all the time. So, since there was nothing in between the negative black and positive white, the assumption is that either a person is black or white. If you are not black, you automatically became white.

It is true to some extent that once a person has a drop of white blood in him or her, that person is automatically identified as white. The reason for this may be due to an attitude that has been reinforced over and over that "white is always the best." There is no place that I am aware that non-whites are classified as whites other than in Africa.

It was, however, surprising to me to ask myself this question before I migrated to the U.S. Why is it that in Africa, the majority still classifies Mexicans or Puerto Ricans (who in Puerto Rico and the United States are considered to have African heritage) as "whites." In other words, Mexicans, Puerto Ricans, and even Caribbean or the Virgin Islanders with predominant white genes are classified as whites. Africans that have traveled or received an education of course know the differences.

However, in African cultures, a person's race is not focused on as much as it is in the United States or Europe (except in South Africa or in countries such as Namibia). To most Africans, the impression demonstrated above may not change since it is not an important concern in determining how an average African relates to another person. In Africa, to be sincere, people deal with others on a personal basis, not on a racial basis.

Africans are very open to accepting people and assimilating them into their societies no matter the color or race of the person. People are not coded or classified by race unless in South Africa or Zimbabwe, where the whites, even though in minority, have the financial power, while blacks in majority, still comprise the poorest in the society. In the eyes of an African, hardly are Asians, Europeans, and Americans treated or segregated based on the color of skin, the person's religion, or their creed. You are either a native or a visitor, and Africans are very hospitable people and respectful of other people's cultures.

BLACK ON BLACK STEREOTYPES

78. Question: I have an African friend, and my sister is married to an African. Occasionally, there is this attitude in him (the African brother) that he unconsciously exhibits, which could be interpreted as African pride—proud of being an African. I wonder if this attitude runs among Africans generally, since some of my friends have similar experiences, or is it just a personal attitude?

Answer:

First of all, the attitude of your African friend is personal. Secondly, there are some Africans that have migrated to the West, not just the United States, and realized that racism is alive and well. Also, amidst other cultures, African traditions and cultures are rich in values and therefore must be embraced, respected, and projected. In essence, some Africans may take Africa's strong moral and ethical values as being above other cultures—something to be proud of and to show off. Is this the case for the majority of Africans? Of course not. Africans are described as very simple and easy to get along with. However, these remarks do not mean that every African has the values they have disclosed. Overall, what is seen is that an average African is proud of his or her culture.

Further, in response to your questions, the attitudes of the two Africans you know are not in any way a representation of Africans in the United States or elsewhere. There is a publicly expressed divide between blacks and whites in America; however, for some, this divide is very deep. Unlike the divide between whites and blacks that is racial, political, social and economic, the divide between some Africans and Africa's Diaspora is cultural and ideological. Some are as a result of competition.

Some believe that Africans as coming over to America to take their jobs. There is rivalry, especially in business or office environments. Also, there is an insignificant percentage of African-Americans that strongly believe that Africans are equally accountable for slavery—especially those that are not well informed or college educated. Regrettably they harbor the 'grievances' silently or express them when in contact with Africans.

Among educated African-Americans, the bias, stereotypes, and attitudes to which I am referring are subliminal, unlike the literal ones. Also among those that have been to Africa, the impression is almost non-existent. The majority of African-Americans, as well as Africans, don't discriminate among themselves or others. The majority realizes that there are more characteristics that connect them to Africa and human race than that divides us—our race, religion, and creed notwithstanding.

In today's global village, diversity is not just about learning about other races but also about looking at us as coming from various backgrounds with different personal experiences and cultures. We must also be seeking ways and means of closing the communication gaps, not just between whites and blacks but also between Africans and African-Americans in the United States. Do not get me wrong, the relationship between Africans and African-Americans is good, considering increasing marriages and the numbers that visit Africa each year or that now live in Africa. However, there are bridges to cross, especially those things that make us suspicious of each other's intentions and directions. Attributed that still plague African tribes and traced back to 'Divide & Rule" colonial policy of administration.

The media images we have of each other have, for decades, run contrary to what we thought of each other. I previously used an example of Nigeria and Cote d'Ivoire, two African countries on the West Coast of Africa, just about 1,000 miles apart, yet these neighbors were far apart from each other for more than a half-century. They see each other differently because of the way colonization framed the nations and separated the people.

There is no time in the 21st century for the blame game. Since we are more exposed to different media now than ever before, it is up to us to open up and learn about one another—about human diversity overall. Travel is affordable and the opportunities that will make us live and enjoy our diversity—whether black, white, or green—are now available than ever before.

A reporter that went to Africa for the first time during one of the U.S. Presidential trips returned surprised by the level of misunderstanding of Africans—not just by whites but by African-Americans. According to him, the journey was an eye opener. It revealed to him a beautiful continent, proud heritage, and loving people ready to welcome any visitor or immigrant with open arms. Africa, he described, is more than anyone has read in newspapers or seen on television.

I explained to an African-American friend that I have been discriminated against by some because of my accent. He remarked, "I was thinking the reverse should be the case." In other words, he felt that I would be less discriminated against as a black person in the United States because I have an accent and was therefore "a foreigner." I told him that discrimination at times does not recognize accent as an advantage. In some places, including among blacks, the more predominant the accent, the more the person may be discriminated against.

All cultures have some experience of one tribe or group stereotyping another. I am not saying that this is the case between Africans and African-Americans, but I want to give you a picture of relationships between groups around the world. Diversity is the slogan of the 21st century, and as we live more in a global village, the need for us to embrace one another becomes very important.

PART VII

SEX, NUDITY, AND SEXUALITY

AFRICANS AND SEXUALITY

79. Question: I wonder what Africans think about us and sex. I learned from a friend in the Peace Corps in Africa that Africans see us in America as sexually permissive. How true is the observation, and how do Africans define sexuality? What does it mean to be sexy in Africa?

Answer:

Daily life in Africa is framed with traditional values. The value system cuts across tribes, and since one tribe may live in more than one country, the overlap of cultures is overwhelming. It means that an opinion on one subject may not change much in several countries, or it may change drastically within the same country. High mobility and easy association among people from diverse cultures enhances the learning process among tribes.

The traditional religion that was practiced centuries before Christianity came to Africa shaped people's conscience and values. In traditional Africa, it is a taboo to talk openly about sex. There is a veil of secrecy surrounding it.

From observing and living in several African cultures, I have yet to find a place where people are not discrete or conservative about sex. In Africa, religion and customs prevail on behavior, including how women dress or express their sexuality. They both require that women pay attention to what they wear and how they dress in public.

An individual's sexual orientation is not a concern for others because it is private. It is a "don't ask, don't tell" belief. African cultures portray sex as something to be engaged in for procreation purposes only" and not for gratification. Through these stipulations, the society hopes that it will "prevent" adolescents from recklessly engaging in sex when they are not ready to deal with the outcome.

Public nudity, even in villages where it once existed, is no longer acceptable culture. Villages that still have men and women nude (some we occasionally see on cable and satellite television

programs in the United States) are located in extremely remote locations. They are sparsely populated and far away from the rest of the
cities and villages in Africa. Since there is no restriction on nudity,
their way of expressing freedom is to dress as they wish and as their
cultures dictate. Subjects involving culture are delicate, and rarely
does the government touch on or engage in politics with anything
traditional or cultural. Doing so comes at a great price. That is why
attempts to legislate or regulate culture have failed—unless such
cultures endanger life, and people believe that it actually does affect
their daily living.

In fact, to the majority of the public, nudity attracts public
outrage, embarrassment to the nudist, and the discomfort of public
stares.

Personal sexual habits and orientations are not subjects of
public discussion. For the new or "next generation" Africans, the
adolescents in particular, the story is a bit different. The wall of silence around sex is gradually falling apart. Yet, these unlocked doors
are nowhere as open as they are in Western societies.

In Tanzania, in the month of July 2001, ten newspapers and
magazines were banned from circulation because the government
believed that the publications were "promoting the spread of STDs"
by exposing youths to sexual innuendoes and images. Other reasons
included violating the traditional values of speaking publicly without reservations, thus violating an African taboo.

The same experience occurred in Nigeria before Tanzania's
clamp down on nudity. One of Nigeria's popular circulating newspapers featured scantily dressed women, but it was forced to stop
the publication of the pictures. The National Film and Video Cen-
sors Board in Nigeria approved 76 local movies for the month of
September 2002, and 70 of the video movies were classified unsuitable for broadcast because of explicit sexual innuendoes and sexual
content. Pornography is against the law, and trading any material or
literature on nudity is a crime. Preventive measures no doubt limit
the circulation of nudity in public, but it is still a lucrative underground business.

Romance novels from European authors have for last thirty
years found market among African young readers. The African cul-

ture restricts native authors from exploring the genre. However, satellite entertainment and cable television have grown over the years. Africa has over 15 million CNN subscribers. Africa's talk shows on radio and TV, MTV, and Soul Train are received live from various locations across the continent. Africa's version of "Big Brother" aired in 2003, and it was broadcast around the continent through satellite television. The program received mixed reviews, but the overall rating of the debut program was good, even as critics disagreed, maintaining that it was damaging to African culture and exposed youths to sexuality.

With information technology at a level unimagined before, sexually oriented materials transmit easily through the Internet, satellite television, and cable news networks. With the airwaves saturated with this information, cultural taboos are attacked on a routine basis. Subjects such as sex, once taboo and avoided in public discussions, are now openly discussed on radio and television shows. However, local stations, even privately owned media, are still very cautious not to violate the broadcasting codes against pornography on the airwaves. The free expression of sex on American radio talk shows, the proliferation of sex bars and saloons, strip clubs, sex on television, and sexual innuendos on advertisements are what may be shocking to Africans.

AFRICANS AND NUDITY

80. Question: I have seen images of some tribal villagers—men, women, and children—clad in native African dresses: some of them are half-nude while others are totally nude. It is my personal impression that African societies accept nudity as way of life. Is this true? What can I learn about African tribes and nudity?

Answer:

I have traveled extensively, writing and reporting news. I have accompanied government officials to launch or promote development projects in very remote villages. I have traveled on several assignments and visited and lived in some of these native tribes. In fact, I never realized the beauty of African traditions and cultures until I came in contact with villagers that still live everyday as their old traditions and cultures dictate without interference from other cultures. For example, the Maasai people of Kenya. It is not until a person encounters villagers that he or she realizes how much our own culture has been "degraded" or adulterated (even with our strong values).

There are different perspectives to life in remote villages compared to city or urban lifestyles. The Maasai and the Himba tribes are among some of the few African tribes that still have their cultures intact. However, our intrusion to their cultures and lands are, unfortunately, trampling and destroying these unique customs. Regrettably, in the long run, it may not be good for the people, and all of us, because the history, tradition, and cultures they are preserving may one day be extinct.

In Ibo tribe today, the language and culture are facing serious threat from other cultures, in particular the Western culture. New generations don't speak the language as frequently as they should. There are no museums or monuments to celebrate the culture, and the worst threat is the westernization of modern Ibos.

The images you may see of nude tribes are in remote tribal villages that express a culture of nudity. In Ibo culture, there is no nudity. Across Africa, there are very few isolated tribes that you can spot on the map where nudity is still their lifestyle.

The Maasai of Kenya and the Hamer people of Ethiopia are examples of tribal people that have free expression of what they wear and what they bare. Dress or no dress, I was overwhelmed by the closeness of some of these tribes to nature. I realized that to Maasai tribal people, the number of assets such as cars, big homes, and other property we have does not measure their happiness. If the money in our wallets or the cars in our garages measured happiness, the Maasai would be very far away from it. That may not be the case. With the Maasai, or Koma people, the level of spirituality manifest in their lives, and their values, made them seem happy and not concerned with lifestyles outside their tribe and how we think of them and their culture.

The Maasai (Kenya), the Mandingos (Sudan), the Hamer tribes (Ethiopia), and the Koma tribes (Nigeria), including pockets of rural tribes, have like many other African tribes fought "cultural imperialism and exploitation." While from a distance, we may marvel at our differences, they equally wonder what exploitation we have brought to them and to their environment. The Maasai have been displaced in the Maasai Mara National Reserve because of tourism, the lure for tourists to the Kenyan section of the beautiful Serengeti plains, and the wildlife that the same region holds.

What you can learn about Africans and nudity in cultures where nudity is still allowed is about human closeness to nature in a sense that everything about nature is natural, but humans have always tried to tamper with that nature. Overall, Africans value nature primarily because nature is significant to the existence of body and soul. Nature has important values, not just for the air we breathe, or the shrubs and herbs that come from the environment for medicinal purposes. Nature, in essence, is life. From myths to folktales, the stories are the same. Just as a person must not be disfigured while on Earth and alive neither should the land be desecrated or polluted. It is believed that humans will be reincarnated, and the land they will occupy must be pure.

In some African cultures, the worst abuse of a woman is to strip and expose her nakedness publicly. In this instance, the nudity portrays the severity of abuses and pains. The case of the nude Delta women—the group of women in Nigeria that used nudity as a communication tool to get their message across against the abuse of their environment by oil companies—is another example where nudity symbolizes the severity of pains and violation. The women exposed their nudity to send a message that oil companies polluting their lands and environment were poisoning the souls and minds of the people. Such expression of nudity means a lot in their culture.

HOMOSEXUALITY: DON'T ASK AND DON'T TELL

81. Question: I was recently in Africa, and I was surprised that certain subjects, such as homosexuality, are never talked about or discussed publicly. How do homosexuals fit into conservative tribal societies? I gathered that customs, traditions, and cultures determine every behavior. Is homosexuality a taboo by definition of all of the above?

Answer:

Homosexuality is a subject that is hardly mentioned in private or in public because it is very uncomfortable to talk about. In short, it is still a cultural taboo to be a gay or lesbian in Africa.

But as we know, consciously and unconsciously, some elements of the Western culture sweeps around the world like a tornado, just as African cultures have for decades impacted other cultures around the world too. But subjects or issues that other cultures are skeptical or 'uncomfortable to talk or deal with becomes open to public on Western front, it does not take time before they filter through everywhere around the world. Such was the issue of human rights, democracy and now gay rights – fast-forwarding at lightening speed altogether another issue; and that is gay marriage. Some subjects that once was extremely difficult to touch or talk about in public, and now 'easily' discussed publicly over the airwaves in Western media and even in conservative religious organizations such as the Methodist and Catholic churches. Some call U.S. impact on issues around the world as the power of great nation's media in the 21ˢᵗ century. Others call it the effects of globalization with one nation, United States, for the mean time the leader of the global village. In essence, what I am saying is that five years ago, it was unimaginable, even in the U.S., that homosexuality would be discussed in the media, it was unthinkable few years ago that a homosexual, not to mention a bishop will be invited to primetime network news program with his male partner to talk about their relationship. To any African, it is an extremity of taboos and a violation of the matrimonial relationship between a man and a woman. However, as uncomfortable as many people are, they are reflecting on these changes, weighing both the negative and other impacts such open cultures may have in the long run on people's attitude towards individuals with this type of lifestyle. In Africa, homosexuality is still regarded as an "abnormal sexual behavior," and it may take a while (if at all is possible) to change that belief.

Africa has on some situations and under certain circumstances resisted Western influences on her cultures. But as history tells us, even when there are conservative societies (majority in fact) that will always resist such Western influences on African cultures, there are other cultures that will welcome these changes, even when it is not talked about or celebrated openly. For now, in Africa, homosexuality remains a cultural taboo that may be very difficult to overcome because of the difficulty societies are resistant to cultural changes in Africa.

In the computer age—with the Internet explosion—dialogues on the subject of homosexuality are open on the web, and since these issues are beyond people in societies where the subject is a taboo to stop, they are catching in on these discussions even as publicly people express their rage that such discussions should be allowed in the first place. People do anticipate, in the next generation, "Africa's many codes of silence" on subjects or issues such as open discussions on sex, homosexuality, women sexual development and problems may begin to unravel.

But we are certain that things always slowly change in conservative African societies. Africa's traditional values, coupled with strong religious principles, add to this conservatism. Individuals may have their liberal opinions (tolerance attitude), but in Africa, where life revolves around community, it is the community that dictates what is right and wrong. Therefore, professing acceptance of what the society considers a taboo is very difficult. The media can bring the subject to the public arena, but individuals talking about homosexuality in public will still be considered an abomination.

Homosexuals could be found in any part of the world, irrespective of race, gender, religion, and creed. Some may speak out about the subject; others still keep the subject out of the public domain or "in the closet of their 'undisclosed secrets." However, in many parts of Africa, culture and tradition have made it impossible for homosexuals to come out in the open, as they do in the West. Any open disclosure of homosexuality is a very risky gamble with personal life, reputation, image, family relationships, and the damages it may be ushering in, that could be avoided by don't ask, don't tell code of silence. These are not experiences that anyone would want to live with for too long. In close-knit African societies, relationships with family and neighbors are treasured and any attempt by a homosexual to come out publicly will ruin these relationships.

In short, no homosexual would want to be ostracized or allow the members of his family to be treated as outcasts or felons. Simply put, there are retributions for being gay and coming out in Africa.

The opposing reaction of the Anglican synod of Nigeria during the ordination of a gay bishop in the United States speaks volume about the descent of the church against homosexuality. Also, African Anglican bishops in Nigeria with over 17 million members (the largest outside England) criticized and registered their dissatisfaction and threatened not to receive the Anglican Archbishop of Canterbury during his trip to Nigeria for contemplating to ordain a gay bishop in Britain. The gay bishop later withdrew his nomination for his ordination.

Internalized and conservative societies see sex, even among married couples, as sacred and private. That is why in almost every African society, hardly are spouses seen holding hands or kissing on the streets. That level of conservatism says a lot about how the society may react to lifestyle that may be considered a taboo.

Zimbabweans were surprised in 2002 when gays and lesbians marched openly and protested on the streets in the country seeking recognition by that society.

TEENAGE GIRLS AND EARLY MARRIAGE

82. Question: I read and heard that most African women marry at very young ages. At what age do most African women marry?

Answer:

Honestly, it is very difficult to say categorically at what age women marry in Africa since cultures vary and it is the one of the most defining factors on marriage in African cultures. As I always emphasized, Africa is not a monolithic culture, therefore it also depends on the tradition of the people, the tribe, the culture, the religion and in what country of Africa. Overall, there are many other factors that determine at what age a woman marries. It also depends on the type or class of family she is born into. In traditional societies, women marry very early, between the ages of thirteen and eighteen.

There is this impression I came about during the period I was putting this project together among my questioners that young women are whisked away and married to men that they don't love. Yes, no doubt there are situations where families determine what type of man a woman will marry or the family their daughter would be married into, but when such circumstances occur and the woman is uncomfortable with an arranged marriage, she could divorce, or flee, from the man. As I write, the culture of arranged marriages in Ibo land, for instance, is gradually phasing away. But in rural tribal villages in Africa, it is still the culture that they believe has more advantages than disadvantages. Marriage is a sacrament and an institution that must be preserved at all costs. Marrying into families where the husband or wife is comfortable with shared values is very important. Such other factors as religion and tribe, and attributes such as hard work, perseverance, and families not prone to inheritable or genetic diseases, and not prone to criminal activities are among the reasons parents arrange marriages for their sons or daughters in some African cultures.

In traditional African societies where education or women going to school is not top on the list of their priorities, they often marry very early. In such societies, the roles of women still remain raising children and taking care of the home. In cultures where women have limited opportunities to go to school, they do more than just take care of the children and catering to their spouses. They also work in family farms.

Africa has come a long way in the cultural revolution. It has also passed through several cultural gestation periods. All aspects of a woman's life have improved from what they were in the 60s, but a lot still remains to be achieved. It is not uncommon to have women's issues discussed publicly. The education of more women has led to a large number of women graduating from high schools. In the Ibo tribe of Nigeria, college and university enrollments are predominantly women. The pattern is not just in cities but also in the rural areas. However, there are tribes where women's literacy rates are extremely low and frightening.

There are laws, depending on states, in Nigeria that mandates compulsory elementary education for children, boys in particular, since the rate of school dropout for boys, compared to girls, is growing faster than projected.

Africa is witnessing an improvement in the age women marry. A look at the overall picture of women and marriage in contemporary African societies shows that the pursuit of higher education, smaller family sizes, and career development affect the age women marry. On the man's side, marriage requires emotional, and financial stability to be able to handle it. Traditional marriage in Africa takes more financial and emotional huddles that some struggle to fulfill.

African cultures do not accept unmarried partners living together, even when it is obvious that they may eventually become husband and wife. Such co-habitation does happen but it is discouraged. And when they do, since "It Takes a Village," parental pressures mount to stop it from happening. The same pressure faces men that marry women considered underage, especially in towns and cities.

Apart from the social stigma (more against women than men) on women that co-habit with a man when they are not married, the church also imposes its own rules and punishes parents (in subtle ways) whose children engage in such co-habitation without officially marrying in the church. The church would be the last to wed an underage bride in the church—and don't forget that the church has very strong influences in every facet of African life, not just on religion alone.

In the rural areas or villages, the median age at which women marry today varies from culture to culture, villages, and towns. Ages range from thirteen to eighteen in rural traditionalist culture and often-conservative societies; eighteen to twenty-six among the middle-class; and between twenty-two and thirty-two among the educated class.

Gradually, African societies are witnessing a growing number of single parents, in particular among educated women in cities. Single-parenthood is not as frowned upon as it used to be, but every society still sees the institution of marriage as key to a strong family and community.

DIVORCE, AND DOMESTIC VIOLENCE

83. Question: Single parenting and divorce, I learned, are very rare occurrences in Africa. Could you tell me about how African societies deal with these social problems? Are there reactions to divorce and single parenthood that are different from what we have in Western cultures?

Answer:

Africa is a very diverse continent with various cultures and value systems. The ways and means that societies deal with single parenthood and divorce vary from one culture to another. As we have seen in previous responses to questions, religion plays an important role in people's moral and ethical judgment and values. Therefore, a person's religious beliefs shape the person's behavior and the individual's reaction to impulses around him or her. Moral and ethical codes are specified by tradition, religion, and an individual's conscience and other beliefs.

It may not serve a good purpose to give a blanket "yes" or "no" answer to your question. For instance, in Nigeria the Ibos are known to be conservatives, and in such a conservative society, the divorce rate is extremely low, but in the same country, there are other cultures where divorce and single parenthood are tolerated.

Single parenting, however, is not a popular culture, and it is facing the same opposition and disapproval by the majority of the people, partly because it is unnecessary and secondly because of the church's enforceable moral standards, which have so much influence on people's lives. In fact, the church condemns single parenthood (unless it is as a result of the death of a spouse), and any deviance attracts punishments that include the withdrawal of the right to receive the holy sacrament of communion. The privilege to be wedded in the church could also be removed. Compared to other tribes in Nigeria, divorce rates and women having children out of wedlock are very low.

On the other hand, there are tribes where single parenthood does not attract the rebuke or disapproval that it does in Ibo culture. The point is that single parenting is not frowned upon or stigmatized, as it is in the South.

In most conservative African tribes, it is a cultural taboo for a young woman to be single and pregnant. There are circumstances where the man or boy responsible for the pregnancy has been persuaded to either marry the teenager or take full responsibility for the care and financial welfare of the mother and child. In some instances, parents have weighed in to take full responsibility of the baby by taking custody of the child.

The divorce rate is dismissingly low in Africa for the main reasons that tradition and religion have established strong moral standards and prescribed rules and order, including consequences that make divorce somehow difficult. However, when compared to the generation of our parents, the divorce rate among new generation of Africans is on the rise. Overall, Africa's divorce rate is still nowhere close to what is witnessed in Western cultures or in the United States. Most divorce cases in Africa still occur in cities compared to villages. And in villages, especially in traditionalist families, a wife may prefer to remain in the marriage, even when the husband has married another woman.

Raising children in African culture is community-based. It takes a village to condemn a teenager that "destroys" her future by getting pregnant without a spouse. In the same vein, it takes the same village to embrace the child born under this circumstance into the community. Uncles, fathers, mothers, big uncles, nieces, and nephews are available to assist a pregnant teenager, even though teen pregnancy is frowned upon and condemned—but of course, they do occur. Teen pregnancy becomes the responsibility of the individual and the society; most importantly, it has serious implications and repercussions. Women forced into marriage following teenage pregnancy are often victims of domestic abuse, violence, and eventually divorce.

The nuclear family provides the guide, the support, and the counseling needed to carry on the weight or problems from marriage. A woman being abused by her husband could flee to her father's home. The husband always atones by coming back to his spouse's home with gifts. He is, in most situations, accompanied to his in-laws by elders in asking for forgiveness from the wife. It is not always that this arrangement works well, but mediation (by family, the community, including the church) has been the strongest approach to resolving marital problems in African societies.

For the wife to come home, the husband must pledge not to raise his hands on their daughter (his wife) again. The husband may decide not to show up at the atonement ceremony. If he refuses to show up, he may lose the custody of his children, especially if the woman has fled with them to her father's village. It is an attribute of self-failure in most African cultures if a man loses his wife and his family through this way. It also brings disrespect, since some may take the separation or divorce as a failure on the part of the man not the woman. Africans see keeping family together as the biggest assets to the community and most assuring success story a man or woman can tell of his or her life. Family, when managed well, is seen also as a status symbol.

TEENAGE PREGNANCIES

84. Question: I was told that families ostracize a teenage daughter that gets pregnant while she is attending school. How true is this? And how do you describe an average teenage girl's relationship with her mother (versus peer pressures)? How big of a problem is teenage pregnancy in Africa.

Answer:

It is not true that parents ostracize teenager daughters that get pregnant. However, in Africa, where promoting conservative religious and social mores are important, having a child out of marriage, or a teenage pregnancy for that matter, is simply breaking a cultural taboo. It is not only an embarrassment to the family of the girl but it also lowers the public respect of the girl's family. How seriously the problem affects the family of the girl depends on the family's good or bad reputation and the moral standard in the family. It depends on how conservative the parents are. However, parents, in cultures where girls are not married at ages of thirteen always feel disappointed, saddened to say the least, when their teenage daughter gets pregnant. There is that feeling hanging around them, and at times, it may be very difficult to take down. There is this moral conscience that tells them they have not done well enough in bringing their daughter to face her world, else she would not have become pregnant at such a young age.

In conservative African societies, "good name is worth more than riches." Parents are proud of having exemplary children and role models. In the close-knit community that is common in Africa, the village looks forward to when their daughters mature and get married. People look forward to participating in those flamboyant, traditional wedding ceremonies, and the community comes together to celebrate and toast their success in raising a responsible daughter—now a bride and soon mother to be. In my tribe, women with children from a fiancée or from a previous marriage (assuming the husband is alive) by custom never celebrate traditional marriage. If there would be a traditional marriage, it would be just ceremonial, not fully recognized since some traditional libations and rituals may be eliminated or not performed.

Traditional marriage ceremonies are elaborate, and good parenting is sort of celebrated during traditional ceremonies, with parents sometimes performing certain rites as their daughter's hand is given away to her future husband. The mother is appreciated the most, for her role in bringing up a responsible daughter. No mother feels proud that she was denied this joy and moment of her life because her daughter was pregnant as a teenager.

Teenage pregnancy brings about social and health problems, but African societies are dealing more with teenagers dying from "abortions" performed by quacks than from teenage pregnancies or teenagers delivering babies. The exposure of teenagers to new information, such as technology, books, and magazines on the subject of sex, is trapping young teenagers and young adults in cities and urban-like populated towns. Today, this generation behaves in ways that their parents never did. Lessons of abstinence are values taught by parents but never imbibed by most teenagers. There is also a collision between conservative traditional values with "liberal cultures" and teenagers in the Internet age. As we are aware, the quest to try what is new often overrides the old ways of doing the same thing, and that is the reality facing African teenagers today as they struggle between invading cultures, religious values, and conservative traditional African cultures and values. Women doing what they want with their bodies, as is the case in Western cultures, compared to African traditional cultures that make a woman conform to traditional values is an example of this struggle.

In some communities, for example, the stigma attached to single parenting does not exist. Therefore, it is acceptable for teenage girls in their subcultures to get pregnant. However, the reality facing liberal societies where there is laxity in observing religious and traditional moral values is that there are always high rates in school dropouts, sexual permissiveness, crime, and other social ills.

In conservative societies, there were incidents of pregnant teenage girls running away from their families because they didn't want neighbors, peers, and villagers to know. Even single, female adults concealed such pregnancies because the society frowns at single parenthood. This tells the severity of the "crime" of a single mother getting pregnant, not to mention a teenager.

In traditional African societies, the mother's role is always to guide and counsel the daughter about the reality of being a woman and about the problems facing women in their societies. Mothers, on their part, are becoming more knowledgeable on how to respond to the psychological needs of their pregnant teenage daughters. African societies still hold abstinence as the best alternative. Good parenting initiatives and the explosion of contraceptives as alternative options have contributed to reducing the problem, but not at the level that is anticipated.

In cases where teenage pregnancy does occur, and abortion is ruled out, parents and grandparents often get involved in raising the child delivered by their teenage daughter or granddaughter.

In rural villages, education is important, and classrooms are not for pregnant teenagers. It is "One strike, you are out." Get pregnant, and you are out of school. After the delivery of the baby, it is still very difficult for the teen mother to go back to school because of the stigma—mockery, cajoling, and embarrassment—that may follow her around for a very long time.

African cultures are all encompassing. There are societies where what I have described is opposite. These are very small, liberal communities and villages compared to the more than 4,000 tribes and subgroups that make up 800 million Africans.

There are tribes where the family of the girl seeks the person responsible for the teenage pregnancy. Whether he marries the teenage girl is not the issue. The issue is that a child raised in the village must have a father or a father figure—a role model. That father figure, like any biological parent, has a responsibility to the community in raising a strong child.

PART VIII

SOCIETY AND ECONOMY

AFRICA: RICH RESOURCES, POOR CITIZENS

85. Question: Africa—with its huge mineral deposits of aluminum, silver, iron ore, lead, gold, diamonds, uranium, bauxite, quartz crystal, precious stones, and petroleum resources, including natural gas—continues to be a poor continent. Why should any nation in this endowed continent be poor? What explanation do African leaders have for the poor state of African economies?

Answer:

I have, in most of my previous responses, spoken on both the good and bad leadership that African people have had in the past as well as in some cases, the present. The irony of good and bad is that mending what has been destroyed (economies of countries with bad leadership) takes time. When a nation is dug inside a hole as a result of bad leadership and policies, new leaders that come after to rebuild already destroyed economies are like athletes racing for a championship. Some are tied with a rope on the legs and suddenly, mid-way through the race, a savior comes in to untie the rope. It is unimaginable that the athlete will catch up in the race, unless through the miraculous zeal of extra hard work, determination, and a consistent plan of action.

Africa, according to many pundits, has had very few " savior" nations after colonization. While nations in Europe and Asia with wars, disasters, invasions, and occupations had one form of "Marshall Plans" to alleviate their pains, sufferings, and exploitation, Africa has had none. Take Western Europe after the World War or the present-day Iraq; adequate funding ($97 billion) has enabled these countries to start somewhere in the race to rebuilding infrastructures.

I have also talked about corruption and the lack of strategies by some past weak leadership in the continent. They were part of the problem, too. Africa is not a poor continent. What is lacking is the leadership and strategies to turn things around. In that sense, it would be unfair to lump Africa's good leaders with the bad. But Africa has, in the past, witnessed some bad leaders, and you are absolutely right—no land and people endowed with such natural and human resources should be poor. The reality is that it is not, and the problems stem from various places—some self-imposed, others as a result of her past and present policies. But whether it is accepted as the truth or not, leadership that has repeatedly failed the people may be more responsible for the state of affairs in Africa than any other cause. However, it would be wrong to paint all leadership with one brush and label all African leaders as failures. The problem is that when the majority of leaders are not doing well, they tend to undermine the good work others are doing. Since the world is linked, some actions taken by industrialized nations weighed down the progress in Africa (tariffs, subsidies, and lack of interest in African products). What goes on in Britain and the United States affects Nigeria. What goes on economically in Ghana or Liberia affects what goes on in Nigeria and the whole region. Therefore, Nigeria's efforts to improve her economy, even with good leadership, would be undermined by what goes on in Sierra Leone or Liberia. That is the reality that has been facing Africa, and it took more than forty years for leaders to realize that this co-operation, which I call economic symbiosis for the survival of these nations, is vital to national and regional development.

Nigeria has, since independence, realized about $400 billion from sales of oil to the world market and yet basic amenities such as good, running water, uninterrupted electricity, and affordable housing remain daunting problems that confront any in-coming administration. A look around the country shows that more of the wealth is in the hands of the few or has taken flight out of the country to private bank accounts overseas. In fact, improper application of wealth and corruption, even as governments in the past and present have tried to stem the virus, has continued to hamper development in the country. Some African leaders, especially committed ones, are doing their best to balance the economic mess of the past; however, it will take time to correct problems that have been allowed to accumulate for three or four decades.

A closer look at Africa's situation goes beyond just selling oil and mineral products. African wars would not be taking place if not as a result of economic, political, and sociological reasons, some of them self-imposed by Africans ourselves through unnecessary and unsettled ethnic rivalries, including the selection or election of who should be leading and what tribe or region such a leader should come from.

Another problem often not mentioned publicly is the "Lack of Trust by Africans on fellow Africans." We don't believe in our capabilities to achieve and accomplish our goals without dependence on external "expertise" or assistance when human resources abound in surplus and waste away in the name of unemployment. Some of these African men and women have the same training and experience as the so-called "experts," but African governments prefer to hire or contract these jobs to non-Africans. The reality of global village is interdependence, including labor and resources, but when such dependence is overwhelming and to the disadvantage of national interest and development of a developing nation, such policy must be reviewed.

The role of leadership is to build trust and confidence. African leadership has not done so. This lack of trust easily exposes Africa's vulnerability to external influences, manipulation, and control—including her resources. With our insistence on not negotiating, cooperating, and collaborating, we allow old problems to rear up their ugly heads and ignite to the magnitude and destruction of lives and properties we witness in conflicts in some countries in the continent. Not to be mistaken is the correlation between poverty, social injustice, and violence. Africa gravitates within spheres of these problems.

Natural resources in Africa are not evenly distributed among nations. Neither is it equally distributed in countries where they are found. Sharing the wealth so that every citizen gets a small share is a huge problem. In Africa, the central government still calls the shots and controls the means of production and wealth, including revenues from the export of mineral resources. Privatization policies in countries such as Nigeria are easing these problems, but in many countries, that is yet to be seen.

The absence of infrastructures, such as good, running water, electricity, and good roads in communities where these minerals have been mined for more than thirty years, and yet nothing to show in terms of development, is an indictment on leadership. Most multinational companies know that in their home countries, the fundamental principles of social responsibility apply to the public, not the government and its officials. They cannot exempt themselves from these social services or else their relationship with the people in the area (not just the government) would suffer.

People are becoming aware of their rights, and they do not want their problems swept under the bridge anymore. People are filled with distrust, anger, and apathy of past administrations that have favored their tribal people in allocating resources to the detriment of other communities. In nations where the wealth is derived, and there are no wars, mismanagement and corrupt practices have encouraged diverting national wealth to personal bank accounts overseas.

African people have, for more than forty years since their independence, been subjected to administrations that have not done enough to improve the lifestyle of people and their economies.

Some agree that unstable governments, lack of strategies to overcome poverty, and corruption are responsible for the deplorable situations most African nations face. They considered past colonization and slavery as some of the most past problems but do not consider them on the top of the list of things hindering Africa's economic growth.

Even with all these shortfalls and different perspectives, critics agreed that forty years after most African countries gained their independence, the period should be enough for African nations to recover from the effects of colonization and slavery and steer its own course towards economic prosperity, with or without the West. They stress that the problem is leadership, pure and simple. Leadership that has failed to assume its seat among committee of nations, at least by working to create a better life for African people and improving rather than stagnating or ailing economies. Leadership, they emphasize, entails gravitating against obstacles, whether self-imposed or external, and there is no justification for Africa in not overcoming the problems attributed to these evils. Leadership should also entail persuading the countries involved with slavery and colonization to "compensate" Africa through a "Marshall Plan." This is important, critics say, since some African leaders have opposed reparations as a means of righting past wrongs.

Talents abound in many forms and in various fields of human endeavor. However, team spirit to coordinate these talents and resources is lacking. Africa continues to suffer from under-utilization of human resources, and it does not improve productivity. African leadership is far behind in utilizing the huge human resources available in the continent to the advantage that will benefit the people. The result is brain drain—experts are fleeing their countries to Europe and the United States where their skills and knowledge are utilized. Africa loses from these developments. What make great nations are not beautiful skylines but human resources. To have a shift in paradigm as far as the development of human resources is concerned, governments needs to invest in education, research, and development in all areas and with an emphasis on science and technology. Leaders must follow through with the policies of successors, especially policies that are real, realizable, and have the long-term goals of improving the lifestyles of the people and bolstering the economy.

Dictatorship brings about confusion, abuse of freedoms and human rights, destroys free market economy, and any existing infrastructures for entrepreneurship and development. When people are not free, they are limited in ideas that they could articulate to nurture development and strategies to overcome poverty. In absence of new ideas and squandered wealth, what is left is a drained economy unable to sustain itself with oil or one source of revenue.

African leadership needs the co-operation and support of the global community to transform the huge African human and natural resources to productivity. Presently, as all attention is on Iraq, Afghanistan, and the on-going War on Terror, Africa must not be left alone in terms of investments by industrialized nations. However, Africa must fight corruption, misappropriation of revenues, and internal security to guarantee the safety of its people and property.

86. Question: What is a "Blood Diamond," and how do individuals and corporations profit from African wars? Who are these profiteers? What are African governments and the global community doing to expose and punish these profiteers?

Answer:

A lot of underground business activities go on in Africa amidst the reports of distressed nations at war. The illegal trade on Africa's rich mineral resources is going on unstopped, even as wars rage in some of these countries that have witnessed recycled conflicts and violence. Most of the transactions in war zones go underground, and the money realized from illegal trading in gold, diamonds, and precious metals is channeled to secret or private accounts and used for purposes that escalate wars. In fact, profits from these activities are channeled for other purposes, such as buying machine guns, mortars, bombs, bullets, rocket launchers, AK-47s, and rocket propelled grenades that kill and maim mostly children and women.

Economic activities are going on in countries where wars are still taking place in parts of the continent. Gold and diamonds were sold in global markets as wars in Sierra Leone and Liberia were going on. It is not coincidental at all that wherever there is war or protracted war in any part of the continent, there is always a trace of gold, diamonds, or other mineral resources abundant in the country. The situation may also explain why the first target of any rebel group or warlord for occupation is a mining field or refinery.

Sierra Leone, the Republic of Congo, Liberia, and Angola were countries where rebel factions fought protracted wars, and each of these wars lasted as they did because they were financed with the profits of war—some of them "Blood Diamonds." War enables illegal business activities to go on underground, including trading in diamonds. The money doesn't benefit the people; it is diverted to purchasing more arms through middlemen or black markets. Of the annual sales of $9 billion, one quarter of the diamonds sold in the open market is from war zones. This is why gems obtained through this way are called *blood diamonds*. In essence, the precious commodity is sold, with no incentives to the people, to fund wars and enrich the war profiteers.

Human Rights and Amnesty International have tracked some of the listed profiteers from the blood diamond trade. One hundred and twenty-five countries and individuals were identified by the United Nations as responsible for funding the Democratic Republic of Congo war, identified by the media as "Africa's World War." We are also aware that diamonds are the major source of wealth for the country. Participants in the illegal trade include people from different ethnic backgrounds and nationalities. The United Nations has also created a black list of people that are engaged in illegal activities, including war profiteers, illegal arms dealers, and other undesirables that cannot move freely from one nation to another.

With the on-going War on Terror, monitoring the illegal sales of arms from blood diamonds has increased. The illegal transit of arms from Russia, China, Czechoslovakia, North Korea, and Eastern European nations has also multiplied.

One important decision made by independent diamond business owners, outside the UN resolution, was to ban selling "blood diamonds." On April 2003, more than 70 businesses engaged in diamond exploration, mining, cutting, and marketing the precious products agreed to label them with the intention of dictating and banning diamonds that may have flown out of war zones in Africa.

AFRICA AND U.S. TRADE

87. Question: What is the United States' trade status with Africa? Is there any data to compare U.S. trade with Africa and the European Union? What is your comment about the current U.S.-African trade relationship?

Answer:

Talking about U.S. direct investment in Africa, it is next to nothing. In 2001, the total U.S. direct investment was as follows: Europe—$726 billion; Eastern Europe—$640 billion; Asia—$217 billion; Central America—$81 billion; South America—$83 billion; and Africa—$16 billion, or about 1.16 percent of the total direct investment around the world.

Trade with the U.S., as well as Europe, is unbalanced in favor of the United States and Europe. Oil accounts for more than 85 percent of the trade. Nigeria alone imports over $2 billion worth of products annually from mainly European countries and the United States. The sale of crude oil from Nigeria remains at 7 percent of U.S. supplies. Canada's supply to the U.S. is about 16 percent, top on the list of countries that export crude oil to the United States.

Africans are seeking fair trade practices in a much-expressed free market economy, including measures to improve the access of African farmers to the United States market. Presently, there is a thick wall in the name of policies preventing African farmers from exploring U.S. markets. Untangling these barriers was one key policy issue that President Bush's visit to Africa was scheduled to address, which unfortunately was never given any attention by the media during the coverage of his trip to Africa.

Africa remains one of the top world producers of peanuts, palm oil, bananas, cassava, tea, coffee, and cocoa, with huge market potential for exports. African farmers, as far as free market economy is concerned, are struggling to come to terms with the reality of breaking into the global market. African goods still remain underpriced. With tariffs on imports, and subsidies by the governments of most industrialized nations, it is practically impossible for African farmers to compete on a global scale. Take the subsidies alone. The United States, Europe, and Japan's annual subsidies to the agricultural sector alone are estimated at over $400 billion annually. Just about the total debt Africa owed to IMF, World Bank, and creditor agencies by all African countries combined. Imagine how African governments still struggling to meet payments on the interest of these loans can afford to invest such an amount in agriculture alone and survive. It is practically impossible. It paints a picture of gloomy days ahead for African economies, unless African governments find economic and political strategies to deal with this problem. African farmers face an unpredictable future if nothing is done to reverse the trend. In fact, under these circumstances, the future of African farmers is bleak as far as breaking into the United States, European, and Japanese markets. In essence, African countries will still depend on oil, gold, or diamonds to meet fiscal budgetary needs.

For now, it seems nothing is going to change the Western government's position on subsidies, but it is hoped that Africa would not be forgotten or dumped into the landfills of global trade politics. In a global village, Africa's poverty translates into global insecurity.

At several arenas, African governments have presented their case. At the 2002 G-8 conference in Canada, it was the first time that African presidents were guests at G8 and Russia meeting. Similar requests have been repeated in several forums, but the West, according to critics, may not be willing to open their doors to African goods other than oil and gas. New Partnership for African Development (NEPAD) initiative is still fraught with obstacles on both congressional and business levels.

AFRICA'S FAST-TRACK ECONOMIES

88. Question: Which African nation has the fastest growing economy?

Answer:

The fastest growing economy for the past thirty years was Botswana in the southern part of Africa, according to the United Nation's Developing Agency. Botswana's economy grew at 9.2 percent on a per capita basis for the last thirty years, according to the study collaborated by the World Bank.

The media and the rest of the world were not paying attention to these growths. However, the headlines became global when the HIV/AIDS epidemic showed up on the country's radar. That was when the headlines suddenly read, "Botswana ranks among the most infected population with HIV/AIDS in Africa."

Botswana still remains one of the most developed economies in the world, with the highest population of people with a good standard of living in Africa.

AFRICA AND A NEW GLOBAL ECONOMY

89. Question: Africans, I learned, are mostly farmers, fishermen, and traders. Are there businessmen and women, professionals, and experts in Africa? The images I see include mainly footage of the poor—people always in distress, war, destroyed villages, urban sprawl, hunger, diseases, and a country always in need of global assistance. Could you explain to me the underlying problems that have placed most parts of Africa in the undesirable economic and political shapes they are today?

Answer:

The image of Africa in the media not only carries negative evaluations but also some degree of fear and anxiety. The most damaging effects of these images are on potential investors, the Americans, and people around the world that wants to visit, reside, invest and do business in the continent.

While it may be true that the media is telling or reporting the news, the over-play of news clips of wars, diseases, and disasters (while neglecting developmental news in terms of business, positive social lives of middle class Africans; rich African traditions and cultures including carnivals, horse races, arts and craft competitions as media show of European cultures) is a really very subjective. When the real Africa is not being told to the world, it amounts to selective stories that are about stereotypes. These stories, when played repeatedly, shape opinions in the minds of viewers about Africa. Rather than improve diversity, these stories endorse separation or disintegration of races.

These stereotypes remain problems that must be addressed by African leaders. They must take stock of how Africa has been portrayed over centuries in the media. They must come up with action plans to address the problem both by their own actions in their respective countries and with the global media networks. Also, news managers, producers, and writers that feed the public with selective, subjective, unbalanced, and shallow analyses of Africa must come to accept that it does no good when subjectivity and unbalanced and biased reporting principles are the rules.

I wrote one foreign correspondent of a major newspaper to tell him that I had covered the same story that he was writing, and that there were misrepresented facts in his story. He thanked me but informed me that his duty was "not to change the world," only to write what he sees. But when I told him that what he "sees" is different from what I'd witnessed and knew to be the truth, he never reversed his stance.

Africa's great empires—Ghana, Mali, and Songhai—all thrived in wealth. Commerce was the center of business activities, since the petroleum that has sustained "rich" African nations today was not discovered at that time. Of course, the Egyptian empire was not alone, since trade and other human activities that linked all African people were taking place at the time, except that transportation was clumsy and movement, restricted.

African resources, mainly agricultural products, continued to be transported by rail from the hinterlands to seaports where raw materials were shipped to service European industries. "Multi-national European companies" like the Niger Company carried out the export of these products. African laborers and merchants provided links to the marketing chain.

Africa, before colonization, had both formal and informal educational institutions. The first University in the World, Fez University in Morocco, was the center of learning and provided formal education, while underground there were numerous institutions of learning, both religious and secular. In the literary world, Africa's literary scholars abounded, and experts in the medical field increased.

Neglected and abandoned was the agricultural sector. In fact, after the Europeans departed, Africa's ruling class practiced what they'd learned—sitting in offices and providing the society with only administrative policies that were short in exploring the abundant human resources through scientific research and technological development.

However, noticeable changes are taking place, but not at the pace critics were expecting. Africa's new leaders are introducing changes in curricula that now, unlike before, emphasize science and technology.

The technology transfer policies of some African leaders in the 70s and 80s flopped because the West and African leaders disagreed over what should be transferred and withheld—what could benefit Africa and lead to technology transfer. The reluctance of developed nations to accept technology transfer as an obligation and prerequisite for investment in Africa was perceived by the West as giving out their competitive secrets on a platter of gold as the price for investment. It never worked. To any competitor that wants that edge, it was practically an impossible request to meet.

Africa has witnessed tremendous growth in the fields of medicine, science, and technology. However, these resources still remain under-utilized. Since the 80s, brain drain is undermining those benefits of reduced costs in utilizing indigenous human resources There is low motivation and little or no investment in research and development (R&D) to strengthen the productivity of African workers still staying in the continent.

90. Question: What is Africa's debt to IMF, World Bank, and other creditors? What are the chances that African countries will be able to meet these loan payments or the terms of these loans?

Answer:

Africa's debt can be viewed from two or more perspectives. Africa's debt to the International Monetary Fund (IMF), World Bank, and the London and Paris Clubs was estimated at $220 billion in 1999; $400 billion in 2003, and it is projected to increase to $600 billion by 2005.

Many have queried the legitimacy of these African loans, especially since most of the loans were awarded during the oppressive military regimes in Africa. Supporters of debt relief for Africa allege that these loans were awarded as handouts to dictators for political reasons and must be written off. They claimed that the loans never benefited Africans; rather they took flight in the name of corruption and embezzlement that ended up, unfortunately, in the same banks in Europe and the United States. This time, in the private accounts of the so-called leaders. The irony of the corruption, as alleged by critics, was that it went on under the watchful eyes of Western loan guarantors and governments that have access to these private accounts. They argue that if money belonging to drug kingpins could easily be recovered, and the accounts frozen, then how could the monetary institutions allow an individual (not institution) to deposit millions of dollars into one account without raising the eyebrows of the authorities or even the bank officials in the West, where most of this money was deposited.

Therefore, the question that many of the critics ask—questions that remain unanswered—is this: Why did the IMF/World Bank and lending agencies award loans to dictators and corrupt officials indiscriminately, knowing well that the money was not properly invested according to the terms of these loans? Critics also sighted South Africa, the white-only government, which accumulated $18 billion in debt and at the same time plundered neighboring nations

in South Africa to borrow $26 billion as a result of apartheid poli-
cies. But lenders disagree, sighting that financial contracts go by
agreements that both parties agreed to honor before the loans were
awarded.

Many African nations have, therefore, found themselves in
this contraption of paying huge amounts on debts from insufficient
revenue. In fact, revenue derived from one source (oil) may no longer be sufficient to meet the needs of the people and, at the same
time, service these loans. Under these circumstances, poverty alleviation initiatives and economic programs mapped out by these administrations as campaign promises translate into empty promises.

In 1999, many wealthy nations promised to cancel the debts
of "Highly Indebted Poor Countries (HIPC). The initiative has not
worked well, as the criteria for selecting the countries still remain
very controversial. As of 2003, 26 African nations received IMF/
World Bank relief of $41.5 billion in terms of loan interest defer-
ment. But when considered against the $10 billion that is required
for HIV/AIDS treatment alone, and that industrialized nations will
spend more than $200 billion every year on agricultural subsidies
alone, the conclusion is that more needs to be done.

Often, people use World Bank debts and accruing interests
to indicate a continent seriously in debt. Africa's situation is more
than paying debts. It is a fact that many nations will end up paying the interest alone as long as their countries remain on the face
of the Earth. Its consequences could be translated into serious economic, political, and social problems ahead for these countries. The
situation explains why global attention must focus on the problem
to avoid creating nations with poor and desperate people—some of
whom are susceptible to undue influences—a position that would
eventually threaten future global peace and stability.

The IMF and World Bank's aim at promoting a uniform international monetary market, currency stabilization, and expansion
of international trade won't work in Africa. Critics conclude that the
ways in which these policies were fashioned, recommended to Africa, and implemented (without consideration to inherent social, political, and economic problems in Africa) remain unsuitable for development. This is because the wrong application of the wrong policies

and their implementations do not address Africa's problems—they aggravate them.

African problems, they argue, are different from Western problems and need thorough studies by independent agencies (including native participants) or those involving Africans themselves. They will thoroughly analyze the problems as they exist in Africa, and not elsewhere, and come out with solutions that are actually suited to tackling these problems. Poor African nations have received promises of debt rescheduling and "forgiveness," but still the future of most African nations, including those affected by the debt relief, remains uncertain.

DRUGS SMUGGLING AND AFRICA'S TRANSIENT

ROUTES

91. Question: There are no African countries that grow or process the plant coca from which cocaine is derived. How do you explain African countries and their connections as transshipment routes for drugs (heroine) entering into Europe and the United States?

Answer:

Drug smuggling and addiction are global problems that no nation can fight alone and win. It requires joint efforts and the complete engagement of the countries where these drugs are grown and processed. The collaboration and focus to fight the war is required of countries that serve as transient or transshipment centers for these drugs to huge markets in Europe and the United States. If we don't engage these nations in the war, all our efforts will be fruitless in fighting and winning the war on drugs.

As we have witnessed in nations that are plagued by drugs, huge resources are spent to fight the war—these same resources are required to prevent the drugs from reaching transshipment centers across the world. It is obvious that when drug transit routes are dismantled, we have prevented some of the drugs from reaching their destinations: the streets and homes of drug users.

As a reporter, I witnessed the battle the Drug Enforcement Agency (DEA) faced from Nigeria's side against drug smuggling in the mid-80s up till the 90s. The security measures in place today have drastically reduced the frequency of drugs moving through West African airports and seaports to Europe and the United States.

The demand for drugs in Europe and the United States drives the market, as arrested and interrogated suspects have claimed. With increased demand for drugs, dealers seek markets across the world. As witnessed with terrorism being exported to Africa, recruits were employed by drug barons to attract the poor, unemployed youths from developing nations. Rather than shipping huge consignments, they use drug peddlers to transport drugs overseas in small quantities.

Africa became an easy transit route because airports were vulnerable and unprepared to deal with the problem. There was little or no surveillance equipment, and personnel were not well trained to do the job of detecting and stopping drug trafficking.

As U.S. and Western European nations increased land and sea patrols, airports not adequately equipped in developing nations to deal with the smuggling problems were easily targeted as routes of convenience for exporting drugs to markets in Europe and the United States.

Some greedy, corrupt airline and airport employees caught up by the lure of money in the business allowed flights originating out of Nigeria, for example, to be used for the illegal shipment of drugs. The use of African airports as transit stations for their connecting routes became the order. Thus, when drug agencies in these African countries finally tightened up security, the business was drastically reduced. Federal authorities in Nigeria commenced serious searches of suspects, using trained dogs and equipment to detect drugs on the bodies of suspects at international airports.

Knowing the huge amount of money a successful trip generates for drug smugglers, new recruits became attracted to the business. It was not until airports became equipped and employed trained staff that a drop in drugs smuggled through airports was reported. Most successes were achieved through the collaborative training efforts of the United States Dug Enforcement Agency and African customs and DEA.

Heroine was the illicit drug of choice for traffickers on these routes because it has more monetary value. It became the dominant contraband routed from Central Asia through Africa, and then transported in smaller quantities to Europe and the United States.

Cocaine and heroine have been drugs of convenience for a very long time around the world. Africa knew nothing about it (at least publicly, as it was elsewhere in the globe at the time), except through the media exposure for the first time in Nigeria in the 80s.

In my days as the airport and senior correspondent of a national newspaper, I reported more than five elaborate events where cocaine and heroine was seized by Customs and Excise officials from smugglers and destroyed by public incineration.

Far from the collaborative efforts on the part of the Nigerian government to fight the problem, authorities in Nigeria were concerned that illicit drugs transmitted through her borders might, if unchecked, create domestic drug consumption problems. Therefore, the campaign to stop the transient route was intensified, and to make a point, some alleged smugglers were executed, regardless of the opinion against the execution at that time.

The easy choice of Nigeria as a drug transit route was possible because of Africa's open borders. Today, the same reasons justify why Africa should not be "forgotten" in the current war against terrorism. Airports in Africa were taken advantage of in drug smuggling because they were easy targets and not as fortified as airports in industrialized countries.

92. Question: What are the significant pollution problems in Africa? What 3impact does this have on rural and urban populations?

Answer:

African cities face more serious pollution problems than rural villages or countrysides. It is yet to be determined what effects polluted environments will have in the long run on the lives of Africans living in villages and cities. Meanwhile, oil and gas explorations entailed clearing the forests and moving heavy-duty equipment that destroy preserved landmarks. The drilling process, and what the process involves before oil or gas is pumped out of deep wells, brings more damage to the environment.

For more than twenty years in Nigeria, just like oil drilling in other African countries, gases were flared on a 24/7 basis, almost all year round, without any concern for lives and property. Africa's blue skies were turned into smog, and treasured village air filled with a haze that blocked shining stars.

Trucks and vehicular emissions, industrial chemical disposals, the dumping of nuclear waste from industrialized countries, poor urban sewage disposal systems, and the dumping of industrial wastes into flowing rivers and streams include some of the pollution types that African people, especially urban populations, face. It is yet unknown what present and future medical complications such bad air and polluted streams and rivers may bring on future generation of Africans.

Migrations from villages to cities for jobs and better living standards have led to overcrowding in urban cities. The migration pattern, coupled with limited resources, has increased the rate of crime, social and health problems in Africa's most densely populated cities. To accommodate the increasing population, human activities, including the construction of apartments and homes, are expanding into once reserved lands.

African economies were agro-based before "liquid gold" in the name of petroleum resources were discovered in the continent. Exploration and drilling involve many activities that absolutely are unfriendly to the environment. For subsistence farmers, the practice of crop rotation and the clearing of bushes by burning have always posed environmental problems.

Proponents of anti-pollution legislation, however, believe that the pollution of Africa started long ago when Europeans, in an attempt to tap resources such as coal and other raw materials for their homeland industries, engaged in activities that degraded the land and the environment. Abandoned caves, formerly coalmines, could be spotted in many African hinterlands. Only time will tell what geographical catastrophe, such as landslides and earthquakes, may result from these manmade caves.

From Nigeria to Namibia and South Africa, great harm continued to be enacted against the environment. Industrial dumps pollute African waters. Similarly, offshore oilrigs that locate on sea and ocean beds add new problems to sea life.

Human rights groups, NGOs, and environmentalists like Earth First and Green Peace have focused attention on these African pollution problems. There were reported cases of deep ocean vessels intercepted on the high seas while smuggling radioactive materials to Africa. They continue to make the headlines. Known cases of such toxic dumping received worldwide media attention when drums of radioactive materials from Europe were dumped in an old man's compound in Koko village, located in Midwestern Nigeria. There was a reported case of a ship that left the United States with toxic waste, but it was rejected, and after a journey around the world, it finally disposed its cargo (in treated form) in Philadelphia in 2002.

There were European companies that smuggled and disposed of radioactive materials in Nigeria. The Koko toxic waste reminded the world that a blink of an eye could result in the disastrous dumping of toxic materials in Africa—and the future consequences may be worse than any epidemic Africa or the world has witnessed.

Regrettably, Africa's pollution problems may not improve soon because governments, for economic reasons, are opening their doors to foreign investors with little consideration to the environmental issues. Companies already operating in African countries, most of them don't keep or observe the same pollution standards as in their home bases, and there is no guarantee that governments would be forcing compliance soon.

Nigeria, for instance, has an EPA, but the agency's roles are limited to supervising and monitoring small, local companies. How these local companies observe and follow EPA policy and laws is not known. It has no enforcement rights as far as convicting big polluters. Instead, the agency has been known recently to enforce the arrest and trial of individuals violating litter edicts and so on.

The reasons for lower standards for big companies is because African governments are scouting, proposing, and willing to table incentives to attract foreign investments to boost their economies. In the name of incentives, goodwill, and good relationships, governments prefer multi-national companies to come in and remain partners—pollution notwithstanding. They want the benefits such corporations bring to the country's economy at the expense of a pollution-free environment.

RELIGION, POLITICS, TRIBES, AND HATE CRIMES

93. Question: In many parts of Africa, there seem to be these huge, unresolved tribal conflicts that once in a while play in Africa's political and social scenes, such as religious intolerance, tribal clashes, religious rioting, as well as other social problems that I have repeatedly read about and watched in the news.
In South Africa, there is still this unsettlement—"Black on black crime"—even after apartheid has ended. In West Africa, there are chieftaincy disputes, land matters, and mutual suspicions, which are leading people to fighting among themselves. Do government policies and poverty play a role in escalating these problems? Since we don't hear or read about the details of what goes on in Africa, do you think that there are other factors that may be responsible for creating these situations?

Answer:

First of all, the problems you listed here never affected all African countries. It boils down to the same impression that I have been dealing with all along with some of my questioners and the media in generalizing African problems. It is wrong to assume that because a problem is evidently present in one or two African countries that the whole continent is enmeshed with the same problems.

Africa, I still express, is not a monolithic society. Every African society is different but linked together by cultures and subcultures that, as I stated earlier on in my previous responses, run across nations.

I am from Nigeria, but in Nigeria, there are more than 250 tribes and other ethnic groups. The differences in cultures are, at times, confusing. As cultures (and subcultures) merge, they come with social and political complications, in particular mutual trusts. They bring about sometimes-unresolved tribal conflicts that take generations to heal. However, on a positive side, African diversity brings harmony and peace. These are some of the problems that get more attention in the media because bad news gets the most attention.

Africa's tribal conflicts existed before the Europeans colonized and partitioned Africa. Unfortunately, some of the tribal problems that were swept under the carpet, and managed prior to colorization, emerged, and in some situations, they were exacerbated as a result of the political strategies of "Divide and Rule" introduced by colonial Europeans to conquer and rule Africans. In the process, tribal harmony and cohesion, which were very important in the development of communities (and the whole nation), continued to leak away. Their wastes continue to pollute tolerance and harmony. The cord of unity that once tied people together was broken, and amending that broken thread remains a serious problem. In this kind of environment, team spirit is difficult to build, and goals are difficult to achieve.

Land in Africa is a "priceless," treasured commodity. It is very important that an individual or community holds strong to property that it has acquired or inherited. Letting it go for any reason is forbidden or perceived as a "weakness." Selling land in villages is sometimes perceived as a sign of personal bankruptcy.

It is asking for troubles and confrontation if "a neighbor" encroaches on property that does not belong to him. Land, when taken away or occupied, must be reclaimed at " all costs." When such property is invaded or lost as a result of war or other reasons, reclaiming the land is not always without reprisals. In some situations, dialogue and negotiations may work; in other circumstances, they may not work. Conflict could escalate, leading to villagers invading an opponents' village and setting an entire village ablaze.

The cultural and political significance of land and landed property does emphasize the need for the owner to protect his or her property, even when it is not put into any productive use. Unfortunately, there is no penalty under any law or statute that mandates the owner to put such property into use when it has been fallow for a very long time.

The amalgamation of states and tribes with no cultural, political, and social affiliations brought about underlying conflicts between tribal people that had previously been underground. European occupiers favoring, elevating, and supporting one tribe to gain political power over the majority added to Africa's conflict syndrome in vulnerable villages and towns. In what some critics describe as psychological war fare, natives, tribes were brainwashed to mistrust each other. Today it is a pattern of conditioned behavior rather than attitude in parts of Africa where rivalry and ethnic conflicts and cleansing have resonated.

In Africa, where politics and religion cannot be separated, political conflicts have become religious conflicts and therefore difficult to curtail. It has also been very explosive when the leader is from the minority group, and the leader is a suspect in using his authority to award privileges or to intimidate others while maintaining authority. The power struggles to undo this disingenuous political construct by people disadvantaged by the system has been responsible in some cases for conflicts in the continent. The struggles to allow power shifts to take place have bred some of Africa's worst political conflicts. It all depends on how politically things shape up; tribal politics in Africa will continue to be relevant in determining peace and tranquility in the continent.

In Africa, social and political problems that have anything to do with faith are lethal. Selfish politicians (pockets of them) have mastered the art of pitting people together with religion as a pretense to exploit the people, their weaknesses, and every political situation that is beneficial to re-elect officials. In fact, the real underlying reasons for conflict have nothing to do with religion.

"Black on black" crime is one of those clichés I see as a way to divert attention from the real social as well as political problems that arise—problems that arise when we isolate, label people, and create an underclass that will always be unable to compete and that will always be pleased to eat the crumbs from the master's table. It is not "black or white," but the situation of apartheid for example, in South Africa, brings a different extreme dimension to the same problem that societies face when one dominant group tends to show superiority over others.

South Africa is not the only nation in the world to emerge from past abuses and conflicts to later function as a decent society. However, deep scars, as evidenced by the reverberating consequences of apartheid policies in South Africa, are always everlasting reminders of the evil apartheid embodied.

WATCHDOGS' BLACKLIST

94. Question: I have watched the news on television and read newspapers; I could count the number of times I have come across African businesses or entrepreneurs doing business with the United States. I say this because this development has discouraging effects on Africa's development, as well as on investments—investors in particular that would want to explore the continent. Does this mean that there are no African companies interested in doing business with the United States or U.S. multi-national corporations doing business in Africa?

Answer:

Pharmaceutical companies, mining, oil drilling, auto companies, and assembling plants such as Peugeot, Mercedes Benz, General Motors, Ford, Honda (both motorcycle and auto manufacturing), and Toyota, to list just a few, all operate huge businesses in Nigeria. However, their stories are absent in the business sections of major U.S. business and general interest newspapers. I would like to emphasize that there are some companies doing well in Nigeria, owned through joint ventures or partnerships with Americans.

Watching and listening to the lullaby of African woes played in the name of news, I volunteered to do content analysis of what news from Africa makes the headlines. The more I sampled news content in pages devoted to positive development news, and the more I reviewed the style of reporting, the more overwhelmed I was by volumes of pages and spaces devoted to African news on wars, diseases, and disasters. I became disenchanted with the style, the narrow depth of stories, and the issues that the media selected to make headlines.

Any viewer of television when President Bush visited Africa, for example, would relate to what I am saying. President Bush's mission to Africa was not just to make promises about HIV/AIDS initiative grants. HIV/AIDS dominated the news while, in fact, President Bush's visit to Africa was more about trade and subsidies that are not in favor of Africa's agricultural exports because of about $200 billion in subsidies U.S. farmers receive from the government. It was about debt relief, oil, the war on terror, regional conflicts, and the progress of Africa's regional political stability, including the assessment of New Partnership for African Development (NEPAD) and African peace intervention forces.

Comparing news coverage during President Bush's trip to Asia in October 2003 with what was reported about Africa when he paid the same visit would demonstrate media biases, subjectivity, stereotypes, and innuendos associated with reporting Africa in the news. The theme was HIV/AIDS. Where was Africa's economic summit in the news in the United States?

When President Bush was in Africa, Nigeria was seeking investors in the multi-billion-dollar rail line. The Sullivan Economic Conference, with more than eighteen African heads of state in attendance—including Former Ambassador Andy Young and former House Member, and only black Republican congressmen, J.T. Watts—received little or no coverage in the mainstream media.

United Nations Secretary General Kofi Annan, in September 2001, disclosed to the world that the "World's top most kept secret" includes the United States businesses that operate in Africa. He remarked that Africa remains the most profitable market for European and U.S. companies, and as scholars and African pundits have known, Africa may be too good for the multi-national companies doing business in Africa. They would prefer to maintain the code of silence about business profits from Africa, lest the market become competitive.

For more than four decades, British multi-national companies have operated in almost every country in Africa, and their history in Africa dates back to colonial eras. The majority of Fortune 500 companies have businesses, partners, affiliates, or subsidiaries in Africa. U.S. companies doing business in Africa came together under the name Corporate Council of Africa. Inaugurated in 1993, the organization comprises more than 160 U.S. companies doing business in the continent of Africa.

It is clear that not every African nation has peace and stability. However, it is true that the environment for operating businesses
in most African nations is present, wars notwithstanding.

PART IX

AFRICA - HIV/AIDS, STATISTICS, MYTHS, REALITY,

AND MISCONCEPTIONS

95. Question: I understand that more Africans are infected with malaria and other non-communicable diseases, and that the death rate from these diseases is higher than the number of deaths from HIV and AIDS. Why is it that nobody talks about malaria and other infectious diseases still taking the lives of children and adults in Africa and the world?

Answer:

HIV/AIDS remains the most dreaded disease facing humankind, not just in Africa but also across the globe. The method and rapid spread of the disease is a serious concern. It has no cure or vaccines at this time. This, and other reasons, explains why there is a serious concern about more people being infected and more deaths, especially in developing worlds. This, among other reasons, may explain why so much attention is given to the epidemic.

The role of the Western media in highlighting Africa's epidemic, and the dissemination of information on these outbreaks, must be commended. Malaria still remains one of the most killer diseases in the world. According to UNDP (United Nation Development Program) 2002 report, about 300 million people are globally affected by malaria. The majority of the infected are from Sub-Saharan Africa. Also, about one million children alone die from malaria every year across the world.

Malaria has vaccines and drugs that can prevent the disease from infecting other people. HIV/AIDS does not. However, the global fears in developing countries where patients can obtain antibiotics over the counter and without a prescription is that diseases such as malaria may become resistant to the parasitic protozoa of the plasmodium that causes the disease—a situation often attributed to antibiotic abuses.

Another problem is the proliferation of adulterated drugs in Africa, estimated at about 75 percent. Since malaria has the ability to reoccur many years after it has first infected a patient, and after many years of treatment, it still posses a great danger to lives in Africa.

In villages, there have been increasing numbers of reported cases of death as a result of infections by other diseases brought about by a weakened immune system. Some say these deaths were from HIV/AIDS; others think that lack of proper health care, poor dieting, poverty, lack of money to buy genuine drugs, and the poor habits of patients not going for medical check ups and treatment adds to the problem. Thus, simple ailments that could be treated or prevented are allowed to magnify, and by the time the patient knows it, already the immune system is completely broken down. Such deaths, when classified as victims of HIV/AIDS, are what trouble some African critics of statistics on deaths from the disease.

Separating deaths as a result of HIV/AIDS or other reasons is difficult. African health workers and UN agencies like the World Health Organization (WHO) have yet to come to an agreement on how to approach this conflicting problem.

Statistics are not the actual problem; the problem is that people are dying as a result of a breakdown in their immune system. Regardless of whether this is caused by inadequate nutrition or by the actual virus that causes AIDS, the real issue is that millions of people are dying. Now, HIV/AIDS deaths in Russia, India, South Asian countries, and in South America are growing at astronomical rates. These health problems need attention and the assistance of the global community to be controlled.

96. Question: Images I see on the television are often of poor village health centers in ramshackle temporary structures, and these facilities never seem to have enough beds or medicine for patients. It seems that there are too few health personnel attending to the many patients with special needs. Watching these clips on television whenever they come up, they suggest that no adequate measures are in place to take care of the infected patients already dying of HIV/AIDS. Also, they do suggest that African governments are not doing enough to prevent the spread of diseases—HIV/AIDS in particular. Is this true?

Answer:

First of all, I totally agree that African governments were not doing enough about the problems of spread, control, or prevention of HIV/AIDS in the 80s and early part of the 90s.

Secondly, it took a little while for health professionals and scientists to study the virus, to understand its history and spread, and to understand where and how to approach the spread of the disease.

In fact, it was not just African governments that were taken unawares with the speed of the spread and mutation of the virus but the whole world. It was not until the disease began to take lives that the enormous task of addressing the problem became a priority of governments and non-governmental agencies.

This reactive disposition has been a disaster for African countries where attention to health care is among the lowest in the world. In fact, health care accounts for about 3–5 percent of the budgetary allocation annually, unlike military and sports, which take a larger chunk of money every year. However, things have changed in Africa in recent times. I do not think that there is an African government that is not concerned with the spread of this disease.

Overall, the health care system is still very poorly funded in the developing world, and Africa's own case is troubling considering that governments are not just dealing with health care but with other problems as well, such as social services and of course paying high interest rates on World Bank and IMF loans. Amidst all these huge problems, health care is still deprived of the actual allocation it requires to match the problems on the sector.

One impressive step in tackling the HIV/AIDS problems is the admission that the disease is "real" and that it is spreading and killing people, irrespective of the fact that the admission came too late.

But many critics (Africans) of the health care dilemma in most African countries dismissed the governments' attention to HIV/AIDS as too late. They agreed that had adequate steps been taken earlier to prevent the spread of the disease when it first came up in the Western world in the mid-80s, Africa would not be in the state it is in today, as far as the number of deaths from the disease.

As I write, the statistics of Africans that are dead from HIV/AIDS still remain a controversy between African governments. Controversy or not, the view of the majority of Africans is that audiences are always shown the worst of every situation in every problem. Does this mean that everything regarding Africa in the media should be good? The answer of course is no. However, objective and balanced reporting gives audiences the flexibility to form their own opinions.

African governments have recently—at least in the last three to five years—confronted the disease by every means available to them. Some countries are still far behind in addressing the problems posed by HIV/AIDS. Overall, I could confidently say that the governments in some countries that were in a state of denial have woken up to the reality and have willingly confronted the problem.

We are aware of the many global conferences on HIV/AIDS, which African governments have initiated, sponsored, and hosted. There is also an initiative by President Bush to add $15 billion to the HIV/AIDS fund. African leaders also played significant roles in reaching an agreement with pharmaceutical companies to relax their strong opposition to lowering HIV/AIDS drug costs, thereby ensuring that affordable medicines are available or at the reach of the poor. Of course, African governments have been involved in the research and testing of medicines and vaccines to control or eliminate the virus.

As is the case in Uganda, the nation's HIV/AIDS initiative for prevention is a clear indication that governments are not just waiting for others to take care of Africans dying from the disease.

I took a trip to Cote d'Ivoire (I was among eight journalists on the assignment) in 1990. We were shown very sophisticated but user-friendly medical equipment housed in a hospital complex at Abidjan. It was new HIV testing equipment that could take samples of blood and diagnose the HIV virus in a matter of seconds.

The problem with Africa's development, including health care, is inadequate contingency plans to control the spread of diseases in times of emergency. In Taiwan, in the month of March 2003 when SARS was identified in the country, more than 1.8 million schoolchildren were out of school as government and health officials monitored the spread of the disease. Such an immediate response to the SARS outbreak was lacking in most African countries. Nigeria, for example, did what was "unexpected," and it took steps to prevent travelers from Asian countries coming into the country and spreading the infectious disease. Incoming passengers from countries with identified diseases were quarantined and placed under observation before they were released into the city population. It worked, and only one patient from Asia died of the disease in a hospital at Abuja, Nigeria.

I have listened to commentaries and pundits talk about the spread of HIV/AIDS in Africa. They have offered different opinions as to why and how the virus spreads so fast in Africa. Some reasons have been genuine, scientific, and reasonable. Others are stereotypical and sometimes incredulous. However, the truth is that Africa's high rate of HIV is not because the people are promiscuous, as some of my questioners have asked and some writers in the media have opinionated. Also, to think that HIV/AIDS is a white, gay male disease is an inaccurate stereotype and a dangerous approach to the problem. Millions are still dying, and there is an indication from the World Health Organization (WHO) that the disease is moving fast to Asia and Russia.

Africa's poor are the most vulnerable people and victims in every African problem and situation. The rich and affluent, with huge wallets, can afford health care at any cost, but that is not the case with the poor in societies where there are little or no subsidies for the poor. Squeezed by the weight of neglect, scared by the high cost of health care, they are also discouraged by government propaganda from patronizing traditional or herbal medical providers. The conflict is the worst problem facing the African health care system. Millions die every year from infectious diseases with known cures, such as measles, tuberculosis, and malaria—not just HIV/AIDS.

African governments, on the other hand, rarely control diseases through the screening of passengers visiting or migrating from around the world to Africa. Foreigners and visitors to Africa are not adequately monitored to determine the origin of certain ailments and diseases. There are no systematic methods used to track diseases, or their spread, to sources inside or outside the continent, even when it is reaching an epidemic level.

97. Question: Is it true that the HIV/AIDS strain that infects Africans is different from the one that infects Westerners?

Answer:

It is true. The HIV strains found in the United States and Europe are different from that found in Africa, especially South Africa and Kenya. There are two strains found in Africa, unlike Europe and the United States.

Eastern Africa has subtypes A & D. Southern Africa has mostly C. Europe and Asia on the other hand has mostly B. Unlike other infectious diseases on the African continent, such as measles and malaria, the HIV subtypes bring to question (including among members of the scientific community) the origin of the virus and how the virus mutations follow the pattern they did.

From pure science, new diseases tend to mutate very fast, and that raises questions as to whether HIV/AIDS is a new disease or if it has long existed in animals, as some members of the scientific community have claimed.

98. Question: Have there been African efforts to curb the spread of the disease or an effort to develop vaccines or a cure for HIV/ AIDS in that part of the globe?

Answer:

In recent times, herbalists have made claims of discovering a cure for HIV/AIDS. Unfortunately, these claims have not been scrutinized enough or subjected to scientific tests. However, the majority of Africans that believe that expensive modern medicines should not be the only dependent remedy to Africa's health care agree that traditional medicines do not need scientific authentication to be used— especially as poor people are dying and government assistance in subsidizing health costs for the poor is far from becoming a reality.

African scientists and groups of international AIDS experts are collaborating towards developing a vaccine for HIV/AIDS. The feat is far from being achieved, but there is expressive belief that the dream would eventually be realized.

In July 2002, NGO's President, Dr Erick Gbodossou, was the lead researcher in clinical and laboratory tests. In what is called a successful result, a three-year study of 62 AIDS infected patients suggested that a brand made from an indigenous herbal preparation of five medicinal plants may be a useful treatment option for African people living with the disease. An international scientific advisory committee oversaw the study, and a diagnostic laboratory in New York conducted the blood analysis.

African nations such as Uganda have provided the world with a model of how government programs can work in reducing infections from HIV/AIDS. There are different African governments and non-governmental organizations with strong initiatives aimed at reducing HIV/AIDS across the continent. The understanding by multi-national pharmaceutical companies to lower prices on expensive HIV/AIDS drugs (which has, for a long time, been beyond the reach of the poor) is a welcome development.

Due to domestic policies, the HIV/AIDS rate has dropped in Botswana, Uganda, Senegal, and Zambia. However, as a reminder, "the deadly seven diseases"—malaria, measles, tuberculosis, hepatitis, diarrhea, respiratory tract infections, and HIV/AIDS—are still with us. Africa still struggles to manage deaths from these diseases.

99. Question: HIV/AIDS has been devastating and demoralizing news for Africa and the rest of the world. Uganda, I gathered, has the highest drop in the rate of patients with HIV/AIDS in the world. How did they do this? Why haven't other African governments adopted Uganda's model to tackling HIV/AIDS?

Answer:

The majority of the people at one time in Africa thought that HIV/AIDS was a "foreign disease." There was no concern that it would touch Africa's soil. Similarly, the Western media's early report of the disease as a "white, gay disease" was not helpful. These stereotypes distracted people and authorities from their responsibilities of monitoring, preventing, and controlling the disease. This is in addition to the neglect that health care faces in these countries.

Africans are very aware of what happens around them through word of mouth; from family members and relatives residing overseas; and through the mass media, with satellite television, satellite radios, the Internet, and cable networks airing around the world. Unfortunately, the local news media are hooked into "Afghanistanism," and foreign news occupies so much space and airtime that local news is sometimes neglected.

What goes on in the United States gets special attention from the average newsreader or television viewers around the world, not just in Africa. Therefore, when the news repeatedly disseminated about HIV/AIDS being a disease that affected a homogenous group of people with certain sexual and drug habits, the news quickly sailed across the world.

The majority of Africans had never heard of the disease at the time, but they knew it existed as a disease "overseas" or "another part of the planet." Unknowingly, and surprisingly, not long after the disease manifested in the United States and Europe, it became apparent in less than 10 years that Africa was not exempt from the disease. Before anybody knew it, the disease started taking lives, leaving tracks of death, especially among the poor—first in cities and gradually, as experienced now, in villages.

Of course, Africans live in a culture where health problems are not pursued with the vigor and attention they deserved until maybe they reach epidemic levels. Africa's HIV/AIDS is on the rise in some countries in the continent because of the delay in response to the disease, poor attention to health care by governments, and the diversion of budgeted funds to other sectors while neglecting health care.

The case with Uganda is interesting and unique because Uganda's approach circumvents all African traditions and cultures as far as "freedom" to talk about sex publicly was concerned. Uganda stayed clear of the controversies described above.

As I earlier remarked, sex is a particular subject that is hardly discussed publicly. It is simply a taboo in every culture I have witnessed across the continent. Private parts, sex, and any other subjects involving intimate relationships between a man and a woman are private and not subject to discussion, even in the privacy of homes. These connections explain how conservative African cultures are when it comes to sex. Whether it has a downside is a matter of opinion, but the majority of Africans agree that it has helped the society rather than the reverse.

Uganda's campaign violated all these rules. The country's campaign went contrary to those conservative principles and emphasized sex education, a curriculum that is forbidden in almost every African middle and secondary school. Educating youths as well as adults about abstinence, safe sex, and the use of condoms became the ultimate theme for the lessons. The theme of the campaign was that abstinence from sex was the better of all choices. Identified as the ABC (Abstinence, Faithfulness, and Use of Condom) formula, the campaign has worked well.

The strategy includes training HIV/AIDS counselors and getting them involved in the education of teenagers about abstinence. Coming from a culture where sex is not discussed with the same freedom as in the United States, Uganda's tremendous move to debunk these taboos was encouraging.

A premier group, TAS, was established with the main goal of helping the infected. The National AIDS Control Program trained AIDS counselors and educated rural communities. Information dissemination using the traditional African means of communication—word of mouth—was effectively utilized. AIDS education among prostitutes was intensified.

Uganda's campaign focused and addressed elements that other African leaders may be framing in their minds but have never addressed. The program worked because leadership was committed, and the people were motivated. As partners, the success story of Uganda's model of fighting HIV and AIDS emerged.

In 1991, 15 percent of Ugandans had the HIV/AIDS virus. In less than a decade, the number has dropped to a mere 5 percent. It is a drastic drop, unmatched in any part of the world. That is why Uganda's example on the war against HIV/AIDS is receiving global attention and positive reviews by world leaders.

PART X

AFRICA: DO'S & DON'TS IN BUSINESS

DOING BUSINESS IN AFRICA

100: Quaestion: What are the basic things I should know about doing business in Africa?

History:

Africa is made up of 53 independent nations with numerous tribal affiliations that cross national boundaries. For instance, in Nigeria, the northern part of the country is Hausa and Muslim by religion. The North has cultural and religious ties with 13 nations in Africa where Hausa language is spoken and Islam is the faith. The Yorubas in Western Nigeria are citizens of Nigeria, but their language could be found spoken by indigenes of five different African countries. The Hausas also have religious as well as cultural ties, directly or indirectly, with 13 countries in the continent where the language is spoken. Tribes are bonded by religion, tradition, and customs and separated by policies of colonialism that have remained part of Africa's challenges till the present moment.

There are also migration patterns by choice or by events of history, such as wars and the search for fertile lands to farm and cultivate. The most common factor for migration patterns is people seeking better and secured environments in which to raise their children. These migration patterns also explain why Ibos of Eastern Nigeria, that were refugees during the Biafran civil war, have communities in Cote d'Ivoire and Gabon. The Ibo migrants carried with them tribal cultures, customs, and traditions to their new lands. They have blended them into existing ones in their host land or their new "homeland."

Therefore, it is not surprising to witness that behaviors, values, customs, traditions, and cultures that existed in one country may be found in another country. Overall, African traditional cultures have mixed for a very long time.

Democracy is taking root in all regions in the continent, faster than would have been imagined. This is in spite of political setbacks in some African countries that have witnessed coup d'états.

Efforts by African leaders in particular to mediate crises in Ivorian, Liberian, Sao Tome, Principe, Sudan, and the People's Republic of Congo demonstrated new political leadership and mediation efforts that may shape Africa's political future.

A recent proposal towards an African Peace Force is the latest of developments that may see order return to conflicting nations in Africa, depending on how committed the parties are to peace initiatives. Africa's new scheme and leadership have new agendas of economic development, freedom (democracy), and emancipation as priorities.

The formation of the African Union (AU) marks a new economic direction from a continent where it seems that all efforts to stir it to economic prosperity have failed. The economic road map that the AU provides is a positive development, but following the road map with the discipline and determination necessary to meet a successful end is another matter. It is what only time will tell.

Attitudes vary—which explains why I decided to list do's and don'ts in business featuring cultures where I have lived or cultures that I have observed for very long periods of time. There are more values shared almost by every African than those separating the people. But the things I express here are not constants—they are different cultures and behaviors of people that stem from their upbringing, their religion, their environment, and their traditions and cultures.

Further materials on African culture can be found in books, videos, slides, and on microfilm at the nearest library.

Languages:

Africa has more than 4,000 languages and dialects. Depending on what part of the continent a person may be visiting, ensure that you have company or a guide that speaks and understands the native languages. It is an advantage to a guest if he has a person that understands and speaks native languages well. Otherwise, don't worry, since an average businessperson in Africa speaks and understands English, French, or Portuguese—depending on what kind

of business you are doing and where they are located on the continent.

Africa's official languages are Swahili, Kinyarwanda (Rwanda), English, French, Portuguese, and Arabic. Other prominent languages and dialects are Hausa, Fulani, Yoruba, Igbo, and Swahili.
(See appendix of African languages.)

Religion:

Africans take religion very seriously. High spirituality is
transparent and manifested everywhere.

It shows in the ways people attend religious services, observe religious events and holidays, or go to services on Sundays
and designated "holy" weeks. It reflects on the ways people talk,
what they wear, and their prayers and praises to the creator above on
moments that warrant them. One of the most interesting aspects of
Africans and spirituality is their resilience to calamities. There are
about 368 million Christians, 324 million Muslims, and 93 million
Animists in the continent.

Negotiation Strategies:

There is no doubt that the more educated an African is, the
more he will look at all options and use objective facts to define
the truth. However, native intelligence rather than academic intelligence is what rules. Most African business people have, in one way
or the other, had contact with non-Africans. No matter how isolated
or remote the village may be in Africa, there is another person, not
necessarily a European but perhaps another African that has contacts or may have lived in the Western hemisphere. As such, lessons
acquired through these interactions and experiences are exposed
when an average African is interacting or negotiating with a guest.
In other words, negotiating with you may not be the first time your
guest has negotiated with a person not from his tribe.

It would be a mistake on the part of a guest to underestimate
an African businessman or woman, especially in regards to his or

her knowledge of the world. The assumption that your host may never have gone to school and therefore may be ignorant would be self-defeating at any moment. The majority of African businessmen or women in Ibo land, for example, have high school diplomas. You cannot outwit him or her in business negotiations on those assumptions.

Traditional Value System:

From North to South, East and West, Africans have different tribal backgrounds and sub-cultures, some liberal, others very conservative. However, all tribes hold strongly to the same value system, which defines what is good and bad. As I emphasized previously, traditional moral values such as honesty, perseverance, love, endurance, forgiveness, integrity, self-control, resourcefulness, kindness, and respect for life exist across almost every culture.

In some societies in Africa, the struggle for survival as a result of economic distress has shifted the paradigm as far as some people observing conservative values and taboos are concerned. Honesty is still transparent, but a few bad apples are trampling on the virtue of honesty. Dubious activities such as 419 scams have suddenly emerged, posing new threats to national security, foreign investments, and the economic survival of any serious nation. Shared value that abhors selfishness, greed, and corruption are eroding faster in urban cities and gradually spreading to villages. The result is the emancipation of wealth in the name of capitalism without consideration of how the wealth was acquired. The tenet of traditional, as well as Christian values that everybody growing up in the village once cherished is gradually vanishing. Thus, values such as trust, ingenuity, and hard work are becoming overshadowed by how many "greens" are in a person's pocket, and not how those greens came about.

The majority of Africans are honest people, and the worst fears confronting genuine, honest businessmen and women in Africa are the actions of a few bad apples in the midst of a whole lot of good apples. These few are damaging the good reputation and trust that have taken so long to build.

Africa has community-based societies. Though individual decisions are exercised and respected in private matters, the person always consults friends, family, and on the extreme choice, elders in the community in reaching some conclusion on vital family matters. Family is very important to Africans, and they count on people in the family for almost everything, including moral, psychological, and financial support.

What one owns belongs to the individual but also brings a shared joy to the community. In countries such as Gambia, what a man owns belongs to his brother and his wife as well as to his sister.

In private business, an entrepreneur is responsible for all decisions that he or she makes. It is not so with matters involving partnership and community-based businesses at large. Overall, family cohesion is very important. It takes a village to raise a child as much as it takes the family, immediate and extended, to give identity and security in order for a person to be successful, including in business.

Across cultures, Africans have an inherent trust in people, at times more than they have in their fellow Africans. This openness is often abused. However, people are becoming more cautious and always monitoring when guests in particular may try to exploit this virtue.

Always say "sorry" when a mistake is made, even when you are not responsible. It has a different meaning from my experience here in the United States. I would always say, "Sorry," for instance, when a customer tripped over a store item on an aisle or shelf in the store where I worked. I was always the first to say "sorry". I have been corrected in the United States by people telling me, repeatedly, "It is not your fault, don't apologize." My culture does not see it that way.

Age is a virtue associated with wisdom. Always show respect to the elderly or the oldest person in a group. Wisdom and education (literacy) have different compartments. However, Africans admire both.

A personal visit is preferred more than any phone call or letter. You could arrange to visit the home for official business, but this is not before you would have established a rapport or have met several times with him or her.

Don't be embarrassed when a question is used to answer a question. There are some African cultures where this is normal; in others, they may be ready to listen, and as such, wait to respond.

Equality /Inequality of the Genders:

Every culture has it own expectation of what roles men and women play in the society. Prior to my trip across Africa, I assumed that my tribe, the Ibos, was the only tribe where men and women had roles defined by tradition—such that man is the breadwinner and the woman, the caretaker of the home. However, these roles are not distinctive or as defined as they once seemed because in traditional societies, including in my tribe, women are dominantly performing those roles that hitherto were attributed to men only.

In Ibo society, women are bestowed with titles in women's categories, but they were equally as important as the titles bestowed on men. In fact, in Ghana, it is the woman that inherits the father's property upon his death. The values and traditions that exist in these cultures define the idea of equality. But behind any successful man in every African society, there is always a strong and powerful woman (the spouse or mother).

BUSINESS PRACTICES

101: Question: What are the significant business practices when doing business in Africa?

Greetings:

As a guest, you will be introduced first, and it is respectful if you greet first. There are various greeting gestures. The handshake is the most common form of greeting. The preferred greeting in the morning is "Good Morning," "Good Afternoon," if it is noon, and "Good Evening" at evening and "Goodnight," if it is dawn.

In some cultures, such as Cote d'Ivoire, Senegal, and Niger, the greeting is by warm embrace and a peck on either one or both cheeks. "Hi" or "hello" is an informal greeting and is in no way a serious greeting. It is perceived as arrogant in some cultures. Better preferred and always most convenient is, "How are you?" Saying it in local dialects or language may spark friendship and creates an automatic spirit of camaraderie.

Men and women shake hands and vice versa. Always allow a woman to bring out her hands first. For men, it does not matter who brings out his hands first. The host, most of the time, brings out his hand first to welcome the guest. Pay attention to this. Africans can stay close to the other person when greeting. They could hold hands after greeting for seconds more after the first handshake. It is perceived as a friendly acquaintance. Take for instance when you are meeting a partner that was introduced by someone previously known to you or through a network of friends, you may expect such a close, warm handshake and the holding of both hands while talking for a few extra seconds. Always introduce your partner. Africans will always introduce everyone around him or her in a conference room during business negotiations.

Appointments:

Africans are very hospitable people. It runs across every tribe, village, and country. An average African could discuss any subject and every topic, from families to the most current events unfolding around the world. Africans love to trust and are scared away when betrayed.

Writing a letter for an appointment is good, but unless you are visiting top government officials or an executive of a corporation, it may not be necessary. Unless there is a security restriction, then write and book for a meeting. It is always best if you can go to the office you want to visit first, and then book an appointment personally or send an office assistant to make the arrangement.

Africans prefer face-to-face meetings for the first time. Face-to-face contact in African cultures is preferred. Meeting in person shows determination and seriousness on the part of the guest. In case you sent a fax, letter, or made a telephone call for an appointment, make sure you follow it up.

Work starts in most offices at 8:30 a.m. and closes at about 4:00 p.m. Depending on the type of business, some offices close at 5:00 p.m., but no later than 6:00 p.m. Most private companies start at either 8:30 a.m. or 9:00 a.m. and close by 5:00 p.m. or later, by choice of the owner.

Essential services are open every day of the week. They are private businesses that open and close late on Saturdays. Offices are open Monday through Friday, except in Muslim states, where Muslims go for prayers on Friday. In cities with predominantly Muslim populations, Friday may be a half day-off, and some offices do close early. Some private companies stay open half days on Saturdays. Sunday is a work free day.

Be early to appointments, and don't get disappointed if the other party shows up 30 minutes or an hour late to the appointment. Family emergencies can shift a business appointment or other reasons; some critics say it is part of the African culture to attend to family first before business and in some instances disrupts appointment deadlines. Many disagree and claim that it is an individual habit and not a generalized behavior.

Negotiating:

Don't expect a breakthrough on the first day of business negotiations. It takes business drive, persuasion, and confidence building to pace up negotiations. Doing business with governments is far
slower because of bureaucratic hurdles than working with the private sector. (The speed of doing business with the government has
improved in recent times in some countries because of the policies
of new leadership to bring business to the standards set by the United States and Europe.)

Don't expect the boss to be the major decision-maker or
the person who determines the success of your negotiations in government ministries or parastatals. There are often thick layers of
bureaucracies and decision-making ranks to get across in getting
things done. Officials may take their turn to initial documents. Find
the link to the person in the organization responsible for approving
your deal. That will make your negotiations faster and easier.

In case of dealing with managers, there is the managing director, and preceding the director is the board of directors and the
minister in charge of the department. It all depends on the size of
your business contract and the amounts that are involved. Some
need "executive" approval, just as others need the managing directors' approval and signatures to be effective. Ensure from the beginning that you are talking to the right person.

Networking before business deals is very important. Different cultures have different names they use to refer to lobbyists (such
as *Imma Mmadu* in native Ibo language meaning, "a well-connected
person"). Such a person, when introduced to you or when you are
able to locate him yourself, will save you time and money, especially when looking at huge contracts. Most multi-national companies
understand this aspect of doing business in developing world, not
just in Africa. Thus, they hire prominent natives and opinion leaders
as directors or consultants, and their assignments include lobbying
on behalf of their companies. It has worked well and will continue
to be part of the business culture, not just in Africa but also around
the world.

Always think twice before dealing with anybody that claims he or she has a connection to link you to government officials that will facilitate contract agreements. Well-connected people are always by referrals. They are silent and, in fact, most of the time the "movers and shakers" of the social, political, and economic frontiers. These men and women can also be reached through subordinates. Find these subordinates or how to reach the contact person.

Business cards are easily available and always give name, title, office, and the home number(s) of the contact. When you are handed the business card, it has more guaranteed contact information than the phone number. Ensure that the listed features, such as telephone numbers and addresses, are on every card. You can visit your African host at his home and discuss official business matters during his private time. Business talks are not restricted to an office environment. It may extend to soccer fields, recreational facilities, bars, or country and nightclubs.

Africans do speak sometimes at very close range, and I noticed that Americans don't. They prefer to remain at a distance. Note that it is always embarrassing to a host when he or she is talking and you suddenly pull back to maintain a distance. I have witnessed this happen on several occasions in the U.S. between two persons talking. Pulling back suddenly from the person talking to you is rude in African culture. In some cultures, it is an insult to pull back at the beginning or during conversations. It is a non-verbal communication that could be interpreted to mean different things. But overall, it is disrespectful to your host. Maintain a distance before speaking rather than pulling back during the conversation.

Some African names are sometimes very difficult, at first, to pronounce. Africans do not take offence when their names are not pronounced correctly the first time. Nevertheless, try to show your host that you know how to pronounce his tribal name. Avoid "murdering" his name by the way you pronounce it. Most African names are difficult to pronounce because native languages have vowels that the English language does not, and their pronunciations are different.

Don't address a person as an African. It is very offensive, shows ignorance on the part of the guest, and it is read that you do not know the people you are dealing with very well. Such mistakes could be misinterpreted as an opportunist that is interested in making money and not concerned with knowing the people he is dealing with. Address a person as a Nigerian, Ghanaian, Senegalese, Libyan, Egyptian, or Algerian, et cetera. An African prefers his native name or baptismal name rather than a title referencing the country where he or she was born.

Africans don't have limitations on topics they can discuss with their guests. You could talk about soccer (football, as it is popularly known in that part of the world). You can talk about wars, but be careful, since you don't know which side your host supports. You can talk about HIV or AIDS, but you will offend the person if you tell him or her that the disease originated from Africa. Telling him about the number or percentage of Africans dying of HIV/AIDS may gain you a look of suspicion and distrust. The majority of Africans remain unconvinced and skeptical about the media for not telling the truth about the origins of the disease and the statistics of Africans infected or dead as a result of the disease. This does not eliminate the reality that the disease is an epidemic taking a devastating toll on lives in the continent.

Telephone lines have multiplied, almost three times in the last decade, and extended into rural areas in places like Ghana and Nigeria. Some villages could equally be reached through regular phones line, but the fastest and most reliable are the GMS satellite phones. Ensure that any cellular phone you have is adaptable to suit a particular nation's approved wavelengths and can receive signals from your location. Tri-mode and GMS wireless telephones are the best. You may be disappointed if you take your domestic handset and assume that it will work automatically in Africa. The cellular phone you have may not be compatible to the local system. In case you have a GSM telephone, you may subscribe locally. Making calls with pre-paid cards is the best bet. You can purchase them locally to avoid delays in setup costs and other bottlenecks that may interfere with your calls. In that way, you don't have to pay connecting fees for regular and cellular phone acquisitions. Also, you could charge your credit card or pay by cash to buy more time.

Public Manners:

If you are eating, don't be surprised if your host is quiet. There are some cultures where you don't talk while eating. In others, you can discuss but not talk. Discussing is different from talking because 'talking' involves engaging in dialogue with a member or everybody on the table on topics not related to the food at the table or the occasion that culminated in the parties coming together to dine; while 'discussing' involves dialogue or general expression of interesting parties about the event or the food often in very low voice. However, it is important that you know what applies to the particular culture of your host.

Detailed private or business conversations are reserved for after meals. Food in some cultures is perceived to be "sacred," and whatever goes into the body must be clean and not violated by "talking" or holding a conversation over dinner. However, there are no standard rules about this etiquette as far as Africans are concerned.

Business Entertaining:

Business launches are preferred over dinner. Dinner can take place at the home of the host. Such meals, when offered at home, allow for business conversations to take place, probably after or maybe during relaxation.

Africans like to pay for the dinner. It is considered impolite for a visitor to pay for a dinner. However, the culture is changing, especially with economic downturns in some economies and the exchange rates, which favor U.S. and European currencies over domestic currencies. It is assumed that dollars have more value than any local currency—and you have more to give than local residents.

Eat only with the right hand, and discuss, don't talk much, while eating. Washing hands before and after dinner is very important and considered hygienic. Always thank your host at the end of a meal, be it at home, at a restaurant, or at a country club. It is an African culture to always express gratitude—including after meals.

Titles/Forms of Address:

Africans across social classes want to feel respected. Therefore, identifying and including a title in both personal and official correspondences is appreciated. It may be a traditional title, an academic title, or a social title. It spells who the person is and what he is doing. It may include honors received, and it goes with the person's name. However, it is not obligatory that you identify the person by all his titles and honors. However, some people are very conscious of their names going along with their titles, honors, and the position they occupy. When you are dealing with a person that is very conscious of his or her titles please do use them appropriately.

There are, however, individuals that do not want their titles to follow them around to be worn on the neck like rosary beads. To such individuals, using their titles may be offensive. Just do a little inquiry to find out what the host prefers. Also, when listening to others address the person with or without his or her title, you as the guest could take this as a cue and decide whether to use the host's title or not.

Oral historians claim that Africans' romance with big titles, tributes, and praises goes back to old African customs. Their explanation is that our ancestors recognized great men in the society in many ways. Some brave men had their titles tattooed on them with indelible inks (traditional marks), which they wear as long as they live. In others, warriors that have performed certain feats, in wars for example are given a badge of honor (not by medals stapled on their breast suit pockets) by marks on their forehead or elsewhere. Women who have shown valor, determination, and exemplary leadership are also honored with titles. It is a mark of respect, honor, and recognition of the importance of the person to the community. To this day, those customs are alive and practiced, not with tattoos or tribal marks on the body but by titles bestowed on these incredible sons and daughters as role models.

In fact, titles and pseudonyms are ingrained in the tradition of African people. It tells who you are (or assumed to be) and what you have achieved for your community, church, or mosque.

Business Gifts:

Africans are very hospitable people. However, you may be sending the wrong signal when you come with a gift at the beginning of a business talk. Avoid this. Gift giving should be reserved till the end of business negotiations, and the reason for giving it must be specified. Many African countries are struggling to clear their systems of corruption and bribery. Nigeria, for example, is a country that has laws in place now against bribery and corrupts practices.

Bribery and kickbacks are problems in most developing countries, and it is more pronounced in some countries in Africa than others. And there are countries where it does not happen at all. Any businessperson must be conscious of this and distinguish when a gift is bribe or a public relations tool. Cooperation from both the giver and receiver is needed to stop any future crimes. When a business deal seems too good to be true, don't offer any gift to get it. Talk to a commercial attaché in either your embassy, the African embassy in the United States, or the Business and Trade departments in the Ministry of Commerce and Trade. Always inquire and confirm the authenticity of the company, what type of business it is doing, and the legitimacy of the operation. It is often when people are desperate that they fall into the hands of corrupt dealings.

Middlemen or people that broker business deals expect some percentages from the deal. It is often termed a "kickback." There are also genuine and honest people in business to assist and network for a guest. Always be careful whom you approach and nominate.

Dress:

Cultural awareness has swept across Africa since the independence of most African countries in the 60s. The love for African dresses and hairstyles has moved steps further. Therefore, Africans love to dress in their traditional attires. In Kenya, Nigeria, and South Africa, men and women still dress for work in business suits. Some African and Western designers have created beautiful dresses from

African fabrics, and these designs can serve various purposes; both may be worn as casual, office, and evening wear.

Cultural awareness has improved including deep reflections on dresses people wear. But cultural consciousness has yet to translate into compulsory dressing codes at government work places. It is worth re-calling that there was a time when traditional attires were not allowed into offices, but that has changed. The change is part of a cultural revolution that started after independence, as I earlier mentioned. People wear traditional dresses to offices in some countries, especially in organizations where strict dress codes are not enforced. Bosses are more likely to dress in traditional *agbadas, dashikis,* or caftan dresses than co-workers. Still, the majority of office employees dress in suits, ties, skirts, and blouses, just like any work environment in Europe or the United States.

Shorts are forbidden for any business meeting, no matter how casual the event leading to the meeting may be. Women prefer modest dressing, either in traditional or western dress styles. Wearing pants to any business occasion or meeting is not prohibited, but in most office environments, it is respectful and more dignifying if you don't wear what the culture abhors. Finding out what is right for each region is important. Occasionally, women can be spotted wearing pants, but it is rarely allowed to work. Modest dressing in clean, simple suits is preferred to tight skirts or revealing dresses. Dresses that promote sexuality or that expose any private parts are embarrassing to wear anywhere, whether to the office or not.

Unlike some other global cultures where you offend people by wearing their traditional dress to a business appointment, Africa's hospitality, which is legendary, sees such dressing as a gesture of friendship.

Gestures:

Do not use your left hand to give or receive anything from your host. It is considered impolite in most African cultures. The left hand is considered, "unclean." Avoid giving anything with the left hand to avoid miscommunication or disconnection with your host.

Eating with the left hand is rare and will draw unnecessary attention, if not criticism. Eating some traditional foods with bare hands is common in most cultures. If it is as a result of culture, please join the dinner table and eat with your bare hands like the rest of the people in the group.

Most of the time, at dinner tables, forks and knives are set on every table, but don't ask for a spoon from your hosts unless they offered that alternative to you. Ask an average African and he will reveal to you that some foods are eaten and enjoyed better when eaten with bare hands. Unless you have built a close and personal relationship, joining your host to eat with your bare hands shows the interest that you have in the culture, which in turn may attract goodwill.

There are cultures where speaking and gesticulation is not frowned upon. However, business is better conducted in an audible voice and always in a calm environment. It is impolite to point at a person with your forefinger. It is most embarrassing if you are speaking to a different person and pointing at another subject whom you have never met before.

Gesturing is a way of speaking, but most business people prefer speaking with their hands steady. Looking straight into your business partner's eyes while speaking may be favored, but don't be upset or read meaning into it when your host doesn't look directly in your eyes while talking. Traditional value systems teach children from a young age in my culture, as well as some other cultures in Africa, that it is "arrogant and rude" to look an adult directly in the eyes while talking with the person. Children grow into adults with the culture. But there are some exceptions. For instance, in my own close family, my parents insisted that we always look directly into a person's eyes, whether an adult or my age mates. This is very different from what I have observed in the United States where looking straight into the eyes of the person talking to you is a mark of boldness, honesty, and seriousness. However, most people, irrespective of learned behavior at childhood, do look straight into a person's eyes during conservation.

Doing business in Africa is more than cash and carry. Business relationship goes along personal relationship and at times relationships that may extend beyond just business. It may over time involve other friends, members of the family or even members of the tribe or community. Therefore the manner of approaching business must be friendly. The respect for the people's cultures and traditions while doing business may foster or mar these relationships. Doing business in Africa is not just about making money. It is more than that. It is about personal and human relationships.

SUGGESTED REFERENCES FOR FURTHER READING

QUOTES

Levi, Virgilio and Christine Allison. *John Paul II: A Tribute in Words and Pictures*. New York. William Morrow & Company, 1999.

PREFACE:

Canadian Mining Company. "2,800 Square Kilometers of World Richest Known Copper Cobalt Deposits...." in 1997 Annual Stockholders Report. Malkior Resources, Inc., 1997.

Carwell, Hattie. *Blacks in Science.* Hicksville, N.Y. Exposition Press, 1977.

"Crude Oil Reserves to Be Raised to 40 billion by 2010." *Daily Trust,* April 29, 2003.

Garrett, Laurie. "Landa-Landa. An Ebola Virus Epidemic in Zaire Proves Public Health is Imperiled by Corruption" in *Betrayal of Trust: The Collapse of Global Public Health.* New York. Hyperion Publishers, 2000.

Robinson, J.P. "I Love my TV (TV Viewing)." *American Demographics* 12(9) (1990): 24–28.

Sahn, D., and D. Stifel. "Poverty Comparisons Over Times and Across Countries in Africa." *World Development* 28 (2000): 2123–2155.

FORETHOUGHT

THE RHYTHM OF AFRICAN WARS

Levi, Virgilio, and Christine Allison. *John Paul II: A Tribute in Words and Pictures*. New York. William Morrow & Company, 1999.

PART I

LANGUAGES, DIALECTS, CULTURE, AND HERITAGE

"African names . . . Communication from Professor Richard Allen." University of Michigan, September 2, 1989. (Also see his articles in the *American Political Science Review,* June 1989.)

Alansan, Mansaray. *A Haunting Heritage—An African Saga In America.* Dallas, Texas. Sahara Publishing, 1995.

Ali, Mazrui. "Islamic and Western Values." *Foreign Affairs,* September–October 1997.

Alpert, Bruce (New House News Service). "Delegation Wants Trip to Open Americans' Eyes—President Embarks on Journey to Africa." *The Plain Dealer,* Sunday, March 22, 1998.

"Battling Malaria: New Weapon From India." *This Day Newspaper,* Lagos. August 6, 2003. http://allafrica.com/200308060357.html. (Referenced: August 8, 2003.)

Charno, Jeffrey (Producer). *Jali Kunda–Griots of West Africa & Beyond* (Book and Compact Disc). Ellipsis Arts Publishers, 2001.

Chung, Amy. *World on Fire—How Exporting Free Market Democracy Breeds Ethnic Hatred and Global Insecurity.* New York. Doubleday, 2003.

Clark, Sandra. "Language Versed in African Sound, Ebonics. Professor Says, Is Derived from Mother Tongue." *Plain Dealer,* March 6, 1997.

Connal, Graham. "The Salt of Bunyoro.... Seeking the Origins of African Kingdom." *Antiquity* 65 (1991): 479–94.

Duffy, John. *The Healers: The Rise of the Medical Establishment.* N.Y. McGraw–Hill, 1976.

Forde, M., ed. *African Worlds: Studies in the Cosmological Ideas and Social Values of African Peoples.* Oxford University Press, 1954.

Greenberg, J.H. *The Languages of Africa.* Indiana. Indiana University Press, 1963.

Mbanefo, Charles. "Nigerians Most Educated of Immigrants in United States." Speech at African Community Association Scholarship Awards, Akron. October 19, 1996.

McClester, Cedric (rev. edit). *Kwanzaa—Everything You Wanted to Know, But Didn't Know Where to Ask.* New York. Gumbs & Thomas Publishers, 1990.

Moore, Francis. *Travels into the Inland Part of Africa.* London, 1738.

New Webster Dictionary and Thesaurus of the English Language. Danbury, CT. Lexicon Publications, 1993.

Norment, Lynn. "Denzel Washington—Cover Story." *Ebony Magazine,* October 1995.

Ojimba, Felix C. *Power of Conscience—The Life and Times of Daniel Obiesie Orjiako.* Ibadan, Nigeria. Spectrum Books, 1999.

Reader, John. *Africa—A Bibliography of the Continent.* New York. Alfred A. Knopf, 1998.

Robey, Melvin J. *African Violets, Gifts of Nature.* Cornwell Books, 1988.

Rogers, J. A. *World's Great Men of Color (Vol. 1).* New York. Touchstone Books, 1996.

Shakespeare, William. "I Speak of Africa and Golden Joys" in *Henry IV,* v. iii. 104. First Published, 1600.

Shillington, Kevin. *History of Africa (Revised Edition).* New York. St Martin's Press, 1995.

Skinner, Elliot P. *Peoples and Cultures of Africa.* New York. Doubleday/Natural History Press, 1973.

Stride, G.T., and Caroline Ifeka. *Peoples and Empires of West Africa.* Lagos. Thomas Nelson, 1971.

WVIZ, Channel 2. "The Rise and Fall of British Empires." Cleveland. Public Broadcasting Service. (Aired June 24, 2001.)

PART II

IT TAKES A VILLAGE

Anonymous & Wire Reports. "U.N. Seeks Help Finding Missing Aides." *The Plain Dealer,* May 18, 2003. A.8.

Barbosa, Rogerio Andrade. *African Animal Tales*. California. Volcano Press, 1993.

Billings, Henry. *Bridges.* New York. Viking Press, 1958.

"Board Declares 70 Films Unfit for Broadcast." *This Day Newspaper,* Lagos. October 10, 2002. http://allafrica.com/stories/200210100309.html. (Referenced: October 10, 2003.)

Burner, P. *Kings, Commoners & Concessionaires*. London. Cambridge University Press, 1982.

Fortes, M. *The Dynamics of Clanship Among the Tallensi.* Oxford University Press, 1945.

"Going the Distance to Ghana." *Sunday Plain Dealer,* March 30, 1997. p. 1.

Igboaka, Simon Richard. "The History of Ihiala People of South Eastern Nigeria." Oral history and unpublished manuscript, 1992.

Michele, Stepto, ed. *African-American Voices*. Brookfield, Connecticut. Millbrook Press, 1994.

Ohia, Paul (with Agency Reports). "Nigerians Happiest in the World—Survey." *This Day Newspapers,* Lagos. October 2, 2003. http://allafrica.com/stories/200310030073.html. (Referenced: October 3, 2003.)

"Poverty Breeds Worst Forms of Child Labor." *Business Times,* Dar es Salam, Tanzania. August 7, 2003. http://allafrica.com/stories/200308080631.html. (Referenced: August 8, 2003.)

Rogers, J. A. *World's Great Men of Color (Vol 1)*. New York. Touchstone Books, 1996.

Rowton, Simpson. "The New Land Law in Malawi." *Journal of Administration Overseas,* vol. 6, no. 4 (1967).

PART III

SOCIETY: SOCIAL ISSUES, LIVING, AND CULTURE

Allan, W. *The African Husbandman.* Oliver & Boyd, 1965.

Baeta, C. G., ed. *Christianity in Tropical Africa.* Oxford University Press, 1968.

"Catholic Archbishop Marries..." *CNN Headline News,* May 28, 2001.

Charno, Jeffrey (Producer). *Jali Kunda—Griots of West Africa & Beyond* (Book and Compact Disc). Ellipsis Arts Publishers, 2001.

Goody, J.A. *Death, Property and the Ancestors.* Cambridge University Press, 1966.

Gray, Richard. *A History of the Southern Sudan, 1839–1889.* London, 1961.

Iyefu, Adoba. "Nigerian Women Most Fertile." *This Day.* Lagos. May 25, 2004.

"Mmegi, First Female Paramount Chief Welcomed." *The Reporter,* Gaborone, Botswana. September 5, 2003. http://www.allafrica.com/stories/200309050722.html. (Referenced: September 5, 2003.)

Qu Robin, Law. *The Slave Coast of West Africa.* Oxford, 1991.

Rogers, J. A. *World's Great Men of Color (Vol. 1).* New York. Touchstone Book, 1996.

"The Moving Kidnap Story of Olaude (Revealed—The Roots of Equiano's Mother)." *Center News—A Magazine for Sustainable Development,* vol. 2, no. 1 (January–March 1998).

Walkin, Daniel J. "African Priest Irks the Vatican Again." *The Plain Dealer,* April 3, 1996.

Williams, Eric. *Capitalism & Slavery.* London, 1942.

PART IV

POLITICS: DEMOCRACY AND LEADERSHIP

Armas, Genera C. (with Associated Press). "Population Boom Likely in Africa. The Future of World Population." Associated Press, July 22, 2003. Also in *Plain Dealer,* July. A7.

Associated Press. "Police Patrols Nairobi After Ethnic Rioting." *Plain Dealer,* Wednesday, October 18, 1995. A23.

Benton, Barbara, ed. *Soldiers of Peace—Fifty Years of the United Nations Peace-Keeping.* New York. Facts on File, Inc., 1996.

Busumtwi-Sam, J. "Redefining 'Security' After the Cold Wars: The OAU, UN, and Conflicts Management in Africa" in *Civil Wars in Africa: Roots and Resolution* edited by T.M. Ali, and Robert Matthews. Montreal. McGill-Queens University Press, 1999. pp 257–287.

Chiahemen, J. "Congo's Kabila Sacks Outspoken Minister." Reuters, 2003.

Chua, Amy. *The World on Fire: How Exporting Free Market Democracy Breeds Ethnic Hatred and Global Instability.* New York. Doubleday, Random House, 2003.

Davidson, B. *Which Way Africa? The Search for a New Society (revised edition).* London and Baltimore. Penguin Publishers, 1967.

Freund, Bill. "Oil Boom and Crisis in Contemporary Nigeria." *Review of African Political Economy,* no. 13 (August–November 1978): pp. 91ff.

Italiaander, Rolf. *The New Leaders of Africa.* Englewood Cliffs, N.J. Prentice-Hall, 1961.

Klare, Michael. "Supplying Repression: US support for Authoritarian Regimes Abroad." *Washington Institute for Policy Studies* (1977): p. 40.

McLean, Mora. "Oil Trade, AIDS, & Democracy—A Few of the Reasons the US Should Pay Attention to Africa." *Plain Dealer,* Tuesday, August 29, 2000.

Ozoemena, Charles. "Nigeria, Others Mobilize to Rout Sao Tome Junta." *Vanguard Newspapers,* Lagos, Nigeria. July 22, 2003. http://allafrica.com/stories/200307220535.html. (Referenced: July 22, 2003.)

"Popoola Identifies Factors Working Against Democracy." *Vanguard Daily Newspaper,* June 23, 2000.

Rosenblum, Mort (with Associated Press). "Report Says World Failed Rwanda." *The Plain Dealer,* Wednesday, February 28, 1996. sec. 8.

Uvin, P. "Prejudice, Crisis, and Genocide in Rwanda." *African Studies Review* 40 (1997): 97–115.

Watkins, K. *The Oxfam Poverty Report.* Oxford. Oxford University Press, 1995.

Weiner, Myron. "The Pursuit of Ethnic Equality Through Preferential Policies: A Comparative Public Policy Perspective" in *Independence to Statehood: Managing Ethnic Conflicts in Five African and Asian States* edited by Robert B. Goldmann, and A. Jayaratnam Wilson. London. Furces Printers, 1984.

Wiking, S. "Military Coups in Sub-Saharan African: How to Justify Illegal Assumptions Of Power." *Uppsala: Scandinavian Institute of African Studies,* 1983.

"Zaire: An IMF Subsidiary?" *The International Bulletin,* vol. 6, no. 3 (February 12, 1979): p. 2.

PART V

STEREOTYPES, MYTHS, AND REALITIES

Chung, Amy. *World on Fire—How Exporting Free Market Democracy Breeds Ethnic Hatred and Global Insecurity.* New York. Doubleday, 2003.

"CNN Opens Its Fourth Center in Africa." *The Guardian Newspapers,* Lagos, Nig. July 29, 2001.

"Coup Applauded by Politicians and Ordinary People." UN Integrated Regional Information Network. September 14, 2003. http://allafrica news. com/200339150589.html. (Referenced: September 15, 2003.)

Crawford, J.R. *Witchcraft and Sorcery in Rhodesia.* Oxford University Press, 1967.

Cross, Theodore. "Black Africans Now the Most Highly Educated Group in British Society." *The Journal of Blacks in Higher Education* (1994): 92.

D'Souza, Dinesh. *The End of Racism—Principles for a Multiracial Society.* New York. The Free Press, 1995.

Grunwald, Michael. "Swazi King Learns His Hints, Makes Peace Over 10th Wife." *The Plain Dealer,* November 6, 2002. A18.

Lacayo, Richard. "Space Case—With New Ideas about Light and Form, British Architect David Adjaye is Ready to Make his Lip Across the Atlantic." *Time Magazine,* Style & Fashion, Special Edition, Fall 2003.

Lacey, Marc. "A Marriage Made in Controversy—Kenyan Activist Scandalizes Nation by Wedding much Younger Man." *New York Times/Plain Dealer,* Sunday, September 28, 2003.

Morton, Margaret. "Tunnel People Emerge. Opinion and Ideas Column." *Plain Dealer,* Tuesday, October 10, 1995.

Parrinder, G. *African Mythology.* London. Chancellor Press, 1996.
Struass, J., and D. Thomas. "Human Resources: Empirical

Modeling of Household and Family Decisions" in *Handbook of Development Economics Vol. 3A.* New York. Elsevier Science, North Holland (1995): 1883–2023.

PART VI

STEREOTYPES, MISINFORMATION, AND MISCONCEPTIONS

Associated Press. "Nigeria—Impoverished Nation Joins Space Age." *The Plain Dealer,* Lagos, Nigeria. Sunday, September 28, 2003. A.4.

Brown, Tony. *Black Lies, White Lies—The Truth According to Tony Brown.* New York. William Morrow and Company, Inc., 1995.

Chinweizu. *The West and the Rest of Us.* New York. Vintage Books, 1975.

Himmelstrand, Ulf. *The Problem of Cultural Translation in the Reporting of African Social Realities.* New York. African Publishing Corporation, 1974.

Koplow, David. *Smallpox: The Fight to Eradicate a Global Scourge.* Los Angeles. University of California Press, 2003.

"N1.5 billion Satellite for Launch September 26, 2003." *Vanguard Newspaper,* August 21, 2003. http://allafrica.com/stories/200308210687.html. (Referenced: August 22, 2003.)

Overholser, Geneva. "Lessons from Civic Journalism." *The Plain Dealer,* September 23, 1995. 10-B.

"Park Police May Quit Giving Crowd Counts." *The Plain Dealer,* Friday, October 20, 1995. 20-A.

Revel, Jean-Francois. *The Flight from Truth: the Reign of Deceit in the Age of Information.* New York. Random House, 1991.

PART VII

NUDITY, SEX, AND SEXUALITY

Allan, W. *The African Husbandman.* Oliver & Boyd, 1963.

Ammar, H. *Growing Up in an Egyptian Village.* London. Routledge and Kegan Paul, 1954.

Giorgis, B.W. "Female Circumcision in Africa." Report by United Nations Economic Commission For Africa Training and Research Center for Women and Association of African Women for Research and Development. Addis Ababa, 1981.

Hansen, H.H. "Clitoridectomy, Female Circumcision in Egypt." *Folk* (1972–73): 14–26.

Kouba, L., and J. Muasher. "Female Circumcision in Africa: An Overview. African Studies." *Review,* (1985): 28(1), 95–110.

Lightfoot-Klein, Hanny. *Prisoners of Ritual. An Odyssey into Female Genital Circumcision in Africa.* New York, Harrington Part Press, 1989.

Megafu, U. "Female Ritual Circumcision in Africa: An Investigation of the Presumed Benefits Among the Ibos of Nigeria." *East African Medical Journal* (1983): 40(11), 793–800.

Ravitch, A. "Preventing VD and Cancer by Circumcision." New York. Philosophical Library, 1973.

Robins, Gay. *Women in Ancient Egypt.* Cambridge, Massachusetts. Harvard University Press, 1993.

Schwartz, G. "Infibulation, Population Control and the Medical Profession." *Bulletin of the New York Academy of Medicine* (1970): 64(11), 964.

Shell-Duncan, Bettina, and Ylva Hernlund, eds. *Female "Circumcision" in Africa—Culture, Controversy and Change. Directions in Applied Anthropology.* Colorado. Lynne Rienneer Publishers, Inc., 2000.

"Traditional Medicine Treatment for AIDS Passes Clinic Tests." http://allafrica. com/stories/200207110016.html. (Referenced: July 11, 2002.)

Weiss, C. "Motives for Male Circumcision among the Preliterate and Literate Peoples." *Journal of Sex Research* (1966): 2(2), 69–88.

Worsley, A. "Infibulations and Female Circumcision: A Study of a Little Known Custom." *Journal of Obstetric & Gynecology of the British Empire* (1938): 45, 686–91.

PART VIII

SOCIETY AND ECONOMY

"Third World Loses $200bn Through Capital Flight." Secretary General Kofi Annan. *Daily Trust,* November 5, 2003.

"125 Companies Named in DRC Plunder Report." *New Vision,* October 30, 2003. Also on the web at allafrica.com:Congo-Kinshasa. (Referenced: October 31, 2003.)

"Africa's Economies." *The Economist,* September 19, 1998. p126.

Annan, Kofi. "Durable Peace and Sustainable Development in Africa." *South African Journal of International Affairs* 7 (2000): 1–2.

Bates, Robert H. *Markets and States in Tropical Africa.* Berkeley. University of California Press, 1981.

Bauer, C. "Public Sector Corruption and Its Control in South Africa" in *Corruption and Development in Africa: Lessons from Country Case Studies* edited by K.R. Hope Sr., and B.C. Chikulo. New York. St Martin's Press, 2000.

Bauer, P.T. *West African Trade: A Study of Competition, Oligopoly, and Monopoly in a Changing Economy*. Cambridge. Cambridge University Press, 1954.

Bio-Tchane, Abdoulaye. "African Challenges: What Must Be One. A Commentary by Director of African Department of IMF." *East African Standard Newspaper,* Kenya, Nairobi. August 24, 2003.

Birmingham, D. *Trade and Conflict in Angola, 1483–1790.* Oxford University Press, 1966.

Clinton's Address to Joint Nigerian Houses of Assembly on August 9, 2000. http://allaafrica.com/stories/200008290137.html. (Referenced: August 2, 2000.)

CNN Headline News (Producer). "Pat Robertson Criticizes Bush for Telling Liberian Leader, Charles Taylor to Step Down." Aired on July 13, 2003 as News clip.

Ellis, Kathryn. "Diamonds are Fundamental to Sierra Leone Conflict, U.S. Editor Says." State Information Programs. http://usinfo.state.gov/regional/af/security/a106501.htm. (Referenced: July 12, 2003.)

"Foreign Investment in Africa." UNCTAD Report on UN Conference on Trade and Development, Geneva 1995.

Freund, Bill. "Oil Boom and Crisis in Contemporary Nigeria." *Review of African Political Economy* No.13 (1978): 91ff.

Gedda, George. "Diplomat Backs Plans for All—African Crisis Team." *The Plain Dealer,* October 11, 1996.

Goody, J.A. "Economy and Feudalism in Africa" in a seminar paper, Institute of Commonwealth Studies, 1968.

Gray, Richard, and David Birmingham, eds. "Pre-Colonial African Trade: Essays on Trade in Central and Eastern Africa before 1900." London, 1970.

Hanke, Steve. "Africa and Economics." *Forbes,* May 28, 2001.

Kapuscinski, Ryszard. "The Shadow of the Sun, Klara Glowczewska, tan. New York and Toronto." Alfred A. Knopf, 2001. pp. 298–305.

Kwame, Anthony Appiah and Henry Louis Gates Jr. "Africa Can Regain Its Glory." *Wall Street Journal,* January 28, 2000.

Lappe, Frances, Joseph Collins, and David Kinley, eds. "Aids As Obstacle—Twenty questions about our Foreign Aid and the Hungry." *Institute for Food and Development Policy* (1980): p.191

Maier, T. "Rev. Pat Robertson's Ties with Zairian Leader Questioned." *Newsday,* May 21, 1995. A43.

Naisbitt, John. *Global Paradox—The Bigger the World Economy, The More Powerful Its Smallest Players.* New York. William Morrow and Company, Inc., 1994.

Njoku, H. M. A. *Tragedy Without Heroes. The Nigerian-Biafran War.* Enugu, Nigeria. Fourth Dimension Publishers, 1987.

Odogwu, B. *No Place to Hide; Crisis & Conflicts Inside Biafra.* Enugu, Nigeria. Fourth Dimension Publishers, 1987.

Ola Akande, Benjamin. "Good News: Nigerian Company Exporting Software to the U.S." *African News Weekly,* July 1995.

Reader, John. *Africa—A Biography of the Continent.* New York. Alfred A Knopf, 1980.

Reno, William. *Corruption and State of Politics in Sierra Leone.* Cambridge University Press, 1995.

Reuters. "U.S., Britain Offer Help Recovering Nigerian Funds." http://cnn.com/world/Africa/Nigeria.lost.funds.reut/index.html. (Referenced: September 20, 2002.)

Reyntjens, F. "Rwanda; Genocide & Beyond." *Journal of Refugee Studies* 9 (1996): pp. 240-251.

Sahn, D., ed. *Seasonal Variability in Third World Agriculture: The Consequences of Food Security.* Baltimore. John Hopkins University Press, 1989.

Sahn, D., P. Dorosh, and S. Younger. *Structural Adjustment Reconsidered: Economic Policy and Poverty in Africa.* Cambridge, UK. Cambridge University Press, 1997.

Sheriff, Abdul. *Slaves, Spices and Ivory in Zanzibar.* London. Oxford Press, 1987.

Snow, Philip. *The Star Raft: China's Encounter with Africa*. Ithaca, NY. Cornell University Press, 1988.

Thorbahn, Peter F. *The Pre-Colonial Ivory Trade of East Africa, PhD*. Unpublished doctoral dissertation, University of Massachusetts, 1979.

"U.S. Aid to Gulf Region, 1991–2000." General Accounting Office. Congressional Research Service. S. Agency for International Development. *United Press International; Associated Press; Plain Dealer,* Saturday, February 8, 2003. A6.

Walter, Rodney. *How Europe Underdeveloped Africa*. Washington, DC. Howard University Press, 1982.

Ward, Margy. "Africa's Debt, Trade, and Diamonds." http://worldwidewamm.org/newsletters/2001/0901/newsletter/AfricaMargy.html. (Referenced: October 10, 2003.)

World Bank. "2001 African Development Indicators." Washington, D.C. World Bank (2001).

World Bank Report. "Botswana, the Fastest Growing Economy in the World." *The Guardian Leader,* May 18, 1994.

"Zaire: An IMF Subsidiary?" *The International Bulletin* vol. 6, no. 3 (February 12, 1979): p2.

PART IX

HIV/AIDS, STATISTICS, AND MISCONCEPTIONS

Clinton Jefferson. "Rate of Mortality from AIDS/HIV Now Highest in Russian & Caribbean Islands." CNN News (Live), July 30, 2001.

Farley, M. "Annan Proposes a Global War Chest to Battle AIDS." *Los Angeles Times,* April 27, 2001.

Garrett, Laurie. *The Coming Plague—Newly Emerging Diseases in a World Out of a Balance*. New York. Harper Collins, 1994.

Iwasaki, John. "History, Culture Makes Blacks Reluctant to Participate in Research Scholars Say." *The Plain Dealer,* Cleveland. Wednesday, August 27, 2003. A9.

Johnson, E., N. Jaax, and J. White, et al. "Lethal Experimental Infections of Rhesus Monkeys by Aerosolized Ebola Virus." *International Journal of Experimental Pathology* 76 (1995): 277–86.

Levy, J.A., L.Z. Pan, and Giraldo Beth, et al. "Absence of anti-bodies to the Human Immuno deficiency Virus in Sera from Africa Prior to 1975." Proceedings of the National Academy of Sciences 83 (1986): 7935–37.

Pecoul, B., P. Chirac, and P. Trouiller, et al. "Access to Essential Drugs in Poor Countries; A Lost Battle?" *Journal of the American Medical Association* 281 (1999): 361–67.

Rosenberg, Tina. "Abstinence Just One Weapon in AIDS Battle." *The Plain Dealer,* April 30, 2003. B9.

Scott, C., and B. Amenuvegbe. "Effect of Recall Duration on Reporting of Household Expenditures: An Experimental Study of Ghana. Social Dimensions of Adjustments in Sub-Saharan African." Working Paper 6, World Bank, Washington, D.C. (1990).

Sher, R., S. Antunes, and B. Reid, et al. "Serepidemiology of Human Immunodeficiency Virus in Africa from 1970–1974." *New England Journal of Medicine* 317 (1987): 450–51. E.

Sidley, P. "South African Leaders Come Under Pressure to Admit HIV/AIDS Link." *British Medical Journal* 321 (2000): 722.

Simon, F., et al. "Identification of a New Human Immunodeficient Virus Type 1 Distinct from Group from Group M and Group O." *Nature Med.* 4 (1998): 1032–37.

Tabor, R., J. Cairns Gerety, and A.C. Bayley. "Did HIV and HTLV Originate in Africa?" *Journal of the American Medical Association* 264 (1990): 691–692.

World Health Organization (WHO). "Malaria, 1982–1997." *Weekly Epidemiological Record* no. 32 (1999).

World Health Organization (WHO). WHO Report 2001. Geneva, 2001.

PART X

DOING BUSINESS—DO'S AND DON'TS

"An African Success Story." *The Economist,* June 14, 1997. p.47.

Gray, Richard, and David Birmingham, eds. *Pre-Colonial African Trade: Essays on Trade in Central and Eastern Africa before 1900.* London, 1970.

Haggins, Jon. *The African-American Guide to Hot, Exotic and Fun-Filled Places.* New York. Amber Books, 2002.

Morrison, Terri, Wayne A. Conaway, and George A. Borden. *How to Do Business in Sixty Countries—Kiss, Bow or Shake Hands.* Holbrook, Massachusetts. Adam Media Corporation, 1994.

Riley, S.P. "Western Policies & African Realities; Anti-Corruption Agenda" in *Corruption and Development in Africa, Lessons from Country's Case Studies* edited by K.R. Hope, Sr., and B.C. Chikulo. New York. St Martins Press, 2000. pp. 137–158. "The Emerging Africa." *The Economist,* June 14, 1997.

Appendixes: Charts and Statistics

Appendix A:

Global Population by Regions & Areas in Kilometers

Country	Area in Kilometers	Population
China	9,326,411	1,284,304,000
U.S.A.	9,166,601	280,562,000
Europe	4,940,999	728,950,000
India	2,973,190	1,045,845,000
New Zealand	268, 894	3,908,000
Argentina	2,736,690	37,813,000
Total	**29,412,785**	**3,381,382,000**
AFRICA	**30, 343,551**	**841,628,000**

*Sources: U.N. Dept. of Economic & Social Information. Guthrie: 1986. p.83.
United Nations World Population. John Reader: Africa: A Bibliography of the
Continent. Alfred A. Knopf. New York. 1998. p.686.*

Appendix B:

World's Refugees:

Regions	Population of Refugees
Africa (including refugees from the Middle East)	3,002,000
Europe	972,800
Middle East	6,830,200
Americas & Caribbean	597,000
Asia & the Pacific	815,400
South & Central Asia	2,702,800
TOTAL:	**14,920,200**

Source: United Nations Dept. of Economic and Social Information & Policy Analysis. 2002.

Appendix C:

Immigrants Admitted as Permanent Residents Under Refugee Acts by Country of Birth into The United States from 1981–2000.

Country of Birth	1981–90	1991–98	1999	2000
Europe	155,512	371,658	21,801	33,106
Asia	712,092	328,705	9,300	13,342
AFRICA	**22,149**	**46,100**	**2,184**	**3,365**
Oceania	22	265	2	24
North America	121,840	161,014	9,086	15,233
South America	1,986	4,627	417	813
TOTAL	**1,013,601**	**912,369**	**42, 790**	**65,883**

Source: U.S. Immigration and Naturalization Service, Statistical Yearbook, annual reports and releases.

Appendix D:

African Refugees including Middle Easterners residing in the Continent.

Place of Asylum	Origin of Most Refugees	Population
Algeria	Western Sahara & Palestine	85,000
Democratic Republic of the Congo	Angola, Sudan, Burundi, Central African Rep., Rep. of Congo & Rwanda	305,000
Republic of Congo	De. Rep. of the Congo, Rwanda, Burundi & Central African Republic	102,000
Cote d'Ivoire	Liberia & Sierra Leone	103,000
Egypt	Sudan, Somalia & Palestine	75,000
Ethiopia	Sudan, Somalia & Eritrea	114,000
Guinea	Sierra Leone & Liberia	190,000
Kenya	Somalia, Sudan, Ethiopia & Uganda	243,000
Liberia	Sierra Leone	60,000
Sudan	Eritrea, Uganda & Ethiopia	307,000
Tanzania	Burundi, Dem. Rep. of the Congo, Rwanda & Somali	498,000
Uganda	Sudan Rwanda, Dem. Rep. of the Congo & Somalia	174,000
Zambia	Angola, Dem. Rep. of the Congo, Rwanda & Burundi	270,000
TOTAL		**2,526,000**

Source: U.N. Dept of Economic & Social Information & Policy Analysis, 2002.

Appendix E:

Refugees: South & Central Asia

Bangladesh	Myanmar	122,200
India	Sri Lanka, Tibet, Burma Bangladesh & Afghanistan	345,800
Nepal	Bhutan & Tibet	131,000
Pakistan	Afghanistan & India	2,018,800
TOTAL		**2,617,800**

Source: U.N. Dept of Economic & Social Information & Policy Analysis, 2002

Appendix F:

Recipients of U.S. Development Aid 1999–2000

Country	Aid in Millions of U.S. Dollars
Russia	$1,154
Israel	$967
Egypt	$799
Ukraine	$282
Indonesia	$194
Jordan	$179
Colombia	$169
Bosnia and Herzegovina	$152
India	$148
Peru	$136

Source: Organization of Economic Cooperation & Development, 2002.

Appendix G:

U.S. Direct Investment Overseas 1999–2001 (in billions of U.S. Dollars)

REGIONS	1999	2000	2001
Europe	$211	$679	$726
South America	$24	$84	$83
Central America	$18	$70	$81
Africa	**$5**	**$14**	**$16**
Asia & Pacific	$62	$205	$217
European Union	N/A	$11	$13
Eastern Europe	N/A	$604	$640
OPEC	N/A	$29	$31
TOTAL	**$320 billion**	**$1.696 billion**	**$1.807 billion**

Source: Bureau of Economic Analysis, U.S. Dept. of Commerce, 2002.

Index

313

ABOUT THE AUTHOR

Primus Chukwuemelia Igboaka was a Senior Correspondent of Nigeria's Daily Newspaper, the *National Concord.*

He graduated from college with a major in Mass Communication. He earned an MBA (in management) from Tiffin University, Tiffin Ohio. He has written extensively and contributed articles to Nigerian as well as U.S. publications, including *African News Weekly* and *Health Referral News* magazine, Beachwood, Ohio. His other book, *"At the Eleventh Hour - Miss World & The Shunting of a Pageant"* will be due by next fall.

He has received several awards, including the National Youth Service Corps (NYSC) and the Lagos State Governor's Award for excellence. As a Senior Correspondent on the beat, *National Concord* won the British Airways Award of Excellence in Airport & Aviation Reporting.

He is knowledgeable about African history, traditions, and cultures. He lives in Cleveland, Ohio with wife, Vickie, and sons Nnaemeka, Ify, and Somto.

www.ingramcontent.com/pod-product-compliance
Lightning Source LLC
Chambersburg PA
CBHW030248290526
45785CB00001B/15